SCHIZOPHRENIA

An Introduction to Research and Theory

GLENN SHEAN
College of William and Mary

WINTHROP PUBLISHERS, INC.
Cambridge, Massachusetts

Library of Congress Cataloging in Publication Data

Shean, Glenn D., 1939–
    Schizophrenia: an introduction.

    Includes bibliographies and index.
    1. Schizophrenia. I. Title. [DNLM: 1. Schizophrenia. WM203 S539s]
RC514.S48   616.8'982   77–26259
ISBN 0–87626–797–5

To Suzanne, Bud, and Erin

Copyright © 1978 by Winthrop Publishers, Inc.
    17 Dunster Street, Cambridge, Massachusetts 02138

10   9   8   7   6   5   4   3   2   1

Contents

Preface

Several years ago, as I began an outline and several chapters of a proposed text on abnormal psychology, I decided to attempt the most difficult chapter—schizophrenia—first. After considerable effort and frustration I discovered that it is impossible to write a single informative and balanced chapter on this complex and confusing topic. Available texts provided further support for this conclusion. It is possible to find articles and books on schizophrenia to support virtually any conceivable opinion on the topic. I, naïvely, decided to write a textbook on schizophrenia that would be comprehensive, informative, and scholarly. This book is the result of three years of effort and thought. It is suitable for undergraduate courses in abnormal psychology (in which the professor chooses to cover some topics in depth rather than many topics briefly) and graduate courses in psychopathology, clinical psychology, psychiatry, psychiatric social work, nursing, and counseling.

I wish to thank the many people, inside and outside mental hospitals, who have helped, directly or indirectly, to write this book. Thanks are also due to Marty Brown, Claudette Cantor, Diana Tennis, Alex Klingelhöfer, Sue Hargadon, and Suzanne Romero for their patience and assistance in typing this manuscript.

Glenn Shean
Williamsburg

Introduction

Schizophrenics presently occupy approximately two-thirds of the beds in mental hospitals and more than a quarter of all available hospital beds in the United States. The incidence of diagnoses of this disorder is so high that it is considered the central problem for contemporary psychiatry. Statistics from the United States Department of Commerce indicate that a total of 444,777 people (counting admissions and readmissions) entered the country's 337 state and county mental hospitals during 1974. Another 100,000 patients were admitted to private psychiatric hospitals. Approximately one-half of all patients admitted to mental hospitals are diagnosed schizophrenic.

The actual incidence of occurrence of schizophrenia in the United States population is difficult to determine, since the diagnosis has proved to be highly variable and unreliable. Epidemiological research suggests that the incidence of schizophrenia in the general population of Western European societies is approximately 150 cases per 100,000 population (Lemkau and Crocetti, 1958). The proportion of any age cohort expected to be hospitalized for schizophrenia between birth and age seventy-five is approximately 1 percent (Norris, 1959). Furthermore, epidemiological research suggests that there may be from two to ten times as many schizophrenics in the community as are hospitalized, and that up to 6 percent of the population could be diagnosed as schizophrenic sometime during their lives (Bellak et al., 1973).

Admission rates for schizophrenia for both sexes and all races are concentrated between the ages twenty through forty, with peak occurrence between twenty-five and thirty-four. Schizophrenia usually appears relatively early in life and in most cases, despite increased discharge rates, probably continues to impair the individual long after discharge. The annual cost of this disorder, in terms of personal anguish and economic expenditure, is astronomical.

The pattern of use of mental health facilities in the United States has changed dramatically during the last twenty-two years. In 1955, 77 percent of all patient-care episodes (1.7 million) were in inpatient settings. In 1973, the inpatient proportion of patient care episodes (5.2 million) had dropped to 32 percent (Taube and Redick, 1976). The shift from inpatient to outpatient care of schizophrenic patients reflects several factors: the proportion of care episodes in large public mental hospitals decreased from 50 to 12 percent between 1955 and 1973; community mental health centers began to play an increasingly important role in mental health services during the late 1960's (they provided one-fourth of all care episodes in 1973); and admissions to day-care hospitals tripled during these years (Keith et al., 1976).

The present trend in the treatment of schizophrenia is toward brief hospitalization followed by discharge to home or to sheltered care with further outpatient treatment. The introduction of several effective tranquilizers during the 1950's helped to make this change in treatment practice possible. Despite the encouraging decline in inpatient population, readmission rates have been rising steadily; by 1972, 72 percent of all admissions of schizophrenic patients to state and county mental hospitals were readmissions (Taube and Redick, 1973). Many patients have entered a "revolving door" of admission-release-readmission to inpatient facilities. While repeated brief hospitalizations are probably less debilitating than prolonged, continuous hospitalization, many problems remain, and new ones have been raised by the shifting pattern of care. It is estimated, for example, that as few as 15 percent of discharged schizophrenic patients are able to function at an "average" level (e.g. are able to work or keep house). Most discharged schizophrenics are likely to be periodically or chronically unemployed and socially isolated. Numerous patient "ghettos" have developed in cities, and in many cases released schizophrenic patients have simply been transferred from hospital back wards to the isolation of deteriorating apartment buildings. Mental hospital populations are declining, but the complex social and personal problems associated with schizophrenia are still very much at hand.

REFERENCES

ASH, P. The reliability of psychiatric diagnosis. *Journal of Abnormal and Social Psychology, 44,* 1949, 272–278.

BELLAK, L., M. HURRICH, and H. GEDIMAN. *Ego Functions in Schizophrenics, Neurotics, and Normals.* New York: John Wiley & Sons, 1973.

KEITH, S., J. GUNDERSON, A. REIFMAN, S. BUSCHBAUM, and L. MOSHER. Special report: schizophrenia 1976. *Schizophrenia Bulletin, 2,* 1976, 510–565.

LEMKAU, P. and G. CROCETTI. Vital statistics of schizophrenia. In *Schizophrenia: A Review of the Syndrome,* edited by L. Bellak, pp. 64–81. New York: Logos Press, 1958.

NORRIS, VERA. *Mental Illness in London* (Maudsley Monograph No. 6). London: Chapman and Hall, 1959.

PASAMANICK, B., S. DINITZ, and M. LEFTON. Psychiatric orientation and its relation to diagnosis and treatment in a mental hospital. *American Journal of Psychiatry, 116,* 1959, 127–132.

TAUBE, C. and R. REDICK. *Utilization of mental health resources by persons diagnosed with schizophrenia* (DHEW Publication No. [HSM] 73–9110). Rockville, Md.: National Institute of Mental Health, 1973.

————. *Provisional data on patient care episodes in mental health facilities, 1973.* Statistical Note 127 (DHEW Publication No. [ADM] 76–158). Rockville, Md.: National Institute of Mental Health, 1976.

WILL, OTTO. Schizophrenia: psychological treatment. In *Comprehensive Textbook of Psychiatry,* edited by A. Freedman, A. Kaplan, and B. Sadock. Baltimore, Md.: Williams and Wilkins, 1975.

ZUBIN, J. Classification of the behavior disorders. *Annual Review of Psychology, 18,* 1967, 373–406.

Part One

The Concept of Schizophrenia

Chapter One

Madness and Schizophrenia: A Brief History

The Earliest Explanations: Origins of the Spiritualistic Tradition

Humans have apparently been confronted with madness in its diverse forms since the origin of the species. The prehistoric world was populated by imaginary beings drawn from human emotions and imagination, some of them images of fears and anxieties. The causes of the changing conditions of daily life were not apparent, so our ancestors assumed that unseen spirits were responsible. Humans hoped to gain some control over events by learning to influence these spirits.

Illness, infirmity, and madness were regarded as misfortunes involving the entire person; no distinction was made between mental and physical or natural and supernatural causes. Priests or shamans assumed powerful status within these societies, partly because of their knowledge of the secrets of exorcism (prayer, incantation, magic, ritual, and sacrifice), which were intended to appease or drive the evil spirit from the possessed person. Cave paintings in France dating back more than 17,000 years portray a figure wearing a bison mask while exorcising (treating) a stricken patient. Shamans also performed a primitive form of brain surgery called *trepanning*. Skulls found from Russia to South America have had holes drilled through them; it is believed the holes were chiseled in an effort to allow "evil spirits" to escape.

Early monotheistic cultures offered similar explanations for human maladies. A description of demoniacal possession in an

3

Egyptian princess of the Twentieth Dynasty is now in the National Library in Paris. The scriptures of the Old Testament show many instances of behavior we would label neurotic or psychotic. Cain fell prey to his destructive instincts; Hannah, the mother of Saul, was a severe neurotic; Saul was a depressive; Ezekiel was disturbed; and David feigned madness to escape captivity. Solutions to these human disturbances were often sought by appealing to the spiritual world.

The early Greeks continued the belief that the gods caused illness, and so their treatment of madness also required the invocation of divine intervention. Temples of Aesculapius (the god of healing) were established throughout the Greek world to treat human disorders. The temples were situated in pleasing surroundings to assist Aesculapius, and sufferers traveled to them to undergo treatments of sacrifices, ablutions, and fasting under the guidance of temple priests. Research suggests that opium derivatives, hypnosis, and suggestion were used to heighten the effects of the rituals. Sham surgery and impersonations of Aesculapius performed by temple priests while the patient was half asleep, are thought to have been a routine aspect of temple practice. A number of votive tablets found at the temple sites tell of the dreams and visions the patients experienced during sleep. In many cases, Aesculapius appeared to them and brought about recovery by manipulation or soothing words. For the most part these tablets describe the healing of what would currently be labeled *hysterical conversion reactions;* for example, functional blindness, paralysis, and aphonia.

The majority of Greeks visited these temples, rather than go to one of the numerous profane healers who abounded in Greece, not only to seek cure but to preserve their well-being. The temples established by this cult of Aesculapius were so successful that they continued well into the Christian era. Belief in spiritual causes of illness, including madness, represents one of the two major historical traditions of understanding madness that continue into the present. The other is known as the *naturalistic* tradition.

Hippocrates and the Naturalistic Tradition

The Greeks developed a system of logic and philosophy that coexisted with and eventually dominated mythological explanations of madness, at least among the educated citizens. As early as the

6th century B.C. some Greek scholars were trying to develop models of understanding based on systematic observation and experimentation. Hippocrates (460–357 B.C.) was among the first to attempt to describe madness in the context of the Greek naturalistic tradition. He maintained that the brain was the "interpreter of consciousness" and explained the various forms of mental disturbance in terms of humors. In Hippocrates' view of human physiology our bodies contain four basic humors. The four elements of the universe, understood by the Greeks to be fire, earth, air, and water, caused the corresponding qualities of heat, dryness, cold, and moisture within the humoral vesicles. If a person were subjected to an excess of any one of these qualities, the natural equilibrium of the bodily elements would be disturbed, and an excess of one element would lead to changes, which, if severe, could lead to different patterns of madness.

Hippocrates introduced the first systematic theory of a physical cause of madness. He also formulated the first system for the classification of madness as illness, differentiating and describing in detail four categories: mania, melancholy, epilepsy, and mental deterioration. His treatment introduced little that was new, and consisted primarily of rest, bathing, and dieting.

Hippocrates' fragmentary model is important in the history of madness because it represents the first serious attempt to combine available knowledge of philosophy, anatomy, and physiology into one system.

Plato (407–347 B.C.) departed from Hippocrates' empirical approach and developed an idealistic, mystical model of madness. He described the soul as consisting of two parts, the rational and the irrational. The rational soul is seated in the brain; it is immortal and divine. The irrational (animal) soul is mortal and is situated in the chest; it is the source of pleasure, pain, and emotion. Plato believed that madness occurs when the irrational soul is severed from its union with the rational soul. He framed a dualistic theory in which mind and body, or spirit and matter, were posited to account for the reality we perceive. Plato believed that madness was a disorder of the spirit and not susceptible to natural law. Subsequent development of Platonic thought was a further refinement of two major aspects: religious or mystical and formal-rationalistic principles. His work did not lead to an empirical attitude or concern for the sensible world, essential to the development of the naturalistic tradition.

Aristotle (384–322 B.C.) was a student, a follower, and an opponent of Plato. Despite his nineteen years as a student in the Academy directed by Plato, Aristotle developed a philosophical system radically different from that of Plato, because he was most interested in biological problems and natural phenomena. Aristotle's interests led to the development of an empirical, inductive approach compatible with the naturalistic perspective. Although he did not concern himself with the issue of madness to any significant extent, his work gave impetus to the naturalistic view formulated by Hippocrates.

The social chaos that followed the Peloponnesian Wars, the cultural heterogeneity that resulted from the military victories of the Macedonians, and the gradual dissolution of the "Greek spirit" resulted in a period of relative quiescence in Greek science and philosophy. The new masters of the ancient western world, the Romans, were practical people interested primarily in the political, economic, and legal structures of their empire. They were primarily borrowers from Greek science and philosophy rather than contributors to it. Cicero (106–143 B.C.), a Stoic, was an exception to this trend. In his writings on madness he emphasized that disturbances of the soul are the cause of madness. He argued that while physical disorders can be distinguished from mental disorders, emotional factors frequently cause physical disorders. In contrast to Hippocrates, Cicero believed that mental disorders are caused by a "neglect of reason" and called upon sufferers to seek cure through participation in philosophy.

Seven centuries after Hippocrates, the Roman physician Galen (130–200 A.D.) attempted an eclectic integration of the Greek scientific tradition with the tenets of oriental mysticism that had influenced Roman thought for several centuries. Galen believed that psychic functions are centered in the brain and developed an organic model of physiology that dominated western medical thought for over a thousand years. Briefly, his theory stated that food passed from the stomach to the liver where it was transformed and permeated by *natural spirits* that are found in all living substances. Air, which carries the *vital principle,* enters the body through the lungs and combines with natural spirits in the heart to produce *vital spirits.* The vital spirits rise to the brain where they are transformed into *animal spirits.* Madness is caused by disturbances of the functions of animal spirits. Dementia and imbecility are caused by rarefaction and diminution of animal spirits, and coldness and excess humidity of the brain. Mania and melancholia are caused by specific humoral excesses.

Christianity and the Resurgence of the Spiritualistic View

The way a particular culture understands and treats madness is an extension of the way it answers questions about the entire range of puzzling phenomena, including natural events, disease, and the purpose of human existence. The spirited world of Graeco-Roman culture began to deteriorate during the later years of the Roman Empire. The threat of barbarian invasions from the north and east, recurrent epidemics, and the breakdown of the old political and social orders generated a renewed sense of anxiety and spiritual infirmity, which led the Romans to turn away from Greek rationalism toward mystical and spiritual interpretations of existence. Speculation centered on salvation and on life after death.

Christianity spread with amazing rapidity in this atmosphere and was adopted as the official Roman state religion by the fourth century A.D. With the rise of Christianity madness was once again understood in a spiritual context. Sufferers were either left to wander through the countryside as beggars or were given shelter in monasteries devoted to providing comfort and prayer for the disturbed and infirm.

Ecclesiastical concern over growing signs of polytheism and occult practices in Europe resulted in an important Church proclamation in 343 A.D., which stated, in effect, that the practice of magic was evidence of communion with the devil. Mental disturbances, however, remained an ambiguous category and continued to puzzle early Christian authorities to such an extent that complex legal and theological problems frequently arose over difficulties in determining whether the "disturbed" were saints in communication with God and spiritual forces, or "possessed" agents of the devil. In cases of apparent possession, incantation, exorcism, and prayer were applied to drive the evil spirits from the afflicted individual. A complex descriptive and practical demonology was developed as the conviction grew that some forms of group hysteria and emotional disturbance were caused by the influence of the devil.

Madness During the Middle Ages

The Black Plague that began to sweep across Europe around 1347 killed over one-quarter of the population within a span of several years. Epidemics of group hysteria, in which people behaved like wolves (lyncanthropy) or tore off their clothes and danced in the streets with spider-like movements (tarantism), swept across Europe. Groups of flagellants, bearing crosses and flogging themselves with nail-tipped ropes, wandered from village to village. The disruption of the social and economic order generated by the decline of feudalism, the beginnings of a new middle-class of craftsmen and artisans, the eastern ideas brought back from the Crusades, and the dawning of a renewed spirit of inquiry and thought that marked the beginnings of the Renaissance, caused the Church to intensify its concern with the sources of heresy. Nonconformity and eccentricity, in this turbulent context, became signs of heresy. A sympathetic tolerance toward madness was replaced by a more menacing attitude as the Church attempted to restore social order by identifying certain forms of eccentricity and deviance as heresy. It declared war on the forces of Satan by condemning as witches large numbers of women showing signs of what would be diagnosed today as hysteric neuroses. Interestingly, stereotypic madness in the form of psychotic disorders was usually not labeled possession.

the witches' hammer

On December 9 1484, Pope Innocent VIII issued a papal bull authorizing two German Dominican monks, Johann Sprenger and Heinrick Kraemer, to write a definitive work (*Malleus-Maleficarium* or *The Witches' Hammer*) on the existence, description, methods of identification and examination, and sentencing of witches.

This work is cited in most psychiatric texts as marking the period of peak influence of the spiritualistic model in western society, and as the worst example of the destructive consequences that can result from a nonmedical view of madness. The growing preoccupation with heresy and witchcraft during this period of social upheaval unquestionably structured the manner in which many disturbed individuals were understood and treated; nevertheless, torture and moralistic abuse of the insane are not the exclusive domain of any particular view of madness. This work clearly shows that the particular model for understanding madness that predominates during any given period (including the present) is very much a function of the existing cultural framework through which people view themselves and their world.

Malleus was a reaction against the growing instability of the established social order, and untold thousands of disturbed individuals, particularly women, were victims of the worldview articulated in the work. It described and considered both witches and warlocks, but concentrated on witches because witchcraft "comes from carnal lust, which is in women insatiable." The doctrine of free will was introduced to justify the torture and brutality used to extract confessions and punish heretics. Witches and warlocks were viewed as having chosen to succumb to the devil and therefore deserving of punishment. The punitive tone of *Malleus* represents the culmination of an antierotic, misogynous tendency in western religion. Witches were the primary scapegoats used to intimidate citizens and maintain the existing social order.

The Renaissance and the Renewal of a Naturalistic View of Madness

Renaissance thought formed the basis for a naturalistic view of humanity. Descartes' (1596–1650) theory of solids, fluids, and animal spirits interacting through the pineal gland provided a meeting ground between body and soul and allowed for the application of the concept of causality to matters of the soul. Physical qualities such as brittle-pliable, damp-dry, tense-relaxed, and the mechanical transmission of movements could now be applied to the mind or spirit. Descartes reintroduced the naturalistic belief that the mind could be understood as a part of nature that parallels the body's obedience to physical laws of cause and effect via the mechanical structure of the movement of the spirits. Eighteenth century medicine extended this belief to the assumption of a unity in which body and soul communicated directly, providing the theoretical basis for the search for natural causes for madness. As the notion of bodily humors lost scientific acceptance during the course of the eighteenth century, the secrets of mental disturbance and physical disease were sought in the body's liquid and solid constituents; for example, tensions which affected both nerves and organic fibers.

During the eighteenth century, scientific medicine gradually developed a set of concepts dealing with madness which no longer concealed moral judgments related to sin. Madness understood as illness became conceptually possible, according to Michel Foucault (1954), in the new order of reason that assumed an objective distance from immediate experience. In this post-Renaissance milieu in which the relations of people with their feelings, with others, and with time were altered, the observer became the object of scientific study.

The eighteenth century, regarded as the age of rationalism and enlightenment, was in fact a multifaceted period of political turbulence and contrast. The American and French revolutions effectively asserted the importance of the individual in relation to the state and marked the beginnings of a new era of concern for the rights of the individual. This concern did not extend to those considered mad. Up until the end of the eighteenth century there was no system of hospitals established exclusively for the insane. They were either locked up with criminals, political dissenters, and the unemployed, in large institutions nominally called "hospitals," or left to wander the countryside.

Most psychiatric histories (Zilborg and Henry, 1941) tie the advent of a broadly based rational and scientific treatment of madness to the activities and accomplishments of Philippe Pinel (1745–1826). Pinel is depicted as the rational, humanitarian, scientific physician who convinced the leaders of the French Revolution that "madness is caused by physical illness." He emphasized the need for sunshine and fresh air in the treatment of mental disorders and courageously abolished the old order of chains, fetters, and dungeons as the lot of the insane. Under Pinel, confinement of the insane became a medical matter. Madness became widely regarded as a phenomenon with natural causes, and so was considered the province of those trained to treat physical disorders. This trend also appeared in England where Tuke established the York Retreat to provide a healthy environment and moral atmosphere for the treatment of madness. The nineteenth century marked the rapid spread of the view that madness was caused by organic disease. German psychiatry, increasingly influenced by the biological sciences, rose to predominance in the field of severe mental disorders during this period. Physicians were traditionally the directors of asylums, and the model of internal medicine was adopted during this period as the proper approach to the study of madness. This model led to a focus on the classification of mental disorders and to the differentiation of diseases on the basis or origin, course, and outcome. The latter part of the nineteenth century marked the beginning of the "era of systems" in psychiatry. New classifications of mental diseases were abundant, but there was no overall framework that would accommodate the multitude of clinical descriptions of specific mental disorders.

Emil Kraepelin (1855–1926) introduced the first comprehensive and generally accepted diagnostic system in psychiatry. He organized the observations of his predecessors into a single system that divided mental hospital patients into broad disease categories (for example, *dementia praecox,* manic-depressive psychosis) with specific subtypes.

The spirit of the age decreed that madness was a disease, and psychiatry was chartered by society to "deal" with this puzzling and troublesome problem. Kraepelin's system followed from the assumption that madness was a disease like any other disease. The causes were rooted in defective organs, heredity, metabolic changes, or internal secretion. Kraepelin's system proved incomplete; it did not provide for the possibility of recovery and did not examine the past experience of the patient. Eugen Bleuler, influenced by Freud's early thought, introduced the concept of schizophrenia in 1911 to correct this apparent lack.

Most psychiatric histories end at this point. Madness is now recognized as an illness and patients receive nonmoralistic, scientific treatment for their disorders in institutions called mental hospitals. There are some dissenting interpretations of historical fact and contemporary reality, however, and it will be useful to look at one of them in detail.

Foucault's Interpretation of the History of Madness

Standard psychiatric histories (Zilborg and Henry, 1941) imply that the persecution that ensued from application of the spiritualistic model was applied to all forms of disturbance and continued until the naturalistic model resurfaced during the late eighteenth century. In fact, Foucault has documented that prior to the nineteenth century the experience of madness in the western world varied widely. During the years 1560–1740, physicians were frequently requested, by church authorities anxious to quell the enthusiasm of overly zealous fanatics, to give testimony that many so-called signs of witchcraft were caused by disturbances of bodily processes. Ever since the work of Hippocrates, some part of the study of madness was concerned with notions of pathology and whatever medical practices they involved. Medical treatment and medieval hospitals with sections reserved for the mad existed but amounted to no more than a small sector, limited to isolated pockets of those forms of madness regarded as curable ("frenzies," "melancholy"). Foucault suggests that madness was widespread, but that it had no solid medical base until the nineteenth century. Madness was not the exclusive domain of either medicine or ecclesiastical authority.

In Foucault's view, a cultural preoccupation with madness replaced the fear of death (symbolized by the leper) in European culture during the late fifteenth century. During this period innumerable dances and Feasts of Fools were initiated throughout Europe; an iconography of madness extending from Hieronymous Bosch's *Ship of Fools,* to Breughel and *Margot la folle,* to the literature of Shakespeare and Cervantes attests to the growing concern with madness. Contrary to the traditional view that madness was understood exclusively as a sign of witchcraft from the fifteenth through seventeenth centuries, Foucault argues that in fact madness was a common experience that was seldom persecuted, exalted, or controlled. He cites historical evidence in support of the view that, up to about 1650, western culture was largely "hospitable" to madness. The mad abounded in urban and rural areas. They sought refuge in hospitals and monasteries and were free to wander the streets and highways.

According to Foucault, the advance of reason during the seventeenth century was associated with a change in social attitude, which eventually led to the establishment of contemporary mental hospitals. The model of confinement, which over a period of several hundred years led to the successful control of leprosy during the nineteenth century, was applied to other social problems. Institutions called "hospitals" were established to contain the spectrum of the socially displaced: the poor, the disabled, the elderly, beggars, libertines, political radicals, those with venereal disease, criminals, and the mad. These "hospitals" had no medical function; people were kept there because they were unable or unwilling to cope with life independently. Each was considered unfit for a production-conscious society. The confinement of criminals, paupers, dissidents, and madmen to "asylums" had to do not with the treatment of illness, but with what was considered acceptable and unacceptable behavior. According to Foucault, this was determined by a person's ability or inability to participate in the production, distribution, and accumulation of wealth. In this context, idleness was seen as the source of disorder, and madness came to be inextricably associated with the issues of social and moral guilt. Madness retained this aura of guilt even as the political reforms and civil guarantees introduced by the American and French revolutions freed thousands who were confined. The proclamation that put an end to arbitrary internment issued during the French Revolution, for example, specifically exempted "madmen and dangerous animals."

The moral treatment advocated by Pinel and Tuke during the early nineteenth century was replaced by a return to a naturalistic physical approach during the late nineteenth century. Darwin's theory of natural selection was used to support the view that madness was caused by disintegrative diseases afflicting only those of inferior heredity. Madness was seen as nature's way of selecting out the unfit; compassion and humane consideration for the insane were pointless. Madness was confined to large custodial institutions. The violent intensity of the measures used to confine, control, and "treat" madness under the guise of medical treatment (icy baths, fever boxes, spinning chairs, lobotomies, and convulsive therapy) suggest that the mad were not viewed objectively as human beings but as the "guilty," as wild animals to be controlled, disciplined, and mastered. The animal in man was not respected, as it had been in the Middle Ages, but was now considered a sign of disease, moral guilt, and genetic inferiority. Madness, existing as a disease within the person, became embedded in a system of moral values confined within the "objective" concept of mental illness as natural phenomena.

The Contrast Between Traditional
Psychiatric Histories and Foucault's View

Traditional psychiatric histories (Zilborg and Henry, 1941) describe the insane as the oppressed victims of superstition, torture, and imprisonment, rescued from abuse only following the emergence of the naturalistic view that these individuals are suffering from disease. Foucault implies, instead, that the historical situation was considerably more complex; that the experience of madness varied widely; that rather than introducing an objective, morally neutral scientific concept, the view of madness as mental illness has profound moral and philosophical consequences. Foucault argues that the contemporary psychiatric model reflects the political and social values of contemporary western society, values which allow us to adopt a detached view of madness as an objectified "it" or thing.

The contemporary model of madness does not overtly condemn madmen as evil or regard them as possessed. The mad may be regarded as childlike, lazy, dangerous, annoying or pathetic, but above all they are regarded as "sick." Madness is to be "treated" with medication and properly controlled through "hospitalization" in order to be "cured." Psychiatrists are concerned with objective, scientific activities understood as forms of diagnosis, prognosis, and treatment, not exorcism, guilt, or responsibility.

Foucault maintains that the contemporary model of madness as mental illness is a reflection of the historical tendency in western society to view the world and people as objects to be manipulated and studied. Such a view, rather than getting closer to the truth of madness, moves farther and farther away from it. Foucault maintains that reason illuminates only some aspects of reality; that reason and unreason are both parts of human behavior; and that existing histories of madness are written from the perspective of an attempt to validate the assumption that reality can be understood in the light of reason. Foucault argues that the contents of madness, the delusions and regressed fantasies of schizophrenia that our culture rejects and attempts to confine, are to be found in everyone's secret dreams and fears. If we insist, as does the naturalistic model, that reason alone can explain human behavior and experience, we have provided an ironic setting for the certainty that the mad person has invested in his delusion.

Foucault suggests an alternative view of madness. Rather than an objectified illness or "thing" he views the phenomenon of madness in terms of social projection. Madness is understood as an attribution of the culture to a particular group that can embody those qualities "ruled out" of reality as threatening to its existence. In this sense the identification of madness during particular stages of cultural evolution is not merely the definition of deviation from particular norms but is a manifestation of what is repressed in that culture. Foucault maintains that exclusion of the leper served a symbolic as well as a medical function; it allowed medieval Christian culture to detach itself from its sinfulness and to externally symbolize its punishable aspects. The role of madness evolved through the Middle Ages and Renaissance to replace leprosy as a mysterious and dangerous phenomenon requiring separation. The exclusion of madness during the seventeenth and eighteenth centuries, along with the emergence of the dualistic medicine of body humors to explain the influence of the soul on the body and vice versa, led to the pairing of medicine and confinement for the treatment of madness. This pairing resulted in a new content of guilt and moral sanctions; madness became a paradox, a moral evil to be treated medically.

Foucault maintains that contemporary society separates itself from the threat of madness by maintaining it at a distance as a medical entity, reducible to objective fact. Madness as schizophrenia has become the symbol of western society's attempt to suppress its potential for Unreason.

We know little about the structure of sanity itself. We know, as Jules Henry (1973) has observed, that it has something to do with our understanding the relationships of time and space to objects, persons and events, and with our relationships with other people and objects. But how does schizophrenic delusion differ from normal illusion? The illusions of security, of safety, of racial, ethnic and personal superiority, of truth, of heaven, hell and divine word, are instilled by our culture and are part of the consciousness of most sane persons. Yet, what is the difference between the "as-ifness" of sane people and that of the schizophrenic? The following chapters will survey various models of twentieth century madness that attempt to answer this question.

REFERENCES

BANNISTER, D. From there to here: a look at British psychology by Peter Evans. *American Psychological Association Monitor, 7,* 1976, 3.

FOUCAULT, M. *Madness and Civilization: A History of Insanity in the Age of Reason.* New York: Random House, 1965.

――――. *Mental Illness and Psychology.* New York: Harper and Row, 1976.

HENRY, J. *Pathways to Madness.* New York: Vintage, 1973.

LEWIS, N. D. *A Short History of Psychiatric Achievement.* New York: Norton, 1941.

SNYDER, S. *Madness and the Brain.* New York: McGraw-Hill, 1974.

ZACCHIAS, P. *Questions Medico-legales.* Book 2, Volume 2, p. 119, Avignon, 1660.

ZILBORG, G. and G. W. HENRY. *A History of Medical Psychology.* New York: Norton, 1941.

Chapter Two

The Beginnings of Definition and Classification

The First Terminology

Physicians were assigned to administer the asylums of the eighteenth and nineteenth centuries. Trained in the methods of medicine, they were charged with responsibility for the maintenance of minimal standards of hygiene and the discovery and application of effective treatment techniques. The medical specialty of psychiatry originated during the early nineteenth century from this group of asylum directors who tried to understand the strange and bewildering variety of disorders they were charged to treat. Psychiatrists attempted to model their young discipline after the highly successful model of internal medicine, emphasizing the diagnosis of disease syndromes as a preliminary step in the orderly accumulation of scientific medical knowledge. They attempted to identify and describe "sympton" clusters within the institutional population. In most instances, these clusters were simply refinements of categories first described by Galen, Hippocrates, and others. Gradually, the general pejorative terms such as madness, lunacy, and insanity were replaced by more specific terms, most with Latin or Greek roots. The terms referred to groups of individuals who seemed to share similar patterns of disturbance. It was assumed that members of a group suffered from the same or similar underlying disease processes.

The word *dementia,* first used to refer to mental deterioration, was modified and re-introduced as *démence precos,* by a Belgian psychiatrist, B. Morel, in 1865. Morel introduced the term to describe a case in which a fourteen-year-old boy evidenced progressive apathy, mutism, and withdrawal, interrupted by periodic attacks of rage against his father. He used the term *démence* to refer to evidence of serious impairment of cognitive function, and *precos* to refer to the fact that in this case the impairment was progressive and began relatively early in life. Several German psychiatrists, working independently, introduced additional terms to refer to subgroups of institutionalized patients who, in their view, shared certain characteristics. Kahlbaum, for example, suggested the term *paranoia* in 1863, to describe a group in which delusions were predominant. He introduced a second grouping, *katatonia* (catatonia) in 1874, to refer to a category of "demented" patients who shared common patterns of bizarre postures and motor disturbance. Ewald Hecker introduced the term *hebephrenia,* in 1871, to refer to institutionalized individuals who evidenced silly, inappropriate, and regressive behavior. The medical assumptions of these early psychiatrists led them to believe that they were in fact identifying organic disease syndromes.

Emil Kraepelin and Dementia Praecox

The eminent German psychiatrist, Emil Kraepelin, was the first to suggest that these seemingly distinct categories were in fact separate subtypes of a single disease, which he termed *dementia praecox.* Prior to 1896 Kraepelin had considered hebephrenia and dementia praecox to be synonymous. Not until 1899, with the fifth edition of his influential psychiatric text, did he conclude that the separate syndromes of catatonia, hebephrenia, and certain paranoid disturbances were in fact all variations of Morel's original démence precox. Kraepelin argued that although the symptoms were diverse, all of the cases evidenced early (praecox), progressive and irreversible mental deterioration (dementia). In Kraepelin's view, undue attention to behavioral diversity would only obscure and delay discovery of the "true" underlying organic disease process. This assumption is expressed in the following excerpt from Kraepelin's textbook description of dementia praecox:

Dementia praecox is the name provisionally applied to a large group of cases which are characterized in common by a pronounced tendency to mental deterioration of varying grades. The disease apparently develops on the basis of a severe disease process in the cerebral cortex . . . (1904, p. 219).

Kraepelin believed that the most prominent symptom of dementia praecox was thought disorder, which occurs most often in adolescence and early adulthood, and progresses toward inevitable dementia.

Although Kraepelin's views changed over the years, he continued to assert that the above combination of causal assumptions and clinical observations were valid bases for postulating a syndrome caused by a common, underlying disease of the brain. Much of the early criticism of Kraepelin's concept focused on his insistence that the disease must inevitably follow a course of progressive deterioration toward dementia. Kraepelin argued, tautologically, that those patients who were diagnosed as suffering from dementia praecox and later recovered must not have actually had dementia praecox in the first place. This argument was based on the assumption that the symptoms of dementia praecox were caused by "a severe disease process in the cerebral cortex." Since central nervous tissue, once damaged, does not regenerate, Kraepelin obviously could not allow for recovery from dementia praecox without giving up his conviction that these syndromes were caused by underlying organic pathology.

In later years Kraepelin (1912) attempted to refine his diagnostic system to better distinguish between the "diseases" of paranoia, paraphrenia, and dementia praecox. Kraepelin emphasized the importance of such distinctions, and came to regard some cases of paranoia as psychogenic rather than organic disorders, and grouped them with hysteria and similar conditions. The diagnosis of dementia praecox, according to Kraepelin, depended primarily on the observation of the following characteristic features: disordered thinking, hallucinations, volitional disturbances, and progressive intellectual deterioration. He introduced the term *paraphrenia* to denote cases intermediate between paranoia and dementia praecox, paranoid type, which were characterized by paranoid disturbances and systematized hallucinatory experiences which occurred at a later age than was seen in "true" dementia praecox. The term *paranoia* was retained to refer to cases characterized by chronic, persistent, and incorrigible delusions in individuals who did not hallucinate and who continued to be capable of clear and orderly thinking, and of volition and behavior outside the realm of their delusions.

Eugen Bleuler and *Schizophrenia*

In 1911, the Swiss psychiatrist Eugen Bleuler published the historic work, *Dementia Praecox or the Group of Schizophrenias.* Bleuler had devoted years of painstaking effort to the observation and description of the symptoms of psychotic patients, and had attempted to apply Freud's psychodynamic theories to the study of these symptoms. As did Kraepelin, Bleuler regarded thought disorder as the defining feature of dementia praecox. Bleuler, however, took issue with Kraepelin on several points: he observed that the intellectual deterioration characteristic of dementia praecox was not similar to that observed in organic disorders, that many patients were capable of selected areas of highly complex thought and function; he disagreed with Kraepelin's emphasis on the inevitability of progressive mental deterioration and argued that not all patients diagnosed as suffering from dementia praecox evidenced progressive deterioration. In some cases the disease stabilized, and in others, patients seemed to recover for relatively long intervals.

Bleuler considered the common ingredient of the disorders to be a split (*schism*) within the mind (*phrenos*) which was manifested in "loosening of associations" and "disharmony among affects," and proposed the term *schizophrenia* to refer to them. Bleuler did not refer to a "split personality"; he intended the term to refer to a loss of balanced integration of disparate mental functions: cognition, emotion, and motivation.

Bleuler divided schizophrenic symptoms into two separate but closely related groups: *fundamental symptoms (Grundsymptome),* present in every case of schizophrenia and not observed in any other disorder; and *accessory symptoms (akzessorischen symptome)* which may or may not be present in any given case of schizophrenia and may occur in other disorders. Bleuler also divided symptoms into *primary* and *secondary* groups. He believed that *primary symptoms* result directly from the underlying organic disease which he thought caused schizophrenia. *Secondary symptoms* were believed to result from the interaction of the organic disease with a person's environment. Bleuler's lists of fundamental and primary symptoms were not synonymous. Autism, for example, was defined as a fundamental diagnostic symptom present in every case of schizophrenia and as a secondary symptom, since it was not believed to be a direct result of the organic disease presumed to underlie schizophrenia.

Bleuler was impressed by the heterogeneity of symptoms associated with schizophrenia, and at times suggested that the disorder might be discovered to be caused by a group of closely related diseases rather than a single organic disease process. He maintained, however, that there were four fundamental symptoms which are present, to varying degrees, in every case of schizophrenia: altered associations, altered affect, ambivalence, and autism. He also maintained that the disease might be present in individuals who never manifest these signs (latent schizophrenia).

the fundamental symptoms

Bleuler described the four fundamental symptoms of schizophrenia as follows:

1. *Altered associations.* According to Bleuler, cognitive or thought disturbances, in which normal associative connections were weakened, are especially important symptoms of schizophrenia. He maintained that as a result of associational disturbances, ideas are condensed and displaced into symbols, thoughts are generalized broadly, and reasoning and logical operations are greatly impaired. Thinking, because of the associational disturbance, becomes illogical, unclear and, eventually, incoherent.

   Bleuler felt that emotions gain greater domination over "the train of thought" as a result of a basic, disease-caused "weakness of associations" that, he maintained, was the precursor to all other psychological symptoms. As wishes and fears, "rather than logical connection," gain control over thought, "senseless delusions are formed and the road is cleared for exaggerated dereistic thinking [thinking directed away from reality and not following ordinary rules of logic] with its turning away from reality, its tendency to symbolism, displacements, and condensations" (1924, p. 377).

2. *Altered affect*. Bleuler felt that affective disturbance was the most striking symptom in the chronic forms of schizophrenia. "In the sanatoria there are patients sitting around who for decades show no affect no matter what happens to them or to those about them. They are indifferent to maltreatment . . . they have to be taken care of in all respects. Toward their own delusions they are strikingly indifferent" (1924 p. 378). Bleuler's conclusions on the pattern of altered affect in less chronic cases were more tentative. He observed that patients were frequently irritable, sensitive, and moody, that the "finer feelings" were more impaired than the "elementary," and that the ethical sense remained essentially unaffected. He emphasized the importance of affective indifference to crucial aspects of life as a symptom of schizophrenia but stated, ". . . one cannot sometimes speak of euphoria or depression or fear" (1924, p. 379). He observed that one of the surest signs of the disease is an affective rigidity, and referred to a defect in emotional rapport as an important sign of schizophrenia.

3. *Ambivalence*. Bleuler observed that the "schizophrenic defect of the associational paths" made it possible for contrasts that otherwise are mutually exclusive to "exist side by side in the psyche." Thus, patients may experience love and hatred toward the same person ("affective ambivalence"), they may want at the same time to eat and not to eat; they do what they do not want to do as well as what they want to do ("ambivalence of the will").

4. *Autism*. Bleuler described autism as the tendency, particularly apparent in severe chronic cases, for schizophrenics to "lose contact with reality," to withdraw from involvement in the external world and to live in an imaginary world of fantasy, wish fulfillment, and feelings of persecution. Bleuler felt that in mild cases schizophrenics might lose contact with reality "inconspicuously in one respect or another." In severe cases, "the dereistic (imaginary) world is the more real; the real world comes to be perceived as imaginary" (1924, p. 389).

the accessory symptoms

Bleuler maintained that the accessory symptoms had been given undue weight in the diagnosis of schizophrenia, and that they in fact function only to complicate the fundamental clinical picture. Bleuler did not consider the symptoms most commonly used to identify dementia praecox in Kraepelin's system to be necessary or basic to the diagnosis of schizophrenia. The most important of the accessory symptoms in Bleuler's system are delusions, hallucinations, and bizarre motor behavior.

associational disturbance

Bleuler attempted to specify a single underlying psychological deficit that would account for the diverse symptoms associated with the disorder. This deficit, *the only symptom that he viewed as both fundamental and primary, was the associative disturbance.* Bleuler's emphasis on the primary nature of the disturbance of the associations is clearly expressed in the following excerpt from his text.

> For us the alteration of the thinking process, or elementarily expressed, of the association, is of special importance, and, as a matter of fact, nearly all the psychogenic symptoms can be derived from it. As far as we can recognize this alteration, it is a dynamic one. Thus, we also see something similar . . . in dreams and lack of attention, and in so called mind wandering. In schizophrenia, it is the highest control which fails where it would be necessary to act, and this again must be referred to as a disturbance of the connections of all the individual functions. With this dismemberment of the connections, it is comprehensible that the logical function of thinking is disturbed by affective needs. . . (1924, pp. 205–206).

Bleuler used Freudian psychoanalytic concepts to interpret the accessory and secondary symptoms, but described the schizophrenic thought disorder solely in terms of its structure without reference to any motivational bases of origin. Bleuler's nonmotivational approach to the description of "the breaking of the associative thread" followed directly from his belief that this *fundamental primary symptom* is the direct result of organic pathology and the basis for all clinical symptoms. His attitude is clearly expressed in his original monograph:

> Psychic experiences—usually of an unpleasant nature—can undoubtedly affect the schizophrenic symptoms. However, it is highly improbable that the disease itself is really produced by such factors (1911, pp. 345–346).

the integration of kraepelinian and freudian models

Bleuler introduced his concept of schizophrenia in order to clarify several issues related to Kraepelin's description of dementia praecox, and to reconcile Kraepelinian psychiatric thought with Freudian psychoanalytic ideas. Bleuler's position on the issue of the relative importance of psychological factors shifted substantially toward an organic emphasis, however, between the introduction of the concept in 1911 and his death in 1939. In 1911 Bleuler claimed that unconscious intrapsychic complexes, as described by Freud, were the basis of schizophrenic symptoms. Delusions, hallucinations, and stereotyped mannerisms—"secondary" or "accessory" symptoms—began to make sense to him in light of Freud's theory. Bleuler presented a rich catalogue of clinical examples. He outlined the process by which unconscious pathogenic complexes in schizophrenia overpowered conventional meanings, language, and thought processes, allowing for the expression of wish-fulfilling actions and fantasies. A problem remained for Bleuler: how to reconcile these observations with his acceptance of Kraepelin's belief that underlying organic processes caused the disorder?

Helm Stierlin (1967) has described how Bleuler adapted A. Semon's nineteenth century associationistic psychology in an attempt to bring about this reconciliation. Following Semon, Bleuler distinguished two basic entities within the human psyche: engrams and their associative links. Engrams are stable once established while their links are variable. According to Bleuler's formulations, associations are formed as a result of experiences. These associations are integrated into clusters which under certain circumstances are hierarchically organized and goal-directed. According to Bleuler, the hierarchical organization of associational clusters is loosened during sleep-dreams and fatigue. This theory postulates that the associative trends compete with one another, those with the greatest affective charge eventually winning out. At this point Bleuler ingeniously connected Semon's theoretical concepts to his medical assumptions by postulating an as yet unspecified disease of the brain, which results in a weakness or deficit in the metaphorical switches which govern and coordinate the associational clusters, a weakness that allows affectively charged clusters to "break loose." This theoretical weakening or "loosening of the associations" was believed to result in a loss of hierarchical structure and goal-directed thinking. Bleuler believed that in severe cases, affects become fragmented and the inner unity of the personality is lost (split).

Bleuler believed that his theory of the weakness of the associative links provided the necessary connection between the organic genesis postulated by Kraepelin, and widely accepted by the psychiatric establishment, and Freud's psychodynamic formulations.

> We can assume a decrease in the associative links which corresponds to the nature of the illness, namely one which is not functional but which is the direct consequence of a direct chemical or anatomical or molecular brain alteration (1920).

Psychoanalytic theory could also find its place in Bleuler's conceptualization, for the loosening of the associations allowed for the free reign of intrapsychic complexes as manifested in the secondary symptoms of schizophrenia.

Stierlin (1967) has indicated how Bleuler's integration of such different viewpoints forced him to reshuffle schizophrenic symptomatology. Bleuler introduced the distinction between primary and secondary symptoms, a distinction which ran counter to clinical expectation and precedent. Loosening of associations was considered primary, and most symptoms previously given greatest emphasis in clinical descriptions of dementia praecox, e.g., delusions and hallucinations, were relegated to the status of secondary symptoms. Bleuler's emphasis on a psychological formulation of the function of secondary symptoms partially demystified schizophrenia and paved the way for a psychological approach to the understanding of many of what had seemed the most alien and bizarre aspects of this condition.

bleuler's retreat from freudian psychology

Bleuler's view that many schizophrenic symptoms are exaggerations of normal patterns best understood in a psychological context, and his recognition of latent forms which never require institutionalization or treatment, threatened the very foundation of academic, Kraepelinian psychiatry. Bleuler incurred the wrath of the group he had set out to support. He was quickly reminded by his academic colleagues that he was on "thin ice." As Stierlin (1967) has indicated, Bleuler continued to vacillate. From 1913 on he began to move away from Freud and toward "respectable" psychiatry. Two years after introducing his concept of schizophrenia he wrote, "Critics should realize that far too much of my theory has been considered Freudian. . . . The illness (schizophrenia) is in my opinion not due to psychic causes, but a great many of its symptoms are; and some of these come about in ways which Freud and Jung have demonstrated" (1913). His increasing emphasis on an organic, Kraepelinian orientation is clear: "Most schizophrenics are not to be treated at all, or at any rate outside of asylums. Expensive treatments, that are of no use anyway, should be cautioned against, above everything" (1924). Still later, Bleuler observed, "The essential cause, which most likely is necessary to schizophrenia, lies in an inherited disposition" (1937). Bleuler's concept of schizophrenia placed madness, as mental illness, squarely within the confines of biological science.

confusions in bleuler's theory

Bleuler's vaguely worded descriptions of his primary symptoms are an important source of diagnostic unreliability. To further complicate matters, Bleuler was intrigued with the notion of latent schizophrenia, a concept certain to foster unfounded clinical and diagnostic guesswork. Latent schizophrenia suggests the insidious possibility that many individuals who do not clearly evidence any of Bleuler's diagnostic signs (fundamental-primary or secondary-accessory) may, nevertheless, be schizophrenic. He wrote: "There is also latent schizophrenia, and I am convinced that this is the most frequent form, although admittedly these people hardly ever come for treatment" (1950). Bleuler seemed to view schizophrenia in its "mild" and "latent" forms as pervasive, and noted that ten of his schoolmates later developed signs of schizophrenia.

Rieder (1974) has indicated two aspects of Bleuler's historic redefinition of dementia praecox as schizophrenia that have contributed significantly to its subsequent disfavor. First, the four fundamental signs set forth by Bleuler as the "objective" basis for the diagnosis of schizophrenia are frequently not easily identified. Bleuler's descriptions of the signs are often vague and contradictory. Observation of the signs requires considerable opportunity for the diagnostician to communicate and empathize with the patient, something that is often impossible in an institutional context. The following quotes from Bleuler's text regarding the identification of primary symptoms underscore this difficulty: "We may of course, at a given moment, be unable to demonstrate the presence of a symptom with the means at our disposal" (1911, p. 284). "Just how prominent the various symptoms have to be in order to permit a diagnosis of schizophrenia can hardly be described" (1911, p. 298). Second, Bleuler, like Kraepelin, confused his attempt to specify the objective signs which are the basis for grouping individuals under the label schizophrenia with the unsubstantiated belief that these signs were indicative of and caused by an organic disease process.

Bleuler and Kraepelin, trained as physicians, assumed organic causes for abnormal behavior, and sought medical explanations and understanding. Their system of classification was an attempt to define illness, not behavior and experience. For these men the overt psychological features of "schizophrenia" were merely surface expressions of an underlying organic disease.[1]

Rieder has observed that Bleuler was inconsistent on the issue of whether schizophrenia is a single disease or a group of separate disorders. Bleuler frequently referred to schizophrenia as one disease:

> The course of the cerebral disorder is chronic, for the most part, but there are also phases of acute forward thrusts or of standstill; the disturbance of the brain determines the primary symptoms (Bleuler, 1911, p. 463).

According to Rieder, Bleuler's integration of causal assumptions with his description of the syndrome has lead to much useless debate over such issues as which "symptoms" really are indicative of schizophrenia, and to prolonged diagnostic controversies over the proper definition of such concepts as *latent, pseudo-neurotic,* and *residual* schizophrenia. These issues arise only when it is assumed that the "underlying disease" is present in the absence of its primary signs.

[1] The introduction of phenothiazines (major tranquilizers) during the late 1950's breathed new life into theories of organic causation and encouraged many psychiatrists to again imagine that they need not devote attention to understanding the psycho-social origins, development, and symbolic content of schizophrenic reactions. The belief has grown that tranquilizing drugs at last allow psychiatrists to return to the main business of physicians, treating illness. As with antibiotics in the treatment of bacterial infection, it is now widely believed that tranquilizers will "cure" schizophrenia.

The Legacy of Kraepelin and Bleuler

Kraepelin and Bleuler made crucial contributions to the study of mental illness. They provided a wealth of systematic clinical observation as the basis for their attempts to formulate an underlying theoretical basis for grouping diverse subtypes into one disease syndrome, and effectively ordered the confusing maze of disease categories which characterized nineteenth century psychiatry. Their concepts stimulated a large body of valuable research, and continue to serve as the framework for contemporary psychiatric diagnosis.

REFERENCES

BLEULER, E. *Dementia Praecox or the Group of Schizophrenias,* translated by D. Zinkin. Zurich, International Universities Press, 1950 (German edition, 1911).

———. Kritik der Freudschen theorien. *Allg. Z. Psychiatrie, 70,* 1913, 665–719.

———. Störung der assoziationsspannung: ein elementärisches symptom der schizophrenie. *Allegmeine Zeitschrift für Allg. Z. Psychiatrie, 74,* 1920, 1–21.

———. *Textbook of Psychiatry,* translated by A. A. Brill. New York: Macmillan, 1924.

———. *Lehrbuch der Psychiatrie.* Stn. ed. Berlin: Springer, 1937, p. 316.

CANCRO, R. A review of current research directions: their product and their premise. In *The Schizophrenic Reactions,* edited by R. Cancro. New York: Brunner/Mazet, 1970.

FULLER-TORREY, E. *The Death of Psychiatry.* Radnor, Penna.: Chilton, 1974.

HECKER, B. Die helsphrenie. *Archiv für pathologische Anatomie und Physiologie und Klinishe Medizin, 52,* 1871, 394–429.

KAHLBAUM, D. K. *Die Gruppierung der psychischen Krankheiten.* Danzig: Kafemann, 1883.

KAHLBAUM, K. L. *Die Katatonie oder das Spannungeirresein.* Hirschwald, 1874.

KRAEPELIN, E. *Psychiatrie. Ein Lehrbuch für Studierende und Arzte.* Leipzig: Barth, 5th edition, 1896.

————. *Psychiatrie. Ein Lehrbuch für Studierende und Arzte.* Leipzig: Barth, 6th edition, 1899.

————. *Lectures on Clinical Psychiatry,* translated by T. Johnstone. New York: Hafner, 1968 (German edition, 1894).

————. *Psychiatrie. Ein Lehrbuch für Studierende und Arzte.* Leipzig: Barth, 7th edition, 1912.

MOREL, B. A. *Etudes Cliniques: Traite Theoretique et Practique de Maladies Mentales.* Paris: Masson, 1853.

RIEDER, R. O. The origins of our confusion about schizophrenia. *Psychiatry, 37,* 1974, 197–208.

STIERLIN, H. Bleuler's concept of schizophrenia: a confusing heritage. *American Journal of Psychiatry, 123,* 1967, 996–1001.

SULLIVAN, H. S. *Schizophrenia as a Human Process.* New York: Norton and Company. Copyright © by the William Alanson White Psychiatric Foundation, 1955.

Chapter Three

Definition by Description

Diagnosis and Scientific Classification

Scientific research is based on the establishment of reliable systems of classification. Classification is intended to simplify, order, and facilitate communication by bringing a group of related observations together into a single system. "The classification of facts, (and) the recognition of their sequence and relative significance is the function of science" (Pearson, 1951). Scientific classification is distinguished from mere cataloging of phenomena by the attempt to group observations according to an explanatory system of propositions which serves as a conceptual framework from which hypotheses about new orders of relationships can be generated. Systems of classification are not true or false, only useful or not useful in explaining our experiences.

Subtypes Based on Etiological Assumptions

In formulating the concept of dementia praecox, Kraepelin classified cases into categories based on descriptions of predominant behavioral manifestations. Diagnosis by subtypes is notoriously unreliable since many patients evidence at one time or another symptom patterns characteristic of each subgroup. Many clinicians reject subtypes as useless relics of the biological disease model, and argue that more is to be gained by studying each patient, his or her life experiences, and inadequacies and pertinent social forces. Because of their historic importance and continued widespread use, the subtypes of schizophrenia are described below.

Schizophrenia, simple type. This subtype is marked by insidious reduction of intellectual and emotional life and social attachments. The withdrawal is not related to discernible precipitating events, begins during early adolescence, and represents a quiet and unremarkable withdrawal into autistic fantasy.

Schizophrenia, hebephrenic type. The name for this subtype is derived from the Greek myth in which Hebe, the daughter of Zeus and Hera and cupbearer to the gods, sipped the wine she was bearing and slipped into a state of silly giggling and exuberance. This subtype is characterized by disorganized thinking, shallow, silly, and inappropriate affect and regressive behavior. Delusions and hallucinations are poorly organized.

Schizophrenia, catatonic type. This category is divided into two types. The excited type is marked by excessive motor activity and excitement, the withdrawn type by stupor, mutism, uncomfortable postures and automatism.

Schizophrenia, paranoid type. The paranoid subtype is identified primarily by the presence of persecutory or grandiose delusions. The onset is typically later in life than most other subtypes, with new cases appearing in patients in their thirties and forties. Excessive religious fervor and a suspicious, hostile attitude are often present.

Acute schizophrenic episode. This subtype is characterized by acute onset, associated with confusion, perplexity, emotional distress, dissociation, excitement, and fear. In time the individual may evidence complete remission or the symptom picture may change into one of the other subtypes.

Schizophrenia, latent type. This category is used to refer to individuals "having clear symptoms of schizophrenia but no history of a psychotic schizophrenic episode" (APA, DSMII, 1968).

Schizophrenia, residual type. This subtype is applied to individuals showing signs of schizophrenia but who, following a limited psychotic schizophrenic period, are no longer psychotic.

Schizophrenia, schizo-affective type. This category is applied to individuals who evidence a mixture of schizophrenic symptoms with pronounced elation or depression.

Schizophrenia, childhood type. This subtype refers to cases in which schizophrenic symptoms appear before puberty. Signs may include autistic and withdrawn behavior, failure to develop an identity separate from the mother's, gross immaturity, and developmental inadequacy.

Schizophrenia, chronic undifferentiated type. This category is used to refer to patients who present a mixed picture of definite signs of schizophrenic thought, affect, and behavior not classifiable under the other subtypes, and who have been diagnosed as schizophrenic for several years.

problems with subtypes

The heterogeneity of individuals diagnosed as schizophrenic has presented a major obstacle to scientific research. Attempts to reduce variability among research subjects by dividing patients into subtypes based on clinical symptoms have not been successful due to the unreliability of subtype diagnosis (Rotter, 1954; Zigler and Phillips, 1961). Critics argue that clinical subtypes are at best only loosely descriptive, that many patients evidence symptoms of more than one category, and that the clinical picture of many individuals changes from one symptom subtype to another within a relatively brief time. Unspecified factors have also resulted in the disuse of some subtypes in recent years. London (1968) for example, has reported that not one case of catatonic or hebephrenic schizophrenia appeared in the first admission records of one large mental hospital during a period of over five years.

Classification Based on Overt Behavior

The concept of schizophrenia was originally predicated upon physical, etiological assumptions. Many contemporary investigators believe, however, that it is both necessary and possible to formulate this concept as a descriptive category that is not tied to a particular set of etiological assumptions. Handlon (1960) has contrasted the referents of descriptive versus etiologic definitions of schizophrenia as "schizophrenia as overt behavior," and "schizophrenia as entity or process not necessarily revealed in overt behavior" (p. 56). The descriptive approach views schizophrenia as no more than a category of behavior which allows scientists and professionals to communicate with one another and to test theories about possible causes of this broad range of behavioral phenomena. The category is considered a necessary first step in the orderly scientific process of hypothesis-testing, empirical observation, and the eventual validation or rejection of theoretical models. In contrast to Kraepelin's and Bleuler's definitions of schizophrenia, the descriptive approach attempts to derive an empirical description of schizophrenia phenomena which is independent of particular etiologic (causal) assumptions.

It should be pointed out that a diverse and extensive group including Goffman (1961), Sarbin (1969), Scheff (1970), Menninger (1959), and R. D. Laing (1967) reject even the possibility of a useful descriptive category called schizophrenia. In their views, the very meaning and derivation of this term implies a model based on at least two objectionable assumptions: that behavior disorders can be divided into distinct and useful categories; and that schizophrenic disorders are caused by aberrant internal (psychic or somatic) processes.

The confused historical evolution of the concept of schizophrenia, and the multiplicity of theoretical models developed to explain this "disorder," have resulted in a welter of conflicting definitions. Contemporary diagnosticians claim variously that basic genetic, psychologic, neurologic, metabolic, or familial indices are the most effective criteria for classifying schizophrenia. There is at present no generally accepted way of integrating concepts and models based on such diverse observational data as social history, prognosis, presenting symptoms, subjective report, biochemical imbalance, and genetic groups into one system of classification. As Freeman (1969) has observed, schizophrenia is to some a disease with recognizable characteristics, to others, a group of poorly differentiated syndromes of multiple etiology, and to still others, a misleading, metaphorical concept which serves only to maintain the illusion that problems in living can be explained on the basis of organic disease.

A descriptive approach to the definition of schizophrenia is further complicated by the fact that schizophrenic phenomena are fluid, changing processes rather than static, qualitative differences. The schizophrenic patient does not evidence "symptoms" fixed in the manner of organic dementia and other physical disorders. Signs may be present one day and gone the next. The clinical picture may change dramatically, e.g., from catatonic to paranoid within a brief time. Signs and symptoms may not be exhibited consistently or uniformly across situations, or from one examiner to another. Furthermore, diagnostic signs are often based on the examiner's ability to interpret the patient's subjective experiences—interpretations considered irrelevant by theorists of different perspective. Despite these objections, many researchers and clinicians believe that it is possible to derive a useful, generally acceptable description of schizophrenic phenomena.

Several approaches have been used to derive a generally accepted descriptive system which will enable clinicians to recognize schizophrenics, including summaries of definitions and descriptions derived from the clinical literature, and statistical studies using cross-cultural designs to evaluate the effectiveness of various signs in distinguishing schizophrenics from nonschizophrenics.

clinical criteria

Freeman (1969) has presented a summary of the clinical criteria most widely used to arrive at a diagnosis of schizophrenia:

1. *Impairment of the capacity to relate to others,* manifested in a general loss of interest in external events, indifference to others, and identity confusion.
2. *Disturbances of speech,* including mutism, neologisms, and jargon-like speech.
3. *Disorders of thinking,* including overinclusiveness and concreteness, but not typified by any one particular pattern of disturbance. Two categories of thought disorganization are encountered in schizophrenic psychoses:
   a. Syncretic thought is so closely bound to personal needs that external reality is not differentiated in thought, and is structured by emotions and drives. A breakdown of the basic self/object discrimination and loss of self-autonomy is characteristic in such cases and is often associated with confused

speech characterized by neologism, fragmentation, and the concretization of meaning.

  b. A second pattern of thought disturbance is associated with logical and coherent communications in which ideas are valued for themselves and are endowed with a magical omnipotent power to alter the environment and/or the self.

4. Thought disturbance leads to the development of *delusional systems*. Delusions associated with syncretic thought disturbance are typically confused, disordered, disconnected, changing in content, lacking in an organized central theme, and divorced from recent or existing relationships. Complex, systematized delusions are observed in individuals characterized by the second category of thought disturbance, i.e., those who do not evidence severe impairment of affect, cognition, or volition. Grandiose, hypochondriacal, melancholic, and persecutory delusions are the most common categories. It is Freeman's view that all delusions have adaptive functions and provide a bridge to the external world. He lists three factors operative in delusional thought: 1) extreme egocentrism reflected in the patient's belief that he is the focus and cause of diverse activities; 2) an omnipotence usually attributed to self; 3) an active denial of facts which would undermine beliefs.

5. *Disorders of perception and self-awareness* include reports of synthesias [confusion of sensory experience], hypersensitivity of sensory systems, and disturbances of perceptual processes. Perceptual disorders in chronic, withdrawn patients appear to be related to a general inattention to external events. Freeman observes that there is substantial evidence that withdrawn patients can become quite active and alert at mealtimes or when offered high-interest items such as cigarettes. External perception in withdrawn patients is conditioned by needs, and appears to be impaired in most cases because social interest is minimal. For many chronic schizophrenics, other individuals exist only as instruments for the satisfaction of personal needs. Auditory hallucinations in which the patient hears his or her own fantasies, thoughts, or wishes are the most commonly reported form of perceptual disturbance.

6. *Psychomotor phenomena* are evidenced in disturbances of voluntary movement, e.g., repetitive movements, unusual postures, and motor blocking.

7. There is no single pattern of *affective disturbance* associated with the diagnosis of schizophrenia. Disturbance may be evidenced in the form of elation, depression, anxiety, self-criticism, and dread in acutely disturbed patients. Flat and inappropriate affect have traditionally been regarded as characteristic of long-term patients.

Freeman has observed, however, that psychotherapeutic studies indicate that there is no permanent, irreversible impairment of affective potential in schizophrenia; it is rather the likelihood and manner of expression which is disturbed.

cross-cultural signs and symptoms

Carpenter and his associates (1974) have used extensive statistical analyses and cross-cultural research methods to derive "unbiased" signs and symptoms for distinguishing schizophrenics from non-schizophrenics. They have devised a simple diagnostic system based on twelve signs and symptoms, the presence of any five of which has been shown to reliably diagnose 80 percent of schizophrenics. The twelve diagnostic symptoms derived by Carpenter and his colleagues are as follows:

Restricted affect	Elation (−)
Poor insight	Widespread delusions
Thinking aloud	Incoherent speech
Waking early (−)*	Unreliable information
Poor rapport	Bizarre delusions
Depressed facies (−)	Nihilistic delusions

* (−) sign given negative weight

subjective descriptions of schizophrenic experiences

Experiences appear to vary in accordance with personal history and the pattern of onset of the disorder. For example, the diagnosis of schizophrenia is applied to many individuals who do not evidence an abrupt transition from apparent normal function to schizophrenic disorganization. These individuals typically have a long history of marginal social adjustment, parental overprotection, isolation, vague thinking, and blandness of affect which gradually—over a period of years—results in bizarre, eccentric, or dangerous behavior, and hospitalization. Detailed subjective accounts of the experience of this process are not available since such individuals are usually unable to be self-reflective and to acquire or re-establish the verbal skills necessary to describe their experiences. Most available material has been derived from a select category of schizophrenics—those who managed a superficially normal life adjustment into periods ranging from late adolescence to middle-age before experiencing a relatively abrupt transition to schizophrenic psychosis. This acute schizophrenic breakdown experience is associated with mounting anxiety, tension, distractibility, fear of personal dissolution (loss of identity), and a sense of loss of direct connection with interpersonal reality.

The Build-Up. Kolb (1973) has provided an excellent composite summary of the acute schizophrenic experience. In his view, no single feature is definitely indicative of an acute schizophrenic reaction. The pre-schizophrenic individual is often described as aloof, unempathic, unrealistic, lonely, suffering from a sense of rejection and lack of self-respect. An overwhelming sense of resentment and frustration and the need for self-protection lead to withdrawal from emotional involvement with other people. Marriage may become a means of "proving" masculinity or femininity, a financial convenience, a way of transferring dependency needs, of expressing anger, or of demonstrating the ability to conceive a child. It will not be a long-term, intimate, shared experience. Individuals in this category often affect attitudes of superiority, and of disdain for convention and social amenities. Hypochondriacal physical concerns are common. All relationships are representative of a pattern of autistic dramatization experienced without full affective contact with life, as though there is a screen between the inner person and interpersonal reality. Increased social responsibility, a real or imagined interpersonal loss or rejection, or personal failure often appear to precipitate the acute schizophrenic "break."

The Break. This "break" is marked by a period of affective disturbance in which the individual is unable to feel and regulate emotions normally. Emotional expression appears to be related to highly personalized internal processes rather than external reality. This period is associated with feelings of vagueness, of unreality, detachment, and depersonalization, which culminate in intense anxiety. In a sense, the limits of the personality have been lost. The patient feels at this point that he or she no longer has the internal personality structure necessary to maintain the basic distinction between self and other. The acute schizophrenic patient may feel that aspects of his or her thoughts and body are alien; and that coincidental external events have an uncanny personal significance. A sense of heightened awareness, of being possessed by strange, alien forces, of being overwhelmed by strange impulses, may lead to ideas of reference [random events assume personal significance] and periods of religious fervor and preoccupation. A strong sense of unreality often leads to thought-blocking, stupor, dream-like states and other attempts to withdraw from this nightmare experience. In such cases, attention is increasingly narrowed and centered on subjective content. Rapid mood changes and affective inconsistencies contribute to an impression of severe personality disorganization.

Perceptual disorders include shifting, unrealistic perceptions of self and others. Inner experiences are projected onto the external world in the form of perceptual images. Emotions, impulses, and guilt feelings are experienced as external voices or images, auditory or visual hallucinations. The schizophrenic individual may eventually find the hallucinations so compelling and serviceable that he or she is unwilling to relinquish them (see the case of Kevin in Chapter 4). The hallucinatory world may become such a cherished, protected (though rarely altogether pleasant) world that the patient never leaves it. Bizarre, impulsive actions may result from a lack of personality integration and harmonious association of affects, motives, and conscience. Negativism, withdrawal and lack of energy have been interpreted as means adopted by the patients to renounce the world with which they cannot cope. Thought and communication may variously appear fragmented, eccentric, amorphous, overly intellectualized, and metaphorical. Communications may be meaningful to the sufferer, but seem bizarre and eccentric to others. Initial excitement and flight of ideas may develop into incoherence. Cases of gradual onset are likely to show a poverty of thought and communication, often associated with a long process of autistic withdrawal and narrowing of attention. Kolb believes that the basis of schizophrenic thought disorders is found in the extent to which associations are directed by internal perceptions and meanings unrelated to or imposed upon occurrences in the immediate environment.

The dominant ideational content of the schizophrenic is typically delusional in nature. Delusions are widely considered to be attempts to establish some order over the chaotic experiences associated with altered sensory and perceptual input and widened categories of relevance predominant during the initial stage of acute breakdown. Delusions appear to serve to subjectively reorganize life situations in a manner which allows the patient to live with frustrations, insecurities, inadequacies, disowned qualities and impulses, and guilt in disguised, projected, and symbolic form. Delusions are experienced as irrefutable facts, and are meaning structures of intense importance to the schizophrenic patient.

Bowers (1968) has formulated the following summary of the sequence of events typically associated with the formation of delusions in cases of acute schizophrenic reaction: (1) impasse, dread, and overwhelming anxiety; (2) altered experience of self and world; (3) the need to "make sense" of the experience; (4) overcoming of the constraints imposed by normal reality guards; and (5) a certain relief and comfort (even elation) experienced with the emergence of the delusional idea.

lorr's statistical approach to classification

Lorr and his associates (1966) have employed complex statistical procedures (factor analysis and cluster analysis) to develop alternative systems for the classification of psychotic disorders. The dimensions obtained from this technique are derived from ratings of interview data however, and are limited by the validity of the initial observations.

The specific first-order factors (these factors are derived on the basis of intercorrelations between specific items) obtained from Lorr's interviews with acute psychotic patients are as follows:

1. *Excitement:* The patients' speech is hurried, loud, and difficult to stop. Mood level and self-esteem are elevated, and emotional expression tends to be unrestrained or histrionic. The patients are also likely to exhibit controlling or dominant behavior.
2. *Hostile Belligerence:* The patients' attitudes toward others are ones of disdain and moroseness. They are likely to manifest much hostility, resentment, and a complaining bitterness. Difficulties and failures tend to be blamed on others.
3. *Paranoid Projection:* The patients give evidence of fixed beliefs that attribute a hostile, persecuting, and controlling intent to those around them.

4. *Grandiose Expansiveness:* The patients' attitudes toward others are ones of superiority. They exhibit fixed beliefs that they possess unusual powers. They report divine missions and may identify themselves with well-known or historical personalities.

5. *Perceptual Distortions:* The patients report hallucinations (voices and visions) that threaten, accuse, or demand.

6. *Anxious Intropunitiveness:* The patients report vague apprehension as well as specific anxieties. Attitudes toward the self are disparaging. They are also prone to report feelings of guilt and remorse for real and imagined faults. The underlying mood is typically dysphoric.

7. *Retardation and Apathy:* The patients' speech, ideation, and motor activity are delayed, slowed, or blocked. In addition, they are likely to manifest apathy and disinterest in the future.

8. *Disorientation:* The patients' orientation with respect to time, place, and season is defective. They may fail to recognize those around them.

9. *Motor Disturbances:* The patients assume and maintain bizarre postures, and make repetitive facial and body movements.

10. *Conceptual Disorganization:* Disturbances in the patients' stream of thought are manifested in irrelevant, incoherent, and rambling speech. Repetition of stereotyped phrases and coining of new words are also common (Lorr et al., 1963).

Additional factor rotations (completed to maximize item loadings) suggest that the acute-psychotic population can be represented by the following six types: (1) Excited-Grandiose; (2) Excited-Hostile; (3) Retarded; (4) Intropunitive; (5) Hostile-Paranoid; and (6) Disorganized. Lorr's types hold promise for increased reliability of categorization [across clinicians and locations] of acutely disturbed schizophrenic patients into subgroups that will facilitate the specification of the contributions of causal variables.

single-parameter classification

Other attempts to reduce variance within the schizophrenic population have focused on three sets of variables: the quality of the patient's pre-breakdown social adequacy (process-reactive); the acuteness (or chronicity) of the disorder; and symptomatology (paranoid-nonparanoid).

the process-reactive distinction

The historic concern of psychiatry with prognosis has served as the basis for the evolution of the distinction between process and reactive schizophrenia. Kraepelin originally chose general paralysis as the disease model for creating his system of psychiatric classification. This model led to the expectation that each disorder should be classified in terms of a specific etiology, a determinate course, and an inevitable outcome. Kraepelin's emphasis on outcome originated from a theoretical-diagnostic base in which diagnosis and prognosis were assumed invariant (Garmezy, 1970). Thus, diagnosis was validated by outcome. Kraepelin and Bleuler, wedded to the assumption of biological cause, emphasized the importance of post-breakdown clinical symptoms as predictors of outcome. In contrast, the psychological perspective of Sullivan (1955) and others led to an emphasis on pre-breakdown social and psychological variables as outcome predictors. Variability of outcome has led many workers to suggest that there may be crucial differences between those schizophrenic patients who eventually improve and those who do not. This has led some investigators (Garmezy, 1970; Langfeldt, 1956; Schneider, 1959) to divide schizophrenics into two groups, differentiated on the basis of such variables as pre-breakdown social history, course of disturbance, and outcome.

Bleuler first adopted the differentiation between "process schizophrenia" and "reactive schizophrenia" in the fourth edition of his textbook (1923). He speculated that these forms of schizophrenia overlap in terms of symptomatology but might have different causes—the former having a chiefly organic etiology, the latter a psychogenic one. This distinction has had mixed results; it has given rise to numerous diagnostic obscurities and etiologic misunderstandings as well as to useful research categories.

Langfeldt (1956) refers to patients characterized by an inadequate prepsychotic adjustment as *process schizophrenics*. He has observed that this group tends to become chronically institutionalized. Langfeldt refers to a second group of patients, characterized by rapid, acute onset of symptoms under circumstances in which the premorbid personality is relatively well integrated, as suffering from *schizophreniform psychosis.* Langfeldt introduced this term because he wanted to emphasize his belief that, although the syndrome might appear to be very similar to schizophrenia, *"it is not schizophrenia."* [The concept of *reactive* schizophrenia has replaced Langfeldt's schizophreniform.] At times, however, other analogous categories are used to categorize groups of patients: true/schizophreniform, dementia praecox/schizophrenia, typical/atypical, chronic/episodic, psychogenic/degenerative.

Garmezy has described the *process-schizophrenic* as follows:

> The patient's prepsychotic personality is a poorly integrated one revealing markedly inadequate behavior in the sexual, social, and occupational areas; trends to social isolation and a lack of emotional responsibility to others are clearly evident. There is usually no acute precipitant to characterize the turn toward psychosis; rather, the onset (usually in late adolescence) is an insidious one without a recognizable and consensually validated stressor evident. Symptomatically, there is a gradual onset of emotional blunting, a withdrawal from life's daily activity; apathy and indifference hold sway, and somatic delusions and marked disturbances in thinking may characteristically be present and maintained for long periods of time (1970, p. 35).

The *reactive patient* is described by Wiener as follows:

> From birth to the fifth year, the maturational and developmental history showed no defects, physical health was good. Generally school and home adjustment was good. Parents were accepting. Heterosexual relationships were established. The patient had friends, and domestic troubles did not disrupt his behavior.
>
> The onset of the illness was often sudden with a clear-cut, understandable precipitating event. Aggression was expressed verbally. Decency was retained. The course was fulminating, with massive hallucinatory experiences, ideas of reference, and mild paranoid trends, as well as sensorial impairment. A thought disorder was present according to some observers, but not others. Response to treatment was good (1958, p. 158).

Phillips (1953) has developed a three-part process-reactive scale by which patients' case histories can be rated according to premorbid history, including items pertaining to recent sexual adjustment, social aspects of recent sexual life, past history, and recent adjustment in personal relations; precipitating factors; and present signs of schizophrenic disorder.

Harris' (1975) abbreviated form of Phillips' original five-section scale is presented below.

Abbreviated Scale of Premorbid Sexual Adjustment

Category	Score
1. Married, Presently or Formerly	
A. Married, only one marriage (or remarried only one time as a consequence of death of spouse), living as a unit	
a. Adequate heterosexual relations achieved	0
b. Low sexual drive, difficult sexual relations, or extramarital affairs, either partner	1
B. Married, more than one time, maintained a home in one marriage for at least 5 years	
a. Adequate sexual relations during at least one marriage	1
b. Chronically inadequate sexual life	2
C. Married and apparently permanently separated or divorced without remarriage, but maintained a home in one marriage for at least 5 years	2
D. Same as C., but maintained a home in one marriage for less than 5 years	3
2. Single (30 Years or Over)	
A. Has been engaged one or more times or has had a long-term relationship (at least 2 years) involving heterosexual relations or apparent evidence for a "love affair" with one person, but unable to achieve marriage	3
B. Brief or short-term heterosexual or social dating experiences with one or more partners, but no long-lasting sexual experiences with a single partner	4
C. Sexual and/or social relationships primarily with the same sex, but may have had occasional heterosexual contacts or dating experiences	5
D. Minimal sexual or social interest in either men or women	6
3. Single (Under 30 Years, Age 20–29)*	
A. Has had at least one long-term "love affair" (minimum of 6	

* The scoring category 0 has been eliminated in the absence of evidence that the single person, age 20–29, will ever achieve marriage. Although a significant percentage of such subjects may eventually marry, no serious scoring error is made by assigning these subjects a conservative score of 1.

Category   *Score*

  months to 1 year), or engagement, even though religious or
  other prohibitions may have prevented actual sexual union
  a. If ever actually engaged 1
  b. Otherwise 2
 B. Brief or short-term heterosexual or social dating experiences,
  "love affairs," with one or more partners, but no long-lasting
  sexual experiences with a single partner 3
 C. Casual sexual or social relationships with persons or either
  sex, with no deep emotional meaning 4
 D. Sexual and/or social relationships primarily with the same sex,
  but may have had occasional heterosexual contacts or dating
  experiences 5
 E. Minimal sexual or social interest in either men or women 6

Abbreviated Scale of Premorbid Social-Personal Adjustment

Category   *Score*

 A. A leader or officer in formally designated groups, clubs,
  organizations, or athletic teams in senior high school,
  vocational school, college, or in young adulthood 0
 B. An active and interested participant, but did not play a
  leading role in groups of friends, clubs, organizations, or
  athletic teams in senior high school, vocational school,
  college, or in young adulthood 1
 C. A nominal member, but had no involvement in, or commitment to, groups of friends, clubs, organizations, or athletic
  teams in senior high school, vocational school, college, or in
  young adulthood 2
 D. From adolescence through early adulthood, had only a few
  casual or close friends 3
 E. From adolescence through early adulthood, had no real
  friends, only a few superficial relationships or attachments to
  others 4
 F. From adolescence through early adulthood (i.e., after
  childhood), quiet, seclusive, preferred to be by self; minimal
  efforts to maintain any contact at all with others 5
 G. No desire to be with playmates, peers, or others, from early
  childhood. Either asocial or antisocial 6

Note. This scale should prove to be of particular value in cases (e.g., single persons) in which formal marital status or sexual adjustment is viewed as an unfair or inadequate estimate of premorbid adjustment.

Grouping schizophrenics into process-reactive subtypes has been found to markedly reduce group heterogeneity. Research indicates that these groups can be differentiated on the following criteria: autonomic nervous system arousal and responsiveness, conceptual functioning, linguistic and associative processes, learning and performance, censure sensitivity, parent perception, and family dynamics (Higgins, 1969). This distinction is of particular value because it is based on relatively objective data and has good predictive validity. Reactive patients have been found to have a higher probability of discharge and brief hospitalization, for example, are less likely to be rehospitalized (Strauss, 1973), and show less psychological deficit at first hospitalization (Higgins, 1969) than do process patients. Recent evidence also suggests that process patients are more likely to benefit from major tranquilizers than some categories of reactive patients (Goldstein et al., 1969). Chapman and Chapman (1973) have reviewed the literature comparing process and reactive patients and conclude that these groups can be reliably differentiated on the following measures: problem solving, proverb interpretation, abstract thinking, and word associations. The performance of process patients is generally below that of reactives on each of these measures.

Garmezy (1970) believes that there are at least two matrices of variables in schizophrenia, the process-reactive dimension, and a genetic component. He suggests that the genetic component is differentially weighted in process as opposed to reactive schizophrenia. Several studies have provided data which support Garmezy's conclusion. Kringlen (1968), for example, found the concordance rate in monozygotic twins for reactive schizophrenia to be twenty-five percent compared to sixty percent for long-term, chronically deteriorated patients. Rosenthal and Kety (1968) have studied the biological and adoptive families of adopted schizophrenics, and report evidence which suggests the presence of differentially weighted genetic components in process as opposed to reactive schizophrenia. These authors found that schizophrenic spectrum disorders were observed to be common in biological family members of chronic and borderline adopted schizophrenics, but that no instances of such disorders were observed for the relatives of acute schizophrenic patients.

The process-reactive dimension has proved to be a useful method for accounting for the heterogeneous behavior of schizophrenic patients. Many psychopathologists have come to regard process and reactive categories as two distinct types of schizophrenia rather than end points on a continuum (Chapman and Chapman, 1974). Despite the promise of this method of categorizing patients, the process-reactive dimension is not a simple one, for it appears to be confounded with such variables as social class (Zigler and Levine, 1973) and symptomatology (Goldstein et al., 1968). Critics also argue that process and reactive types represent extremes on a continuum but fail to adequately characterize the majority of schizophrenics, who fall midway along the process-reactive continuum (Freeman, 1969).

the acute-chronic classification

A second procedure for classifying schizophrenic patients is to group them according to the length of time which has elapsed since they were first officially diagnosed as schizophrenic. *Acute schizophrenia* refers to the initial or early stages of the schizophrenic experience, but the term is often broadened in research studies to refer to patients with less than three years of hospitalization. *Chronic schizophrenia* is used in research to refer to individuals who have remained institutionalized for a total of six years or more. This system of classification permits greater objectivity of grouping since both categories can be defined in terms of numbers of years of hospitalization. This distinction is hampered by the poor reliability of clinical diagnosis and is limited by the lack of reliable information, other than official diagnosis, as to the time of onset of schizophrenic behavior.

Chronicity has also been confused with the process-reactive distinction in the literature. The common practice of judging acute versus chronic on the basis of the rapidity of symptom onset as well as length of hospitalization has contributed to confusion with the process category.

Broen and Storms (1968) have observed that chronicity in schizophrenics is associated with change toward growing detachment from both external and internal stimulation. Research evidence indicates that long-term and short-term schizophrenics can be distinguished on measures of cognition, intellectual functioning and perception (Broen and Storms, 1968; Draguns, 1963), but it is not clear why they differ. Are these differences the result of fundamental differences between groups or of the indirect effects of long-term institutionalization? Chronicity has been demonstrated to relate negatively to probability of discharge and successful adjustment to life outside the hospital (Brown, 1960).

Chapman and Chapman (1974) have observed that chronic schizophrenics show more severe thought disorder and less efficient intellectual functioning than acute patients. They note, however, that chronic schizophrenics with several years of hospitalization do not become less accurate on most intellectual tests after several years of additional hospitalization. It is possible that the most outstanding feature associated with increasing chronicity in schizophrenics, progressive withdrawal from interpersonal communication and contact, is an artifact of prolonged institutionalization.

the paranoid-nonparanoid distinction

A third grouping is based on observations of symptomatology. Research suggests that the paranoid-nonparanoid dimension may also be a valuable clinical distinction. Paranoid schizophrenics have been demonstrated to be superior to nonparanoids on measures of intelligence (Payne, 1961), reaction time (Court and Garrvoli, 1968), and attentional processes (Silverman, 1964). Paranoids have also been demonstrated to be less distractible than nonparanoids (McGhie et al., 1965). Paranoid schizophrenics show different patterns of hospitalization (Strauss, 1973); they tend to be hospitalized for relatively brief periods. The paranoid-nonparanoid distinction has been valuable in the search for symptom clusters related to drug response. Judd (1973), for example, has reported evidence that reactive nonparanoid patients, in contrast to reactive paranoids, may not benefit from phenothiazine medication. Research suggests that paranoid patients generally show fewer signs of cognitive and behavioral deterioration than do nonparanoids.

criticisms of overt behavior diagnosis

The purpose of classification is threefold: to facilitate communication, to assist in the discovery of causes, to assist in treatment and control (Spitzer and Endicott, 1969). The descriptive systems presented in this chapter have attempted to improve reliability of communication between scientists and professionals by providing empirically derived summaries of behavioral signs. Carpenter's system, in particular, shows high reliability across a range of diagnosticians. The descriptive summaries presented by Freeman and Kolb provide a richer descriptive picture but lack evidence of statistical reliability. It is paradoxical that each of these systems, despite the determination to avoid etiological assumptions, is in fact based on a model of classification (diagnosis) that implies cause. All assume that these behaviors are best understood in terms of a medical framework, rather than a social, psychological, or economic one. Descriptive diagnostic systems are based on behavioral observations that are considered "symptomatic" of an illness category.

At this point it may be helpful to consider Cancro's (1975) discussion of the distinction between diagnosis and classification. He points out that a diagnosis is a statement about what is assumed to be the cause of a person's problems at a given time, in a particular context. It is an effort to combine general knowledge about a category of illness with specific knowledge about an individual as a means of helping that person. Classification is quite different. It is an attempt to organize data into a comprehensible system based on our particular cognitive framework (the way we think about the phenomena observed). Classification imposes our understanding on data by ordering it in a particular fashion. Classification and diagnosis are the same only if we assume a biological-illness model.

Cancro has argued that the current diagnosis of schizophrenia as a single disease is not helpful. He claims that the variation is too great for this broad category to include only one disorder or type of illness. He suggests that schizophrenia has some limited diagnostic usefulness only when considered as a group of end states arrived at through different pathways from different conditions. The category cannot be independently validated, however, and so does not increase our understanding of the process. We can only conclude that for unspecified reasons the individual's previous adaptation to his or her environment failed at the time of the psychotic break and that a process of achieving a new steady state was initiated. There is no agreement as to whether schizophrenia is this process, or, as diagnostic categories imply, the end state itself.

An important criticism of the diagnostic systems formulated

by Kolb, Carpenter, and others, derives from their focus on a set of symptoms within a brief time period, symptoms that may change from one social context to another and over time. Critics argue that the systems ignore readily attainable life history data on the individual's social adjustment prior to diagnosis. Let us consider patients X and Y as examples. Both may be diagnosed schizophrenic because they manifest bizarre delusions. Patient X completed fifth grade, had a long history of childhood emotional difficulties and poor social adjustment, had never worked or dated, and lived with his eccentric, aged parents until his bizarre behavior was brought to the attention of the police. Patient Y, on the other hand, was married, the father of several children, and held a responsible position for over fifteen years prior to his schizophrenic break, which was associated with the accidental death of his son. Both patients receive the same diagnosis in Carpenter's system, yet life history data suggest that there are important differences between them that probably relate to the relative significance of different causal factors, and to what courses of treatment are most likely to be successful.

According to Cancro, the concept of schizophrenia is too broad and is based on too limited a sample of observational data to serve as anything more than a preliminary construct that must in turn be replaced by more specific classifications based on process as well as sign.

The history of the concept of schizophrenia is marked by a series of fluctuations in emphasis and perspective. The definitions of schizophrenia used by contemporary psychiatrists, despite increased clarity of definition and diagnostic reliability, present static, cross-sectional views of individual lives. The primary diagnosis of schizophrenia is still based exclusively on immediate signs of disturbance. This approach ignores the possible adaptive function of these behaviors as well as the circumstances and processes of their development. The symptomatic focus of psychiatric diagnosis inevitably leads to confusion in attempts to discover cause because any behavioral end state can be arrived at from a number of different initial conditions and through a variety of pathways.

Until investigators can identify independent validating signs appropriate to their particular level of focus (blood tests, for example, or measures of thought disturbance); the process-reactive and paranoid-nonparanoid dimensions appear to offer the most promise for clarifying the present muddle of schizophrenia research. Despite the problems of a dichotomous system of classification, and the confouding of these dimensions with such variables as length of hospitalization, social class, and intelligence, both have facilitated the reliable differentiation of subgroups of schizophrenic patients on a large number of useful indices (Higgins, 1969). Overall ratings of patients according to pre-breakdown social, sexual, and vocational history, precipitating factors, and present signs, have been the most useful. This approach suggests that the most fruitful course to follow in future research is the differentiation of subgroups of patients who show signs of severe or mild disruption of inter-personal function and differ in pre-breakdown characteristics which predict recovery rate and degree of recovery (Goldstein, 1973). Development of improved scales for rating patients will un-doubtedly facilitate future research.

REFERENCES

BLEULER, E. *Lehrbuch der Psychiatrie.* Berlin: Springer, 1923.

BOWERS, M. Pathogenesis of acute schizophrenic psychosis. *Archives of General Psychiatry, 19,* 1968, 348–355.

BROEN, W. E. and L. H. STORMS. Lawful disorganization: the process underlying a schizophrenic syndrome. *Psychological Review, 73,* 1966, 265–279.

BROWN, G. W. Length of hospital stay and schizophrenia: a review of statistical studies. *Acta Psychiatrica Neurologia Scandinavia, 35,* 1960, 414–430.

CANCRO, R. Genetic considerations in the etiology and prevention of schizophrenia. In *Schizophrenia: Biological and Psychological Perspectives,* edited by G. Usdin. New York: Brunner/Mazet, 1975.

CARPENTER, W. T., J. S. STRAUSS, and J. J. BARTKO. The diagnosis and understanding of schizophrenia. Part 1: Use of signs and symptoms for the identification of schizophrenia patients. *Schizophrenia Bulletin, 11,* 1974, 37–49.

CHAPMAN, L. J. and J. P. CHAPMAN. *Disordered Thought in Schizophrenia.* New York: Appleton-Century-Crofts, 1973.

COURT, J. H., and E. GARIVOLI. Schizophrenic performance on a reaction-time task with increasing levels of complexity. *British Journal of Social and Clinical Psychology, 7,* 1968, 216–223.

Diagnostic and Statistical Manual of Mental Disorders, Second Edition. Washington, D.C.: American Psychiatric Association, 1968.

DRAGUNS, J. G. Responses to cognitive and perceptual ambiguity in chronic and acute schizophrenics. *Journal of Abnormal (and Social) Psychology, 66,* 1963, 24–30.

FREEMAN, T. Symptomatology, diagnosis and clinical course. In *The Schizophrenic Syndrome,* edited by L. Bellak. New York: Grune and Stratton, 1969.

GARMEZY, N. Process and reactive schizophrenia: some conceptions and issues. *Schizophrenia Bulletin, 2,* 1970, 30–67.

GOFFMAN, E. *Asylums.* Chicago: Aldine, 1968.

GOLDSTEIN, M. J. Premorbid adjustment and paranoid status as significant variations in schizophrenia research. Paper presented at the Annual Meeting of the American Psychological Association, Montreal, Canada, 1973.

GOLDSTEIN, M. J., J. M. HELD, and R. L. CROMWELL. Premorbid adjustment and paranoid-nonparanoid status in schizophrenia. *Psychological Bulletin, 70,* 1968, 382–386.

HANDLON, J. H. A metatheoretical view of assumptions regarding the etiology of schizophrenia. *Archives of General Psychiatry, 2,* 1960, 43–60.

HARRIS, J. G. Abbreviated form of the Phillips Rating Scale of Premorbid Adjustment in Schizophrenia. *Journal of Abnormal Psychology, 84,* 1975, 129–137.

HIGGINS, J. Process-reactive schizophrenia. *Journal of Nervous and Mental Disease, 149(6),* 1969, 450–465.

JUDD, L., M. GOLDSTEIN, E. RODNICK, and N. JACKSON. Phenothiazine effects in good premorbid schizophrenics divided into paranoid-nonparanoid status. *Archives of General Psychiatry, 29,* 1973, 207–211.

KOLB, L. *Modern Clinical Psychiatry.* Philadelphia: Saunders, 8th edition, 1973.

KRINGLEN, E. An epidemiological clinical twin study on schizophrenia. In *The Transmission of Schizophrenia,* edited by D. Rosenthal and S. S. Kety. New York: Pergamon Press, 1968.

LAING, R. D. *The Politics of Experience.* New York: Penguin, 1967.

LANGFELDT, G. The prognosis in schizophrenia. *Acta Psychiatrica Scandivanica,* Supplementun, *110,* 1956.

LONDON, P. The major psychological disorders. In *Foundations of Abnormal Psychology,* edited by P. London and D. Rosenthal. New York: Holt, Rinehart and Winston, 1968.

LORR, M. (Ed.). *Explorations in Typing Psychotics.* New York: Pergamon Press, 1966.

McGHIE, A., J. CHAPMAN, and J. S. LAWSON. The effect of distraction on schizophrenic performance. (1) Perception and immediate memory. *British Journal of Psychiatry, 111,* 1965, 383–390.

MENNINGER, K. Psychiatric diagnosis. *Bulletin of the Menninger Clinic, 23,* 1959, 226–240.

PAYNE, R. W. Cognitive abnormalities. In *Handbook of Abnormal Psychology,* edited by H. J. Eysenck. New York: Basic Books, 1961.

PEARSON, K. *The Grammar of Science.* London: Dent, 1951.

PHILLIPS, L. Case history data and prognosis in schizophrenia. *Journal of Nervous and Mental Disease, 117,* 1953, 515–525.

ROSENTHAL, D. and S. S. KETY (Eds.). *The Transmission of Schizophrenia.* New York: Pergamon Press, 1968.

ROTTER, J. *Social Learning and Clinical Psychology.* Englewood Cliffs, N.J.: Prentice-Hall, 1954.

SARBIN, T. On the futility of the proposition that some people be labeled "mentally ill." *Journal of Consulting Psychology, 31,* 1967, 447–453.

SCHEFF, T. J. Schizophrenia as ideology. *Schizophrenia Bulletin, 2,* 1970, 15–19.

SCHNEIDER, K. *Clinical Psychopathology,* translated by M. W. Hamilton. New York: Grune and Stratton, 5th edition, 1959.

SILVERMAN, J. The problem of attention in research and theory in schizophrenia. *Psychological Review, 71,* 1964, 352–379.

SPITZER, R. L. and J. ENDICOTT. Diagno II: further developments in a computer program for psychiatric diagnosis. *American Journal of Psychiatry, 125,* 1969, 12–21.

STRAUSS, M. E. Behavioral differences between acute and chronic schizophrenics: course of psychosis, effects of institutionalization, or sampling biases. *Psychological Bulletin, 79,* 1973, 271–279.

SULLIVAN, H. S. *Schizophrenia As a Human Process.* New York: W. W. Norton, 1968.

WIENER, H. Diagnosis and symptomatology. In *Schizophrenia: A Review of the Syndrome,* edited by L. Bellak, pp. 107–173. New York: Logos Press, 1958.

WITTENBORN, J. R. *Wittenborn Psychiatric Rating Scales.* New York: Psychological Corporation, 1955.

ZIGLER, E. and J. LEVINE. Premorbid adjustment and paranoid-nonparanoid status in schizophrenia: a further investigation. *Proceedings, 81st Annual Convention, American Psychological Association,* 1973, 477–478.

Chapter Four

Five Persons Called Schizophrenic

In insanity we do not discover anything new and unknown; we are looking at the foundations of our own being, the matrix of those vital problems on which we are all engaged . . . it makes no difference to the facts whether these disturbances are called dementia praecox or by some other name.

—C. G. Jung

The case histories and interviews included in this chapter are composites based on material gathered from numerous sources over the past eleven years. These portraits were drawn to represent a reasonable cross-section of persons labeled schizophrenic. They do not represent a random sample of the millions of Americans so labeled. The multiple and ever-changing diagnoses, the continuous juggling of prescribed tranquilizing drugs, the recurrent cycle of admission, medication, diagnosis, and return to unchanged life circumstances that were experienced prior to admission, are facts of daily life, however, for thousands of "schizophrenic" persons.

The student should read these case examples carefully, for they provide the ground from which all theoretical perspectives are to be understood. The cases are depressingly common. These are individuals who have been institutionalized in most cases more than once, as are most patients diagnosed as schizophrenic. The background material on each individual is brief, limited in scope, and focused on specific events, as it is in most hospital records and psychiatric social histories.

WINSTON AND THE STARSHIP

Winston, a twenty-eight-year-old black man, was born in a small farm community, the youngest of a family of seven siblings and five half-siblings. His family was poor and managed financially only with the help of welfare. His father was killed in an auto accident when Winston was five and his mother has worked as a motel maid since that time. There is no reported history of mental illness in the family. Two brothers have been hospitalized for alcoholism. Winston was described by his mother and sister as a quiet, religious child, a loner who was most interested in radio kits and electronics. Winston reportedly wanted to be a preacher, and read the Bible frequently. He was described as a happy child and an "ideal" teenager who excelled in school. He was, however, troubled by frequent nightmares during his senior year of high school, but managed to win a full scholarship to a prestigious eastern university. Winston had successfully completed three and one-half years of an engineering curriculum when one day, in the midst of final exams, he received notice from his selective service board to report for a draft physical. Two weeks after reporting for the physical Winston was picked up on the streets adjacent to the university acting frightened and con-fused. Upon hospital admission he stated that he was "Christ dying on the cross in order to save the world from evil." The diagnosis was *schizophrenic reaction, catatonic type,* and Winston was started on heavy dosages of tranquilizing medication. Winston's family believed that several factors might have precipitated this break: receipt of notice for the draft physical; his recent breakup with his steady girlfriend; and worry over his mother's worsened heart condition.

Winston was released to his family five months after his initial hospitalization. Shortly thereafter he began pacing the floor restlessly, reciting scientific information from his college courses, and stating over and over that "the starship is coming." He was re-hospitalized in a private psychiatric hospital three weeks after his discharge. This time the diagnosis was *schizophrenic reaction, paranoid type.* One week later he was transferred to a state hospital where his diagnosis was changed to *schizophrenic reaction, catatonic type.* He stated during a staff interview at this time that God had chosen him for a special purpose and that he was endowed with supernatural powers. He described his recent expe-riences while at home as a "crucifixion" and referred repeatedly to the admitting physician as a Russian spy with the KGB.

One month later Winston informed a staff psychologist that his ideas about being God were all in the past and that he believed that he must have gotten sick from studying too hard and worrying about the draft. He was released to return to college that January, one year after his initial hospitalization. The release note stated that he was no longer confused, agitated, or delusional but that he seemed to lack the motivation to attempt to organize his life and plan for the future.

Winston failed all courses that semester. He returned home with the explanation that he felt that his body was "not present," and that he was unable to keep track of time; days seemed like seconds and seconds like days to him. He complained of dreams about the apocalypse, global war, famine, pestilence, and disease, and became increasingly depressed. Within days after returning home, Winston became obsessed with the idea that warts were growing all over his body, was agitated, and began to engage in endless dissertations on his plans to create an advanced society to rescue earthlings from evil. He was returned to the hospital within two weeks. The diagnosis was *schizophrenic reaction, acute undifferentiated type.* He remained in the hospital for almost one year without visits home. Staff members described him as hostile and agitated during much of his stay. Winston was prescribed six separate major tranquilizers and heavy doses of multivitamins [during the three-year interval since his first hospitalization]. He was released after eighteen months to live at home with his mother, and found employment as a bus boy in a restaurant. Winston visited an outpatient clinic for injections of tranquilizing medication regularly throughout his release. Eighteen months after his release Winston became agitated, hyperactive, could not sleep, began reading the Bible constantly, and experienced periods of uncontrollable laughing and crying. He was readmitted to the hospital with a diagnosis of *schizophrenic reaction, paranoid type.* He was described as very hostile and difficult to manage on the ward; he claimed to be the "Son of God," and refused all requests and directives, such as taking medication, attending activities, or going to bed at the appointed time until "ordered by God."

Winston has been hospitalized continuously for over three years at present; his diagnosis for the past two years has been changed to *schizophrenic reaction, chronic undifferentiated type.* His most recent summary note described him as a "withdrawn, delusional, unsociable, active homosexual" who is "resistant to treatment." He continues to believe that he is the son of God, and recently refused a physical examination because "his Father does not allow him to have physical exams." The most recent recommendations of the ward psychiatrist were to "continue hospitalization and increase medication."

The following interview took place five and one-half years after Winston's initial hospitalization.

An Interview with Winston

W: Insanity is caused by seed, eating. Eating human seed, sperm.

I: Seed eating?

W: Seed, human seed, the sperm. It gets lodged in the brain and causes a shift—a shift in time in the brain, you get lost in time and can't communicate. And that causes the person to remain here in the hospital.

I: So eating human seed, which is sperm that will get lodged in the brain, causes a shift in time.

W: Causes a person to get lost in time. And to acquire the personal characteristics of another person, the disposition, the personality of another person.

I: You get lost in time and then you acquire the personality of other people?

W: Both things happen, yeah.

I: What sort of people?

W: Whoever gives the seed—see, the seed contains the heredity of a person to be born from that seed. And it's all by chemical identity—the chemical identity of a new person. When the seed unites with the egg—when the sperm unites with the egg that's where you get the two hereditary factors from the two parents. But the sperm by itself can contribute to the heredity of the person in the brain—just the unwinding of chemical bondings.

I: And when you were in college you felt that your professors . . .

W: That's what is, what was happening at every college. They were thinking that they could learn how to reclaim my form by seed. Because each seed can receive radio messages from God's brain and because at the same time they thought that it would all work—the stored stuff would all play out to them and give them different personalities and education. It never worked though. It couldn't work cause there was no way to separate the individual from the knowledge that they thought they were getting.

I: So they tried to do this in universities to get people to . . .

W: . . . just wanted them to swallow the seed just to get educated.

I: Because the seeds receive messages directly from God?

W: From the God family. When he was projected out to them. The white group had been educated because they were educated by God's brain putting out messages to them specifically by the universe which is the highest thinking cell in my head.

I: By the what?

W: The universe, which is the highest thinking cell in my head.

I: The universe?

W: That's the highest thinking cell in my head. The first cell.

I: Are you the only person who has that cell?

W: That's right. There's only one of them and it's two billion years old. And it's in my brain—my subconscious.

I: Two billion?

W: Two billion—that's how long people have—that's how long the God family has been around—two billion years.

I: How do you know that the universe cell is in your brain?

W: Because it announced itself to me by a message from God to me that stimulated my whole brain.

I: How did you experience that message?

W: Everything around me disintegrated by radio—except for myself and my speaking voice and I was the only thing left. And I knew that because the universe is always the first thinking cell and the only thing left and everything else disappeared.

I: Everything disappeared and disintegrated around you? All your senses?

W: Everything except for my voice. This happened to me while I was in bed resting. And it was like a dream but it was just an escape into my subconscious—into the universe which is my subconscious. It's a microscopic cell and there's nothing else around but that. It couldn't happen for real—it could only happen that way to show me that I was the universe. It didn't happen automatically. Things didn't have to disintegrate, but there it went. That was everything, everything had to do with that, you know, to preserve me.

I: You're the universe—inside of you?

W: That's right.

I: Inside you?

W: There's another concept of the universe too—the whole of everything. There are two concepts of the universe. One is the highest thinking cell and the other one is everything—all of the matter, all of the space that has ever existed, expanding forever.

I: Does anyone else have the universe inside of them?

W: No, I'm the only one that has it, and the God family, that would be six individuals and they will have highest thinking.

I: The God family has six individuals in it?

W: It will have six individuals. It will have my father and my mother and myself and my wife and two children—a boy and a girl.

I: Does the God family exist now?

W: It does. They're just waiting in orbit above the earth in a stationary orbit waiting to come down when the time is right, picking me up and taking me back to heaven—it will take a million years to get there.

I: Why have you been put here?

W: To kill all the people that persecuted me when I was an infant, with my radio brain, and to protect all the good people, who will be protected by me. Those who never swallowed seeds and didn't have to go crazy.

I: So you've been put here to kill off the people who persecuted you when you were an infant?

W: That's right. For five years they persecuted me as an infant and they even tried to do it throughout my whole lifespan. But they've always been countered since 1492, when I was born again in the universe with the universe taking over everything.

I: And you're here to protect the people who haven't swallowed seed?

W: That's right, good people who want to expire in the last two seconds of their life without feeling pain. Anyone that has swallowed seed will have to have abject pain when they die because they've been fed seeds from the Smith family and they deserve all the punishment because they were the first ones to punish me. They murdered me for five years, in every conceivable way that they could. Smith is my family name only because the family that I lived in was disguised. And when I leave for heaven I will be changed from that into my perfect self and will have no hair on my body except for my head—my eyes will be blue and my skin will be a dark tan—and my hair will be gold the way it was when I was born as an infant. My body will be sealed. I will have no penis and no anus. I will eat perfect food and I will never have to worry about having a bowel movement or excreting. I will have a perfect body—my height will be 6'1", my father will be 6'4", and my brother will be 6'10"—a perfect family—that's what it could have been like on earth if God decided to allow it.

I: So the Smith family is the family that began to persecute you during the first five years.

W: They were the ones having to do with being paid off for say $25 to murder me off. Everything had come to an end on earth you know to perfect the universe. Everything on earth had to come to an end. Everything on earth would have been moved to heaven or else everybody would go to heaven and would expire peacefully if they never swallowed seeds or never had any antagonism towards the God family. Everyone that swallowed seeds killed themselves off because of the way the seeds operate. They cause you to feel air and space and punishment and pain forever—expanding for a million years, when you die off if you swallow that seed.

I: Who hired the Smith family to persecute you?

W: The white people did because they thought it was necessary to kill God so they could continue to exist as they like to with all the sexual perversity they wanted. That sexual perversion was the whole cause why everything went crazy within the white race and they can kill the first three and they can get the niggers—the Negroes—to do anything that they want them to do for money. Just that small sum of money, $25 at that time seemed like a fortune, that they were paid to get rid of me. And I was dead for five years practically. Dead but just receiving more and more punishment—they beheaded me, carved me up, burned me, and hung me, every conceivable thing that they could do to punish me. That's why I'm here, to get even with them. And I could do it easily with my radio brain without giving them a scratch or scar that can be detected by anyone. Just my mere presence causes them to feel pain, the same pain they caused me to feel—intense pain for five years. And they would experience this for a million years in two seconds time when they get down to their time to die I'll get them. They were deliberately deceived to think that they could continue to swallow seeds so that they could live forever, because anyone who swallowed seeds can't get a chance to die out all year long. They can never die because once they reach expiration at one point in their brain—another seed gains consciousness in another part of the brain. They have not—it takes one signal to your consciousness in order to die out. A single signal to the consciousness to die out. When everything comes to an end on earth everything will fold right up. There will be nothing left at all. Nothing on earth left at all except for the good people who I will take to heaven and the good people who expire perfectly on earth in two seconds experiencing everything that the God family could have experienced. That is the reason why things have been made equal. The God family is setting an example for the whole human race so that they could get into their rhythm and experience the same thing that they would experience knowing that if it's good enough for the God family it's good enough for anyone.

I: So you've been sent here to save people who haven't swallowed seeds?

W: That's right.

I: Are they all black people?

W: No, there are some whites. The whites who bought seed within the cell are distinct from the mass of the white people who persecuted me, are called Caucasian, and that's white people who will never have a chance to know what happened to them when they die. They're the ones who never swallowed seed and never had any antagonism toward God—would rectify themselves if they never had any false hope. Heaven was never planned for white people. It was planned for the colored race. I know of two colored races that have achieved enough of everything to justify saying that—they were the Chinese and the Nigerians and they are with my father and they are perfect in heaven on the starship.

I: What of the Smith family, are they black or white?

W: They're niggers. They ate white seed and black seed. Once they have done that they are classified as niggers. They're neither black nor white, they have blacks and whites in them. They had a chance to become a colored family before they swallowed seeds. There are members of the Smith family who will not die, the children—some of the children— and they will not have to expire and feel the pain, they will expire perfectly, they will not feel the pain or the ecstasy, they will have experienced everything. It only takes two seconds to do it in. It would seem just as long a time as if he had lived it out for real. Only with a tongue could there have been a justice so that they would have expired perfectly. And it was all stored in my brain. It took me a million years to put it together. I came here filled up with a message and enough information to have made it possible for every living soul on earth to have expired without feeling pain or to have ascended to heaven. But because of the things that happened to me in the first five years after I arrived on earth it became impossible for white people to expire without feeling the pain and agony that they had caused me to feel. If I had lived out my life span perfectly I would be thirty-three years old now. That's why they say that Jesus Christ was thirty-three at the time that he expired. Everything about Jesus Christ is a myth that Hebrews made up. They thought that since I had a realizing mind, and I could make man by following magnetic fields, that there would be other gods that would evolve on earth that would also be able to do this. The Jews thought that if they told enough people about it and made enough rules and published enough bibles that they would convince the people that they were the "chosen people of God." That they would be the only people to go to heaven, that they would be provided for—everybody else would have to suffer. And they fooled people by writing a Bible and making it unchangeable. Everyone who reads the Bible I've got to say that they didn't read it with a critical eye and the proper kind of judgment. Any person who reads the Bible literally will be deceived. And won't have a chance to be saved. There's good in the Bible but the Jews never intended for the Bible to do anything but to deceive the whole human race so that they could proliferate themselves across the face of the earth.

I: You can make people suffer through radio waves?

W: That's right, from my own brain.

I: And you make the Smith family suffer?

W: It's all stored within their memory. I'll tell my father a story and each time I think about it I get the feelings he feels one more spurt of pain. And then I have them feel it instantly—store it in the subconscious mind and it will all play out to them. I store it in consciousness at a higher level than they are able to reach. When they catch up to themselves it will all play out to them in two seconds time. And they will be punished as much as they punished me and more—as much as they can forever. It would have been worse for them even if I had never made my advent—it would have been worse—everything would be wild. I synchronize all the brains that can't see how to communicate so that they can see a need to expire because of the fact that they were already eating seeds and were storing up pain constantly by having all that air space in their brains. That was planned for them if they hadn't expired on time when I had a chance. They tried to make a white family with the identical memories in it—that's the Smith family.

I: They tried to do what?

W: Make a white family with the same memories in it—with a counterpart, one to one, person to person, a white family with a black, a white for each black in the Smith family. They made it at that crazy institution. And, they had hope that the white family would have the same thing that the God family would have had. Thinking that my former foster mother would have the opportunity to realize next she turned into the wife of God. She thought that she was my mother. I was born perfectly in heaven a sealed male—no penis, no anus. I could have been perfect and grown out to a full height and lived on in heaven apart from real people. But I elected to come down—to take a million-year voyage when I was an infant down to earth to straighten things out. To make it perfect for as many people who had wanted to make way for themselves, and who had preserved themselves by not swallowing seeds. It could have been perfect for the whole human race.

EUNICE AND THE REVOLVING DOOR

Eunice was first hospitalized for mental disorder over thirty years ago. She has been in and out of hospitals ten times since then.

Eunice was born the second of six siblings, and raised in the suburbs of a large midwestern city. Her father had a secure managerial position with a business concern and was described as a good provider. Eunice, according to her parents, was a reserved, quiet, congenial child who helped her mother raise the younger siblings. She was described as an industrious person who enjoyed helping with housework, made friends easily, and was very interested in men during adolescence and early adulthood. There is no reported history of mental illness on either side of the family. Eunice suffered occasional asthmatic attacks as a child; her physical history is otherwise unexceptional. Eunice often complained that she felt inferior as an adolescent and had "spells" during which she lacked confidence. She was an average student and graduated from high school, at age eighteen, ranked in the middle of her class. She was employed as an office clerk in three different businesses during the seven years following graduation from high school. During this time she lived at home with her parents and dated one man steadily for over six years. She quarreled with her family at times and periodically felt that they were all against her and talked behind her back. Her family attributed these "spells" to her monthly periods.

Shortly after her twenty-fifth birthday Eunice abruptly broke off with this young man. She stated that she felt that she was inferior and not good enough for him. She became depressed following this breakup, quit her job, and brooded around the house for several months. She later returned to work and began dating a married man. Within two months she began to complain that the office staff was gossiping and complaining about foul odors emanating from her body. She began to express fears that someone was going to hurt her. Shortly after learning of the marriage of her ex-fiancé, Eunice quit her job. She stayed at home all day, refused to talk or eat for days, and began shouting accusations that her family was against her. She began to accuse her family of controlling and reading her thoughts from a code transmitted over the radio.

Eunice was hospitalized in a private psychiatric clinic for the first time at age twenty-five. She was described as suffering from a "profound psychotic state" by the admitting physician. She stated during the admission interview that she "had no feelings" and needed some "nerve medicine." Eunice was diagnosed as suffering from *dementia praecox, paranoid type,* and received a series of fifteen electroconvulsive (electric shock) treatments for her disorder. She was discharged as "improved" after six weeks in the hospital. She returned to work shortly thereafter, but quit two months later because she believed her coworkers were gossiping about her "disgusting" body odor. She stayed at home for nine months, was quarrelsome and anxious, and continued to accuse her family of plotting against her. Eunice was committed to a large state institution eleven months after her previous discharge. She was described as angry, sullen, demanding, uncooperative, and withdrawn by the admitting physician.

She stated that "a boomerang" caused her to be committed to the hospital. "It may sound crazy to you, but if you knew all the things they [her family] have been doing to me for so many years you would understand. I have been inflicted with mental pain and cruelty. There have been two different sides and I have been caught between them." She refused to elaborate on this statement, stating that she had nothing more to say. Her diagnosis again was *dementia praecox, paranoid type.* One month later her diagnosis was changed in staff conference to *dementia praecox, catatonic type.* The following dialogue, transcribed in her case record, documents the diagnostic issues considered by the staff in deciding this matter.

Dr. Thorpe: On admission this patient expressed vague ideas of reference, stating that "people were against her." She was negativistic and rather sarcastic, and the interview was unsatisfactory. At staff today she was detached, had difficulty in expressing herself, and evidenced thought blocking in her replies. She was evasive and sensed her confusion but was unable to do anything about it. She showed blocking, silliness, and vague paranoid ideas about radios, electricity, and mental telepathy. I believe that her diagnosis is *dementia praecox, paranoid type*, and her prognosis is poor.

Dr. Bell: I agree with Dr. Thorpe.

Dr. Cohen: I agree with the diagnosis of *dementia praecox,* however, I prefer the sub-classification *catatonic type.* She is apathetic, her speech is very indefinite but not circumstantial and she does not show inappropriateness of affect. Her paranoid trends are noticeable at this time only because it is early in her illness.

Dr. Fox (hospital director):   In reviewing this case before coming to staff, I had thought that she was a *dementia praecox, paranoid type;* however, at staff today she appeared apathetic and quite catatonic. It's a flip-up to know whether she has paranoia or catatonia, but I rather agree with Dr. Cohen.

Dr. Cohen: The prognosis is poor and I believe the catatonic symptoms will increase as the disease progresses.

Dr. Vogler: Based on this patient's history of apathetic periods, of complete indifference and withdrawal, then her response to shock and resuming work mixed with her response during the interview here, I tend to classify this patient, in my opinion, as *catatonic type.*

Staff Diagnosis: *Dementia praecox, catatonic type.*

Eunice began a series of electroconvulsive treatments with *gran mal* convulsions several days later. She reportedly evidenced rapid improvement, became friendly, smiled on the ward and did not again spontaneously express delusional ideation. She was discharged to the custody of her parents three months after her second admission.

Eunice was returned to the hospital on court order less than one year later. She complained that her family was spying on her and broadcasting her thoughts over the radio. She had lived at home during the previous year without attempting to find work and had grown increasingly negative, hostile, and withdrawn. She reportedly would not speak but wrote extensively in her diary. She began to hear imaginary voices, believed her telephone was tapped, believed airplanes were flying low over the house to leave spy messages for her, and accused her family of using a code to testify against her. She refused to eat meals with the family and was particularly antagonistic toward her father and one sister. Eunice's family complained that she had become increasingly irresponsible and unmanageable at home, wandered the streets at night, and kept company with "unsavory" characters. She was placed on sub-shock insulin (convulsive) treatment and furloughed three months later.

This cycle of admission, hospitalization, convulsive therapy, and discharge to the custody of parents was repeated four times within the following three years. On each occasion her parents signed a routine form authorizing the staff of the hospital to use any medical or surgical treatment, including shock therapy, which in their opinion would be beneficial in restoring their daughter to good mental and physical health. They also agreed to accept full responsibility for any adverse results therefrom. Eunice's psychiatrist concluded after five years of such treatments that electric shock and insulin coma had no effect on her paranoid ideas, hostility, and argumentative manner. He did note that she seemed to enjoy the routine that goes with the insulin patient's regimen: organized activities, light work, play, and no responsibility. He recommended transorbital lobotomy (brain surgery) to her family on the basis that this procedure would make her "easier to handle and to get along with at home" even if it did not alter her paranoid ideas.

Five and one-half years after her initial hospitalization Eunice was referred for surgical treatment—transorbital lobotomy. The parents received and signed a routine authorization form for this procedure. Eunice was put under anesthesia with electro-shock, the points of the leukotomes (pointed probes) were introduced under the eye, aimed parallel with the bony ridge of the nose, and driven to a depth of five centimeters. The handles were separated widely, returned half-way, and driven two centimeters deeper. The handles were then crossed over the nose and separated to a total of fifty degrees. The handles were then elevated and a fifty-degree excusion was complete on each side. There was no bleeding. Recovery from surgery was described as routine. The pathways connecting the midbrain (associated with emotional arousal) had been permanently severed from the frontal cortex (associated with complex cognitive function).

Eunice remained in the hospital for four months following her lobotomy. She was furloughed to her parents who stated that she seemed to get along well during her first several months at home. She kept busy around the house, washed dishes, ironed, cleaned house, did yard work, and appeared to be in good spirits. One year later Eunice entered one of her "moody spells" and grew increasingly tense and irritable at home. The family decided to return her to the hospital. Eunice was described as hyperactive, loud, and demanding upon admission. She demanded a court hearing, accused her family of controlling her thoughts after receiving secret messages over the radio and telephone. The admitting physician believed that Eunice should be tried on Thorazine, one of the new tranquilizing drugs. She improved quickly on the new medication, and was released to her parents' custody two months later. She returned to the hospital six months after that, under court order, because of a recurrence of her "persecution complex." She was furloughed four months later, lived at home, visited an outpatient clinic monthly for medication, and worked for a charitable organization. She remained out of the hospital for over three years before readmission.

During the past sixteen years Eunice has been furloughed and returned to the hospital six times. She has been prescribed eight different major tranquilizers and multivitamins. Her diagnosis has been changed five times, from *catatonic,* to *paranoid,* to *chronic undifferentiated,* and back to *paranoid.* She has lived thirteen of the past sixteen years of her life in a mental hospital. She currently believes that she is married to Frank Sinatra, has a large family—all movie stars—is a billionaire, the "true American girl" and "Ike's real woman." Her parents died several years ago. She became very angry and abusive of patients and staff at that time and has been on heavy dosages of medication ever since. She was recently placed in a boarding home, but was returned by the sheriff one month later. She was described as excited, agitated, and incoherent on admission. Eunice believed that her grandchildren came to visit her in the nursing home and all of them were on fire. She simply tried to save them "when people interfered." Her most recent progress note states that Eunice is "tidy but uncooperative, delusional, and hostile." Her prognosis is "poor."

Excerpts from an Interview with Eunice

I: How are you today?

E: I'm going home tomorrow for good. I've been discharged. I think you know that. I've got kin people all over the world.

I: Where will you stay?

E: I'm a psychologist. I'm very religious too and have a reverend husband. I was a doctor in Houston, a medical doctor. I'm an ex-movie star.

I: Are you?

E: I've been coming to the hospital for over twenty years. I'm a billionaire and I don't want to pay you any more money to get out of the hospital!

I: You're a billionaire!

E: I expect that you already know that. You're trying to get my money. I own you and this whole hospital. I get the Supreme Court and the FBI to bring me up to date each morning. And I f-u-c-k the reverend every morning and every night. He knows how rich I am. My husband has given me everything I want.

I: This is your hospital?

E: The state doesn't treat me right. They've tried to make me sick. The doctors move me around from building to building, they lock the doors and they have the keys!

They try to make me carry patients, you know f-u-c-k-i-n-g. I can't tell you how wealthy my family is. They try to get my money. They put me in here, lock the doors, shove me around, read my mail, and give me old fashioned clothes. They move me around all the buildings to make me sick. I've got children, they're movie stars. One married movie stars. I'm a grandmother. Ike loves me.

I: Ike! How do you know?

E: The newspapers and television told me. His picture was always smiling at me on the front page. And the King of England too.

I: President Eisenhower and the King of England are in love with you.

E: Yes. Mamie wouldn't let me marry him but the president was wonderful. The government and my lawyer had to protect me.

I've been discharged from here and the doctors are trying to move me around to all the buildings and make me sick again. The doctors feed me all kinds of medicine and examine me and move me around. They can't see me though because I have a friend in the Pentagon and he says smoking is my only crime. They won't tell me the truth about these doctors.

When I'get out of here I'm going to get pregnant. I have a strange urge to get pregnant. It's a woman's instinct to want to hold babies to her breast.

HARVEY, A HOSPITAL WORKER

Harvey was born over thirty years ago, the fourth child in a poor black farm family of thirteen children. He had a history of asthma attacks beginning at the age of five years that diminished in frequency as he grew older. He began his formal education at the age of five and attended a country school until the eighth grade. Harvey reported that he enjoyed school and received average grades. He repeated the seventh grade, and dropped out at the age of sixteen to find work. He worked for several years in a sawmill, on a farm, and as a construction worker. He had four brothers who were also construction workers, as was his father. The brothers were described by a social worker as "slow" and "withdrawn," but "otherwise in order."

Harvey suffered a blow to his head and subsequent eye infection during his eighteenth year. He was treated at a city hospital, released, and directed to return to the hospital for further treatment. Harvey elected to avoid the followup treatment and, subsequently, became "noticeably upset" according to his father. Harvey believed at this time that the "corruption" of the wound had invaded his brain. He complained frequently of headaches, and believed that his brain was "bubbling."

Several months later Harvey was committed to the state hospital on a petition signed by his father. At this time it was reported that the patient had been acting "strangely" during the course of the previous year and that he was "depressed" and "suspicious." During observation at a municipal hospital prior to his commitment, Harvey reported that he had been experiencing visual and auditory hallucinations. He had also become despondent during this observation period, and reportedly had requested a tablet which would "kill him within minutes." He related at this time that he frequently dreamed about people being killed and calling to him for assistance. Harvey mentioned that he could not tolerate noises because they would "affect" his stomach. He was diagnosed as suffering from an *acute brain syndrome.*

Three months later the ward physician noted that Harvey showed difficulty in expressing himself but was well-oriented. At this time Harvey reported having heard people outdoors yelling for help and shouting his name; some of them spoke in foreign languages. He believed that he had been delivered to the hospital as "punishment" but did not specify exactly what he might deserve punishment for. Ward personnel reported that Harvey seemed to have "ups and downs" on the ward but that the "downs" comprised withdrawal and apathy rather than depression. Harvey was described as frightened, tense, and restless during the first few days of his hospitalization, leading staff members to speculate that he might have been experiencing auditory hallucinations. It was noted that he answered questions promptly and was capable of sustaining a conversation. His judgment was considered to be accurate, and it was believed that he was developing insight into his problems. The examining physicians did remark that Harvey was exhibiting a "certain apathy and superficial euphoria which is quite inappropriate to his condition."

Information about the patient was provided by his father, who visited the hospital (accompanied by a neighbor) shortly after Harvey's admission. Although, according to the social worker, the father "knew nothing of the developmental history of the son," the problems apparently began when the patient complained of stomach pains. Following these complaints the patient had gone to a hospital but had not received treatment, made noises at night that kept other family members awake, mentioned the possibility of overdosing on medicine to kill himself, and threatened a neighbor with a knife while "jabbering unintelligibly." The neighbor who accompanied the father offered the information that the patient was considered to be a menace in the neighborhood because of his bizarre behavior. Harvey had once returned from work in a taxi, jumped from the car without paying the driver, and declared that he was being chased by someone. On another occasion, Harvey had stumbled and fallen through a glass door. One of the patient's sisters later reported that he drank homemade wine and that he would frequently complain of headaches.

Harvey escaped from the hospital four months after his admission

A social worker was dispatched to the patient's home shortly thereafter, to determine his whereabouts and condition, and found Harvey laughing as he sawed wood. The patient's mother maintained that there was nothing amiss with him except that he would talk in a foolish manner— "always talking about making a lot of money." Harvey reported having headaches and stomach pains; he apparently believed that he had ulcers. The patient confided to the social worker that he had killed two Chinese men and one Caucasian man, but without being at the scene of the crime. The patient believed that he was mentally sound but needed an operation on his stomach.

The mother's only complaints were that the patient slept frequently, acted indolently around the home, and talked even more "foolishly" after drinking alcoholic beverages. On the basis of the observation that the family was reasonably satisfied with the patient's presence, the social worker recommended that the patient be allowed to remain at home.

Harvey was returned to the state hospital two months later. He complained of hearing voices. These voices, he stated, were sometimes coming from afar, and occasionally said such phrases as "shoot him" or "hurt him"—referring to the patient. Harvey also believed that he sometimes heard items about himself on the radio. The interviewing physician remarked that the patient seemed to be suspicious during the interview and possessed no insight into his condition. He was diagnosed as *schizophrenic, paranoid type.* Tranquilizing drugs and occupational therapy were prescribed.

Three months later, Harvey was receiving 150 milligrams of Thorazine (four times daily), and he was described by the ward physician as cooperative, polite, and candid in reporting his auditory hallucinations. Shortly thereafter Harvey was transferred from his ward to the criminal ward because of an alleged involvement in the rape of a female patient. Harvey vehemently denied the allegations. His hospital grounds privileges were suspended for more than a year because of the incident.

One year after his readmission, it was recorded that the original diagnosis of *acute brain syndrome* was in error, and that Harvey had actually suffered a schizophrenic break prior to his first admission. At this time he was transferred to an open ward and placed in a work assignment.

Two years after his readmission, Harvey was physically healthy but still psychotic; he reported that he needed "special food for special chemical reactions" in his body. One year later the annual summary note stated that Harvey was cooperative and well-behaved. His medication was changed twice that year.

Ten years after his second hospitalization, Harvey was granted a one-week furlough but, prior to arriving at home, he began to hallucinate, was picked up by the police, and returned to the state institution. Shortly thereafter he escaped from the state hospital and was returned. Upon this return he was reported to be extremely delusional, disoriented, and incoherent. Harvey has remained in the hospital continuously for over fourteen years. He has been given eight types of tranquilizers. About eight years ago, his diagnosis was changed from *paranoid* to *chronic undifferentiated type*. Harvey holds a part-time job on the janitorial staff of the hospital, and is described as an "excellent" patient, "always very cooperative and helpful." He shops in town, periodically drinks a few beers on the weekend, and considers the hospital his home.

An Interview with Harvey

I: Have your views changed since I last talked to you?

H: No. I can't study my mind. I can't study a word. If I see something big, if I see it in my mind I spell a word and it drops big. If I studied a big motor or something, it would drop—so I don't study my mind because it would build up.

I: I don't follow.

H: The motor, or a house, or a world. If I study it, it may drop. A tree or car, I drop cars all the time. A bulldozer fell out of my mind you know, so I stopped fooling with it.

I: It fell out of your mind?

H: Yeah. Anything will fall. If I get a notion to study a car or tree or something, anything might fall. I got a building mind. I got more bulldozers and things in my mind right now. I'll tell you Doc, my building mind is so big it can make anything you want to build. But people that don't have no building mind, they could put down a little food or a tract or something like that, if they get electrocution into their minds—they can reach off the abyss you know. I went over the whole world putting down beans and meat. My body dropped food all the time. It builds the trucks traveling along the highways. My mind is real smart, real smart, real smart, man.

I: How did you get such a special mind?

H: I work. I build worlds. I build worlds. This is a world that we are in. I build all kinds of worlds, all kinds of distance too. But I came back and put a plan down for my home with records, chairs, refrigerators, and stuff like that. I can throw a building, build a footing right through the mud, falls right in place, right in place.

I: So you build other worlds and live in them.

H: I don't live in them. They want me to stay here so they can get their food and stuff. Some people get hungry you know. They want me to stay in my station, at home. My mind works all the way across the universe, or whatever they call it. It puts down meat, beans, and bread all the way across to the other side. There are plenty of people out there.

I: Lots of responsibilities.

H: I build planets. I could be the first man that ever lived, but sometimes my mind hurts. Somebody took my mind and ground it up. They're always killing those boys that build worlds. I go around the creation place building worlds. I set the sun up, but they killed me.

I: Someone killed you?

H: Yes, a missile crushed me. I can't remember what is outside, outside of a building. I don't fool with that. I don't try to remember that.

I: So you don't pay attention to what is going on outside the building.

H: No, I don't. All I do is walk around and eat. Sometimes I cut wood or paint my house. I was burned up three times. Those sons of guns were the most dangerous men I've ever seen, they were afraid of me—they didn't know I was teaching and they got afraid. They burned me three times. They took the body off because the body was working too much. They didn't know about the body. A body is level, you know, it will work to a certain point then it will stop and level. I figured it out. I take old radio battery acid medicine for my body. I take that to keep my books and things.

KEVIN, THE THEOSOPHIST

Kevin, age thirty-seven, was one of four siblings born to a wealthy eastern family. His father died when Kevin was four and his mother remarried two years later. Kevin's siblings include one brother ten years older, a twin brother, and a younger sister. He was described as an exceptionally bright student, quiet, very close to mother, and relatively isolated from children his own age. Both parents agreed that Kevin had not evidenced any noticeable signs of emotional disturbance during childhood or adolescence. There was no previous history of mental illness reported for either side of the family.

Kevin was raised in a large eastern city. He attended private boarding schools, and spent summers at the family home. During childhood and early adolescence Kevin was "closest" to two aunts who filled him with a strong sense of pride in his "aristocratic" family origins. He graduated *cum laude* from prep school and enrolled in an "ivy league" university. His academic performance was well below what it had been in high school. He apparently had difficulty making himself study without the regulation and structure of the prep school environment. Kevin was referred to a psychiatrist for consultation during his sophomore year. The psychiatrist say Kevin twice and prescribed mild tranquilizing medication. Kevin graduated after four years with a degree in modern languages and joined the army, where he was stationed in Germany for three years as a legal clerk. He received an honorable discharge and citation of achievement from his company commander after three years of service. His commander described him as "indispensable but over-dedicated." Kevin has fond memories of army life, and says he has often regretted leaving the service. He lived at home for six months after his discharge, applied to the Foreign Service, was turned down, and worked as a retail clerk in New York City for several months before he quit his job and returned home. Kevin bought a house and lived alone on his modest inheritance for several months. He planned to rejoin the army if his application to the Foreign Service was rejected a second time. He had no friends or social contacts during this period, and became increasingly engrossed in studying the Bible.

Approximately one year after discharge from the army, Kevin was arrested on the rooftop of a large hotel. He stated that he had gone there to jump off in response to voices telling him that this act was necessary for "the salvation of the world and the purification of the devil." He was taken to a psychiatric hospital where he was described by the admitting physician as markedly unkempt, apathetic, passive, and depressed. Kevin stated that he had stopped eating, sleeping, and defecating about one week prior to his hospitalization, and that he was being persecuted by the devil and the police. He believed that his nervousness was associated with a recent decision to stop masturbating. Kevin stated during the admission interview that he believed his mother and father had died and that he heard angels and his mother talking to him. When informed several days later that his parents were in fact alive, and on their way to visit, he stated blandly, "Then they have arisen." The parents felt that Kevin's rejection by the Foreign Service was the turning point in his mental condition; since that time he reportedly had become more and more withdrawn and unrealistic.

Kevin remained in the hospital for four months. His diagnosis on admission was *schizophrenic reaction, catatonic type,* with some paranoid features. Several weeks later his diagnosis was changed to *schizophrenic reaction, acute undifferentiated type.* Kevin received three different brands of major tranquilizers, thyroid extract, a series of thirteen electroconvulsive treatments, five sub-coma insulin-convulsive shock sessions, and "superficial psychotherapy" during his six-month stay in the hospital. At the end of this period, a pre-release note stated, "He became more alert and somewhat catatonic following convulsive therapy but his hallucinations seemed to increase. He remains markedly seclusive and isolated." In March of the following year Kevin was discharged as "improved," and was immediately transferred to a large state mental hospital. His diagnosis was changed there to *schizophrenic reaction, schizo-affective type.*

Kevin has remained in this hospital continuously for the past twelve years. He has settled into a daily routine of visits to the patients' library, several hours of occupational therapy classes, and piano playing. He has not ventured off the hospital grounds unescorted in several years.

Kevin has received eleven types of major tranquilizers, multivitamins, minerals, electroconvulsive therapy, and insulin shock therapy during his hospital stay. His diagnosis was changed to *schizophrenic reaction, chronic undifferentiated type* three and one-half years after his most recent hospitalization. At that time the summary note stated that Kevin evidenced a total lack of interest in grooming and social interaction, that he reportedly heard telephone conversations in his head, and was grossly delusional in all interactions. A note written after ten years of continuous hospitalization stated that pronounced auditory hallucinations continued in spite of prolonged dosages of heavy medication and close ward management. The staff psychiatrist suggested "more probing into the cause of this condition, so that effective treatment measures can be instituted." A recent summary note states that Kevin requires "further hospitalization and increased medication to treat his psychosis." He is described as cooperative on the ward, as occasionally helpful—cleaning and running ward errands—and as harmless to property and people, although he "periodically kicks and screams at people who are not there." He continues to engage in "prolonged conversations with hallucinatory figures."

The following are excerpts from two interviews with Kevin.

An Interview with Kevin

I: Who brought you here?

K: The police is what brought me to the hospital and that's all I know.

I: And no one's ever told you why?

K: I began seeing visions in the wall and things like that. Although it didn't prove to be mental illness, it could be religion.

I: Have you ever heard voices?

K: Yes, all the time. It started ten years ago this month, really, and I have heard voices ever since. I believe there are people really speaking to me. I believe I have extrasensory perception or something. I don't believe it is hallucinations.

I: What sort of things do you hear?

K: I hear people talking to me and I talk to other people. I hear two kinds of voices, really. I have conferences with people about religion and things like that, and then on the other hand I get beaten up by the voices of other people. I have always had this counter-balance with voices.

I: How can you be beaten up by voices?

K: Oh, it's what they say, they say horrible things.

I: About you?

K: Yes, and they ask questions. They interrogate me. Interrogation is painful.

I: What sort of questions do they ask you?

K: They want to find out questions about my religious knowledge.

I: What sort of terrible things do they say about you?

K: Well, they don't really say terrible things about me, and one thing is I really don't remember what they say. They talk about their behavior, it's just bad behavior that they do.

I: Can you give some examples?

K: As I say, I just listen to the voices. I'm kind of acting as a confessor to them, helping to work out their problems.

I: So you listen to the voices and their confessions and go into religious conferences.

K: I don't talk at all in the religious conferences, don't talk at all about their bad behavior, I talk about my latest discoveries in theosophy. There is no doubt that my philosophy is revolutionary.

I: Can you tell me a little bit about it?

K: Well, I really don't remember it, mainly so I'll keep the secret. I've just developed a complete code for Christians on how to lead a Christian life from the sayings of Jesus Christ in the Bible. And what really impressed me the most about the sayings of Jesus Christ is how complete an idea of how to behave is given. It wouldn't seem the same to you because the sayings are very deep.

I: So you feel that most people cannot recognize the depth?

K: I don't think anyone has ever studied the sayings of Jesus Christ as I have.

I: When do you intend to reveal what you have discovered?

K: I reveal it when I have my ward talks with people. I reveal everything, I say it out in speeches just as fast as I learn it, and I think it is being taken down in books by the people. I don't write myself but I am a good talker, but I think what I am saying is being taken down by people.

I: So these voices, when you are in conference, really they are being transcribed by someone?

K: I think they are. Life is too short for me to ever repeat a word.

I: Why are the voices trying to upset you?

K: Well, I think those people are sick. Don't you think they are sick?

I: Well, I don't know what they say . . .

K: Well, I think they are sick and I am helping them with their problems. It's just as bad as undergoing torture. But I've learned now to take it so I don't suffer anymore. After ten years of suffering with it I've learned how to handle it.

I: Can you visualize these conferences as you are having them or are they just voices?

K: It's all voices, I've never had visions before. It's all voices. I never discover them. It could be anybody. I don't know much about them either. I have theosophical ideas to discuss. I think it's ESP. I don't think it is hallucinations or anything. I think it is ESP. After all, in religious work. . . .

I: But people have labeled you as being mentally ill?

K: I think they have. They have been very careful to keep a secret from me on what they think.

I: You mean no one has ever told you whether they think you're mentally ill?

K: No one's ever told me. It's what they have told me that I think is intended as a blind when they told me I heard voices. For instance, Dr. _____ said that I might have to stay in this hospital forever cause I hear voices. I might have to stay in this hospital forever, but it won't be because I hear voices or hallucinations.

I: What do you think will be the reason?

K: I have no idea, it might be a mental illness, but I'm not a psychologist so I don't know a mentally ill person when I see one. I might be mentally ill, but I don't know about it. No one has ever ever told me. The voices have never really told me the truth. So I can't believe a single thing I hear. I'm married, for example, but I have never seen my wife or children, so I can't be sure it is true.

I: You have been married and had children? How did you manage that while in the hospital?

K: Masturbation.

I: By masturbation?

K: Yes, it will produce children.

I: How does it?

K: Well, I think it gives a sexual reaction to a wife which fertilizes the egg. I don't believe that you have to shoot semen into a woman's uterus and fertilize eggs. I don't believe that. I think you can get a mental sexual reaction that will fertilize your eggs.

I: How do you give a woman a sexual reaction?

K: I masturbate.

I: So you masturbate and develop a fantasy about the women you like?

K: She helps by talking to me. Kind of a sexy talk.

I: I see, so you hear her voice?

K: That's correct, it was voices, and then I masturbated and she had the children.

I: Have you ever seen her in visions?

K: Yes, I have seen her in visions, but I don't know who she is.

I: Was she a very nice person?

K: Yes, of course. I'm not married to her anymore. She didn't like me and asked for a divorce and I granted her one and alimony.

I: So you have custody of the children?

K: Yes, I am bringing up ten children.

I: Ten children? You must have your hands full.

K: Well, I don't do much for them, they're very independent.

Interview with Kevin: One Year Later

I: One of the topics I did want to talk with you about this morning is your work.

K: Sure, I'm anxious to talk about that. My work made a lot of sense to me. Only recently have I stopped finding new projects and things like that and kind of stabilized with the old things and going around with them . . . which delighted me.

I: The last time I talked with you, you were engaged in working out a system of theosophy.

K: Well, I don't know about that now. I've gotten so vague about what I'm doing. I just kind of go from one project to the next. I don't know. I'm kind of vague about what I'm doing any more. I mean I want to do something—it had a name—but I never found out what theosophy was or philosophy or anything I'd want to do was. I told the lieutenant I was getting interested in criminology. And I'm getting interested in police work and things like that.

I: In what sense?

K: Well I, uh, I think I'm doing a lot of police work. I think I can do it as well as anybody now. I hope that someday I might even go down to the office and get assigned to it. But, uh, Dr. Yates said he couldn't assign me as yet, but I told the nurse that I was interested in police work—over my voices. I guess that is pretty unorthodox, I don't know what they'd make of it. But police work is what I'd do with my voices. And I'm just training at it by doing it.

I: Police work is where you do all your voices?

K: Well they come along with misbehavior, misbehavior for me to check out and important things like that. You know I've always complained that the voices were misbehaving so. But it's boiled down to police work, dealing with them. You want to ask me about my work so I simply have to mention police work because that's what is interesting to me right now. I do it in occupational therapy and everything.

I: Even while you're sitting in "OT" [occupational therapy]?

K: I know it, and then I put it down and go on with my voices—I'm always busy with my voices or something.

I: Can you be specific about what sort of police work you're doing in terms of your voices?

K: Well I don't know much—I've never been through police school. I would have liked to go, but I couldn't, didn't really go. And now I'm here and don't plan to go. And, uh, I really don't know much about what it consists of. I don't know much about formal technology and technical terms and things like that in the police. I've never been exposed to things like that.

I: I know you're still learning, but can you tell me a little bit about what sort of investigative work you're doing in terms of voices?

K: Oh, well all I do is check out what the voices say and report. That's basically what I do. I check out what the voices say or what the patients do on the ward, for instance. And report—I mean I do report it over my voices and I report, I report to the police department over my voices and they know about me over voices. It's that secret. I don't wear a uniform on the ward or anything like that because I don't want to be caught doing it—no telling what would happen. It's *dangerous and secret.*

I: So you're afraid that if people were aware that you were doing police work that they may . . .

K: Oh I don't know what would happen. It'd be dangerous.

I: Can you give me an example of what sort of things you checked out or investigated?

K: Well, yes—misbehavior. The voices do bad behavior. They do crazy talk. When the voices start doing crazy talk, it's the most horrible thing.

I: Can you tell me what they say, for example, when they're doing crazy things?

K: They do spoonerisms. And malaproprisms. And mispronunciations. They've lied, and they think I talk like that so they think they can afford to do it. I think they're trying to pass as lunatics or mental patients or something like that, and I don't quite know why. I think that's why they're doing it, but at any rate it amounts to plagiarism, plagiarism—and that kind of a thing is a serious felony.

I: So you believe that they're envious of your status of being in a mental hospital?

K: I believe that's why they're doing this crazy talk. But anyway it's an awful thing to have to listen to and it is as serious a felony as plagiarism—I think they could get them for plagiarism at least for doing it.

I: You mean they're plagiarizing your thoughts?

K: Plagiarism and brutality and posing—posing as a mental patient, impersonating a mental patient. All those things are serious felonies.

I: So you're doing an investigation in order to have them convicted of these?

K: I can't begin to say what would happen to them. One thing I can do—I'm very talented at getting confessions from people.

I: Mmmmm.

K: But what I'm mainly interested in is cursing. What I'm really a specialist in at the police is cursing. And when I say "felony" it's really, it's really a variety of cursing except there is an element of brutality in it and the brutality is just about the worst thing in it. They're, they're really committing brutality that I know about and there's a lot of brutality even on the ward. It's connected with cursing. I know more about cursing than I do even about brutality.

I: So the voices are cursing a great deal?

K: They are cursing a great deal and that's why I'm really obliging the police. I know about cursing. That's what I made a kind of specialty of in my works.

I: And the voices curse a great deal in order to sort of upset you?

K: I . . . I'm not quite clear really on whether they're trying to upset me or not. They do upset me. It might be that they just want to do it and aren't aware of upsetting people. I . . . I don't know much about that. It's probably someone else's work or something.

I: I see. So it may not be intended for you?

K: Well I . . . I know they do want me to hear it because I'm the person they're talking to. But it . . . it might be, as I said, for their own selfish ends or something without much concern about what I thought of it. if they knew that I was reporting it to a police department they'd probably be a little discouraged. But I don't want them to know that.

I: How do you report it to the police department?

K: I do it over my voices, and I believe that they're capable of tapping my memory banks. It is that erudite. I think they can get things from me that I've just heard and remembered in my subconscious. I think they can get reports from that. Because they have erudite technology for doing things like that. Police have very erudite technology. I suppose you know that.

I: Mmmm-hmmm. So you believe that the police can tap your thoughts in your memory bank, and so on, and get the information from you?

K: I believe they can do that because it has to be awfully secret. I don't want anybody catching me reporting things to the police. Because if they accuse me of being a "tattle tale" or something, I'll be in serious trouble even with the attendants. I . . . and not many people know that I'm trying to do police work. But that is what I'm trying to do, so it's mainly what I have to talk about.

I: Well, what was it that led to your disillusionment with theosophy?

K: Well, I don't know much about theosophy. When I did that, it was a long time ago. I was probably just learning it. I don't remember much about theosophy. I'm not even sure . . . I don't know what, I really don't know what theosophy is. I probably thought I was doing it, but I might not have been. I . . . I seem to remember that a few years ago I did have an idea of what I was doing in science and so forth, but I've never been clear about any of the sciences and what they consist of, and I'm not doing anything very scientific in the police.

I: Mmmmm. This sounds like an awfully important undertaking for you.

K: Well, I like to work. One thing I just love to do is work and I like to keep busy working—in fact, it's important to my health because if I don't work I'm going to get disturbed. I have to work all the time or be disturbed. I've found that out.

I: Is that right?

K: A disturbance is terrible, I'll start yelling and screaming and dancing around and everything. I'll have seizures if I don't go on working.

I: So you must keep busy for your own health?

K: I must keep busy. I'm that addicted to work. And work is a nice habit, I think. Everybody approves of work, really. But, so few people would like to do it, I find. Even people in jobs don't, I think, like to work as much as I do. Sometimes I think that some kind of work mania is what I'm probably here for. At least that's the only thing I can think of that I could have as a mental illness—some kind of work mania.

I: A work mania.

K: A work mania is what I think . . . I must have . . . no kind of mental pain.

I: What about the periods when you're disturbed, do you think that maybe that has something to do with it?

K: But that's not what I'm here for because I just get therapy for that. I don't keep disturbances any longer than I can help it, because I yell and scream and I don't like to yell and scream because it's—look, it's kind of frowned on in my building. I can do anything but scream, it's so horrible.

I: What sort of therapy do you get for the screaming?

K: I do self therapy. I don't quite know what it is, but I . . . I get self therapy for it. Uh . . . I'm getting to . . . I can therapy other patients. I'm also operating a little business of therapying other patients, now, because of giving myself self therapy, because I didn't get any from the hospital, I give myself self therapy and now I know something about therapy that most people don't know—especially for disturbance and things like that. I've helped out a lot.

I: What have you learned in terms of your own self therapy?

K: Well, it's hard to say, but I know what to say to people to calm them down and get rid of their disturbance. That's what I can do, I can get rid of their disturbance by talking to them and explaining things. Sometimes I think an explanation helps in disturbance.

I: What?

K: Sometimes I think that an explanation helps the disturbed. And I'm good at them.

I: Do you do this through thoughts or do you actually speak to the people?

K: I speak to the people over my voices. I never did speak to them on the ward. They might get violent or something. They might get violent if I spoke to them, but I speak to them over my voices and they can hear. They don't want anybody to know that they're disturbed. It's all terribly secret.

I: Do you know anyone else who can speak to people through their thoughts, or are you the only one?

K: I don't know how many people can do it, but I've heard of the patients—I've heard doctors tell me about other patients that talk over voices. I don't know how common it is . . . It, well, it does seem to have sexual overtones. And I wouldn't like that either. In a Freudian kind of way they probably have sexual overtones, produce a web-like pattern of leaves or something like that . . . was kind of distorted. It probably does have sexual meaning. It's probably one reason why it's so disturbing.

I: Mm-hmm. Do you find sex a disturbing topic or experience?

K: I don't get much of it and I don't have much to do with it (sniff). I've had very little sex in my life. Nobody's ever really allowed me to have it. It's been kind of suppressed. I've never been allowed to have much. They didn't want me to have it at home and so forth. I've been kind of undersexed. I mean I think I am sexually adequate, but as far as practicing it, it has never really come my way. People never pay much attention to me. They pretty well let me go my own way.

I: Mmm. So you felt as though your parents didn't want you to have sex?

K: Well, I suppose that's true, but what I really don't like is the way people—I've had sexual brutality worked on me and things like that. I've had a lot of that over my voices especially—dirty things people have said to me, and so forth, over my voices. And that's the kind of thing I really did object to. And as far as the nice being taken up, as being taken up sexually by nice people well, they've kind of ignored me.

I: So there have been sexual brutalities over the voices perpetrated on you . . .

K: And the good sex has ignored me.

I: Can you give me an example of what you mean by sexual brutalities that the voices practice?

K: Well, yes. Pornography and cursing and dirt and jokes and things like that—anything that will tend to give you some kind of horrible sexual reaction.

I: So, you've decided to do police work on these voices?

K: Well, that's what I . . . I am doing police work on them. I admit that I have to hear it to do police work. And I am doing police work on it. It's just part of this endless report that I am preparing. And if you can believe voices, I can tell you something about who's hearing my reports. Well the Pope, the Pope is interested in this. The Pope in Rome is interested in my reports. He's probably going to do a little excommunication on them. At least that's what he said over my voices. You would be surprised at the famous people that talk over my voices.

I: You mean the Pope is going to do an excommunication on you?

K: Not on me. But on people that I've reported.

I: I see. Who are some of the famous people that you hear?

K: Well, the Pope and God and Jesus Christ and angels—just to name the religious field. Then all kinds of famous movie stars and the people, people in government and politics—heads of state all over the world and so on. That's the kind of person that—and artists and historians and philosophers and people like that—that's the kind of people that talk to me.

I: And some of them engage in sexual brutality?

K: Well, those don't. Those don't, those are the famous people, I'm not talking about them. These obscure people—well, they're not obscure now. I expect they're really rather high criminals now. They're probably involved in some kind of pornography racket . . .

I: No one ever asked you about your voices or the work you're doing?

K: Nobody ever asks me about the work I'm doing. In fact nobody pays much attention to me, including the attendants. They never find out about me. Well, if they do, they're doing it very secretly. They've never asked me questions. The doctor doesn't talk to me. Nobody asks. But this is about the first time anybody has asked me for talk.

I: So the most important part of your life at this point is this report and the work you're doing on it?

K: That's right. Work is what I'm all about now. And having been through college and everything . . . and I . . . I told, I told Mr. J. that I was doing criminology and I think it's certainly true that I'm doing criminology and the police—that's my big science. I don't see that you can say theosophy or anything like that for what I'm doing. I think it's probably mainly criminology. And criminology is basically what I'm doing in the police. What I, what I know of what criminology is—the study of crime or something, I guess. That seems to be what I'm doing: the study of crime . . .

I: The most important purpose that you have in your life now is to continue with this police work?

K: I'll never complete it, because it's just an endless job like any job. It just goes on like, like inspecting soup at Campbell's soup—the soup keeps coming on forever.

I: I guess there's no end to a job.

K: There's no end to it. There'll never be an end to my report. As I said, I'd be disturbed if my work stopped, so I'm glad. I'm that trained for work . . .

I: What sort of pleasures do you have in life?

K: Well, I get an awful lot of pain. For work and so on. I get an awful lot of pain. And I pull up the bag and I—I like it all right. As much as one can like pain. I don't get much pleasure. Sometimes I think pleasure—the pleasure of working—it's just the pleasure of working, that's the only pleasure I get. And any pleasure that's more violent than that I think would tend to upset me. I suppose I could get a bit of it, but really I don't like it now, and I turn it away. When people are nice to me and talk nicely to me I do get pleasure, but I don't like it much, because I'm unused to it and I tend to turn it away and go on with a very disciplined life. I lead a very disciplined life.

I: So you feel as though too much pleasure would upset you?

K: I get more discipline than I do pleasure.

I: Pleasure would disturb you?

K: Well, either would disturb me. It's just not my way. My friends—I have suddenly started talking to friends in Spanish over my voices. And they give me pleasures because of the nicest things; I would just love them. But as for being mushy with them or anything like that I'd never do it. They might like to do it from the way they talk, but I don't.

I: Mushy?

K: Well, romance and emotion and things like that. I talk romantic and emotionally with friends in Pittsburgh.

I: Were these people you knew from your past?

K: Yes, and people like that. I never knew them, but they come on and talk with me now—people I never knew. They're interested in me in Pittsburgh.

I: People in Pittsburgh are interested in you?

K: They're interested in knowing what's become of me as they haven't talked to me for thirteen years that I've been here—I've been here for about—I've been out of circulation for about thirteen years now, and they haven't talked to me since then in Pittsburgh, so I've kind of lost interest in them and I'm very different from them now and if they're going to take up an emotional reward, I know I'm not going to like it because violent emotional pleasure is something I definitely don't want. Not only that, but I can be raped with it. Um, those people in Pittsburgh that talked to me weren't raping me with it, they were just being nice and kind and kind of loving and considerate and so forth, and I don't even like that much because I'm very stern with people now because I don't want to be emotional with people—I'm getting kind of crotchety in my old age.

I: Are you?

K: I'm getting kind of crotchety in my old age.

I: In what sense could you be raped with pleasure?

K: If anybody would try to get violent emotion out of me and especially someone that I didn't like. Some people that I don't like think that they're going to be emotional with me in spite of the fact that I don't like them, but I will be darned if I'll be emotional with people that I don't like. And that's what I call rape. I call it a rape if they're emotional with me when I don't like them. It's perfectly possible—and they think religion preaches it—love your enemies or something, but I don't think religion ever preached *that,* and if it did, I want no part of it. In fact I don't think religion preaches much emotional love. I think that religion preaches something in your heart that you don't feel, just a love in your heart that you don't feel, and I love really, I love a lot, because I'm a good Christian, but as for emotional pleasure, that I don't get.

PAUL: SCHIZOPHRENIA OR RELIGIOUS CONVERSION?

Paul was raised in the suburbs of a large city on the west coast. He was the second of four siblings, two boys and two girls. Both parents were professionals and the family lived comfortably. His mother returned to work when Paul was nine years old, and the children were supervised by a maid. Paul has fond memories of her and describes his childhood as active and happy. He attended Catholic schools through high school, although he began to question and reject church doctrine during early adolescence. He had several close friends and dated actively. Paul's excellent academic record enabled him to enroll in a prominent university; he graduated four years later as a philosophy major with average grades. He began using drugs while in high school and had taken hallucinogens (mescaline, LSD) between twenty and thirty times before he graduated from college. Paul had smoked pot three or four times a week for six or seven years.

The summer following his graduation from the university, Paul traveled to the West Indies with a friend. He had several experiences there which dramatically altered his sense of himself, his existence, and the meaning of his life. First, Paul was swindled out of his money by a native "friend" who easily charmed him into "briefly lending" all of his money. Paul was forced to live off the land and the charity of the islanders for several weeks until he contacted his traveling companion and wired his family for money. Several days later, his friend was attacked and killed by sharks while skin diving. These experiences shocked Paul into a "dream-like" state in which he questioned all previous assumptions about life, and often felt detached from immediate experience. He returned to the United States, and drifted between family and friends. Paul felt alienated from the lives of the people around him. He began to see the lives of his family and friends as sterile, as "illusory attempts to protect themselves from death through the anesthesia of material possessions." They seemed to be "cutting themselves off from life in order to save it."

During this period Paul met several persons who were into the "Jesus movement." They began preaching their beliefs to Paul and eventually invited him to join their musical group and move into a communal apartment. The group often took LSD together and participated in shared transcendental experiences and direct communication with God. Paul shared in these experiences, and became convinced that his friends taught him the "true word of the Lord."

> I turned one hundred and eighty degrees in my thinking and put the Lord in charge: I no longer believed that I was the source of my energy. I could see that the Lord was the source of everything and that I was nothing. So the other fellows in the house and I agreed that it was time for me to cultivate a personal relationship with God and to practice making his will mine. So I went out to speak the word of God, to offer people the realization that there was a meaning to their existence, that there was a source of life that maybe they had forgotten.

Paul began knocking on doors, talking to people about God. He entered an apartment complex in which soliciting was expressly prohibited. He was warned by the manager and replied: "I'm sorry but if it's the Lord's will, then I have to go in there." The manager called the police, who arrested Paul. On the way to the police station Paul attempted to jump out of the moving car. The officers decided to take him to a psychiatric hospital for observation. The admitting psychiatrist described Paul's behavior as "excited, inappropriate, and restless." He noted that Paul was delusional and hallucinating: "Patient thinks he hears messages from God and states that he will do anything the Lord asks him to do." Paul was diagnosed as suffering from an *acute schizophrenic episode* precipitated by drug abuse. This diagnosis was upheld in a diagnostic staff conference several days later. He was placed on a locked ward for seventy-two hours observation and given a moderate dosage of tranquilizing medication. He was transferred to an open ward after three days. He continuously asked to be taken off all medication, and was accommodated after three weeks. A doctor's progress note written one week later noted: "Surprisingly, after the effects of the medication wore off, the patient's actual personality was found to be extremely alert and pleasant; however, over-religiosity continues to be present in his discussion." A nurse's observation note written one month after admission described Paul as "coherent, relevant, expressive, friendly, and spontaneous. He relates quite well." Six weeks after admission Paul was furloughed, his "schizophrenic symptoms" in "good remission." Paul has continued with his involvement in religion since his furlough two years ago, and has had no further formal contact with mental health personnel. The following interview took place one week after Paul was admitted to the hospital.

An Interview with Paul

P: On the way to the police station, I was talking to the man about the Lord, and then for awhile I was praying and I had been saying all day that I would die for the Lord if He wanted me to. It is just what He did for us. He died for us so that we might have life. And I felt that the least I could offer was to spread his word and to risk my life for Him. Many people didn't understand why I would risk my life for something I haven't seen. But I do see the Lord in everything around me . . . in the trees I see the Life.

In taking these leaps of faith, I could see that the Lord is the one who knew best for me. I realized that I did not know, I could not predict the future. Therefore, I could not tell what would be good or bad for me. I could not tell the ultimate consequences of any action I would have.

In putting myself entirely in his hands, I realized that he knew what was best for me. He would take me on the path no matter how dangerous I felt it might be. So the Lord said, you know, well he didn't say, I had a feeling inside that, well, O.K. you said you'd die for me.

Well, the car is going forty miles an hour. Open the door and jump out. So, not doubting that the message was from him—again it wasn't a little voice or anything. It was just a feeling. I said, 'Lord, if it is your will I will do it.' So, I opened the door and started to go out the door and the policeman caught me and pulled me back in. Naturally, I was a little bit scared. My heart was beating and I started sweating a little bit, but I realized right there that the Lord was testing my faith. This is how I interpreted it. There is a story in the Bible, Abraham and Isaac, where Abraham was told to kill his only son, a son that he had waited a long time for. And Abraham said, 'O.K., Lord, I will sacrifice him for you.' So, Abraham was just about to stab him and an angel stopped him. And the Lord said to Abraham that he believed that he definitely had the faith and he rewarded Abraham.

So, I did feel that in this case the Lord was testing my faith. There is a possibility that I was testing my faith cause I doubted in it, but ultimately the action was planned by God, to put me here. The action served to put me here which I feel also was planned—part of God's plan, part of his will.

So the policeman, after pulling me in, then started assuming that I was crazy and started calling up the State Mental Hospital to see if I had escaped from there. And they asked me, 'Why did you try to jump out of the car?' And I told them that I did feel that I was doing the Lord's will and he was testing me and he saved me because I did believe that he would take care of me.

So, I was brought to the hospital and put on a locked ward. Naturally, it's assumed that since I was brought there by the police I was insane, so I was treated as such. When the doctor would ask me a question, I could tell in his eyes, the way he acted towards me that he assumed that I was insane. I knew from psychology courses that when a person is labeled insane that any action—just about any action—any remark he might do is labeled in that context, you know, as being insane.

So, when I was being interviewed, I was asked about why I was brought here and everything. I told him, 'Yes, I believe that the Lord is inside of me and I believe that the Lord communicates with me.' So, he writes on his sheet, 'This man believes that Jesus Christ is inside of him.' You know. Sounds insane, but I believe he is in all of us.

So, it was taken out of context, you know. The one sentence written by itself could be taken as insane. Then I said I believed that God communicated with me, and he wrote, 'He hears God's voice.' Well, not in the common sense of the word. I don't hear him, but I *feel* his presence.

So, when I got on the locked ward after being admitted to the hospital, I just got completely into exploring the environment and exploring the people there. And it was an incredible experience . . . being locked up, being labeled insane and most of your behavior interpreted as being insane. So I found as I was on the ward what the constitutions of these people were. You know, many people—I had assumed that all of them would be insane, but many were not. Many were put in there for other reasons—because they decided they didn't like the penitentiary, because the hospital was known as being sort of an easy way out of things. And they would pretty much get to do anything they want, for if one knows where to look, one can get drugs, one can get women, one can do just about anything they can on the outside only you have to be back on the ward at a certain time.

A lot of people are there just because they have a twitch on their face or some other relatively minor but bizarre behavior that irritates relatives or doesn't quite fit into the average normal American range of behavior.

So, I saw this oppression plus I saw a number of people who obviously did need care. They were confused, they didn't know how to deal with the thoughts going within their heads or didn't know how to deal with their own behaviors.

I was pretty distrustful as to what the doctors could do for them, especially after the experience on the locked ward. I saw that there is very little personal care given.

After I was taken, well, I was taken before staff. I had been in the hospital four days and still hadn't seen a doctor except the admitting doctor, who asked me set questions, and they gave me a physical—a minor physical—and then led me up to the ward. O.K. Four days I was in there without any real personal attention. So I could have been just arrested on a trumped-up charge, which I felt like I was. Really, I saw no reason for me to be put in jail for preaching the word of Jesus, that and attempting to jump out of the car. Well, here they were going to protect me. They were going to put me in a mental hospital because I had attempted to jump out of a car. They were going to protect me for the rest of my life, I guess, from destroying myself, which I surely wasn't out to do in the first place . . . So, here I am on a ward and yet getting no care for whatever my illness may be interpreted to be.

Finally, after four days, I went before the staff and there were psychiatrists, nurses, staff, social workers. I walked in and naturally I was a little bit nervous. I had never been even able to stand up in a classroom at grade school or high school or anything and talk in front of the class without getting a little bit nervous. And here I knew I was going in to be judged by other human beings. In a very short period of time, they were going to tell me whether I was sane or insane. They were just viewing me in this one little room for a very limited amount of time, asking a very limited number of questions. So I was nervous. Even though up until then I felt no desire—no strong desire—to be released from the hospital, because I did feel that the Lord had me there for a reason. And I was seeing that reason every day, I was taking up new perspectives and experience was just broadening my mind, broadening my perspective on the American culture. I was talking with types of people that I had never been in contact with before, and I probably wouldn't, in other instances, have been able to arrange it myself. So I walked into the room, and questions were asked and I knew that since I already was in the hospital, I was assumed insane and, therefore, I knew that there was a possibility of, no matter what I said, it would be labeled in that vein. So, when I went in, I was nervous. I ended up rambling like I am now, and the doctor would cut me off right in the middle of a question. I would ask him, 'Well, O.K., do I have as much time as I need to answer this question, because I could think of causes way back that brought me here. I could think of many reasons . . . what led to my behavior, my belief in Christianity, and so on.' And he would stop me right in the middle and go on to another question, so I didn't feel like I had really had a chance to answer what he was asking me.

So, I was led back to the ward and then I was put on an open ward, and then that evening I was given medication—Thorazine, Stelazine, and for what reason I don't know. Naturally, I was nervous in the meeting, but I did think that it would be assumed that a patient would be nervous walking in front, knowing that his fate was to be handed down from this panel of experts, so to speak.

So, I was given the medication, and I didn't want to take it. I saw no reason for me to take it, but I did. I was watched very closely. So, I took it and that evening and the next day were just hell, because the medicine quickly, well, I guess over about a half-hour period of time, started to depress my breathing. My throat became very dry. One, I had to consciously breathe, and plus, it was uncomfortable, you know, my throat was dry. It felt like my tongue was swelling up.

Gradually, I became very, very listless. I could barely keep my eyes open. I didn't feel comfortable sitting down, standing up, lying down. I couldn't read the Bible, which I had been really thankful to have the opportunity to, so here I could do nothing except just exist.

I felt like I was trapped within my own body. Emotionally, I tried to fight it but, then I realized again that this was part of an experience that God was showing me. So that I was able to carry through it without having to be enraged or fighting back, you know, fighting against the attendants or something, but I felt angry. I felt disturbed, knowing that this happens every day to large, large numbers of people in mental hospitals all over the country, they are given medicine, so to speak, to cure them. It's just used to pacify. Knowing all this, but still at the same time feeling that the Lord would take me through the experience . . .

I: When you say trapped inside your body, how do you . . .

P: Well, I could not really control my body. I couldn't stay awake. I couldn't move around. I just was not able to control my body. My mind was trapped within this flesh. Again, I learned from it. I learned that the flesh is really separate. My body would not respond. I would stammer. It required a total effort to put thoughts together and to get them out of my mouth. So, it was hell.

I: You just really couldn't think.

P: Well, I could think, but I couldn't put it in words. I had the feelings inside, but it was a real effort to get them out. And, since it was such an effort, sometimes I would just not bother to get them out, because it would be so hard, and I knew that the drug affected my behavior and served to further convince people that I did need help. When actually, it was the effects of the drug.

So, I would try to explain this to people when I was talking, but by the time I finished explaining why I couldn't really get across to them what I wanted to say, I was out of energy and I couldn't get into what I wanted to say.

I wasn't sleeping very well, because I would fall asleep and then wake up in the middle of the night. Well, first of all, the beds are very uncomfortable because they are sort of banana shaped—the springs have lost their tension. So they are uncomfortable. But, then, no matter what position I was in anyway, my body was uncomfortable because of the medicine.

My throat would dry out in an hour. So, about once every hour or two, I would have to get up and get some water or something to lubricate my throat, because I was having trouble breathing.

And when I'd go to the cafeteria and try to eat, my hands would shake and again, I would start to wonder whether or not this shaking was because of the medicine or because I started to pick up behavior seen in other patients.

Finally, I got to a building where the doctor did not believe in giving everyone medicine. I tried to get my case across to him as well as I could; that I did not need the medicine and I wished he'd take me off of it for awhile, so that I could return to normal and it would take two and one-half days just for that one dose to wear off. I would have had two doses, but the following morning, I felt so bad on the medicine that when they gave it to me the following morning I put it in my mouth and then spit it out in the drinking fountain. And I just felt that one dose was enough—thank you! I have learned from it and I don't need any more of it. Many people do feel that the effects of the medicine are deleterious to their progress, to their mental health.

You know, I asked numerous doctors if they have experienced the effects of the medicine themselves—if they have taken it so that they know the effect and most of them say 'No.' Whereas I feel that they can never really know what the medicine is doing unless they experience it themselves.

I: How do you find the other patients on your ward?

P: Well, many people have been there—there are chronic patients. They have been in and out because they found it a haven from the rest of the world. Many of them are Christian. Many of them believe just as strongly as I do. Maybe they don't carry it out in their actions. But I have been able to talk to them and tell them that their faith is important. They have just been in and out. They say how they could get along in that environment. They saw that it's a haven. So whenever they get in trouble on the outside again, they might have themselves committed, or they come back in again for a vacation because they really can't afford one any place else, and here they feel like they have some rest and can get their thoughts together, in order to avoid the problems they have on the outside.

Many people don't have the illusion that they are going to be cured. They just need a little bit of rest. Some people are in there, as I said, because they are criminals trying to avoid—well, I don't know that in my building, I can't really say that. A number of people are definitely in need of some help from—some care—but at the same time they don't believe that the doctors are helping them.

I: What help do they get?

P: I'd say a large number of people get help from the other patients. Patients are the ones that are willing to sit down and talk with you—other patients—and also that their behaviors are sort of either ignored or passively accepted by the other patients, so many of the patients do not feel as strange as they do on the outside world. They can talk and interact with other patients, who are also outcasts from the society and they don't feel as strange as they do in the outside world. They can talk and interact because of the one little defect they have.

I: You really see this place as a haven for people?

P: Many people don't want to be in here. They are stuck here by relatives, and things, and they feel oppressed. They feel there is no reason for them to be here—just like one girl was telling me this morning, she said, 'You know, all my life people have been telling me I am crazy. Just because I like to maybe sit outside at night and pray out loud to the sky. I look up to the sky and I pray to God and people say I am insane. This is why I am here now. My social worker sent me here feeling I would be helped. She is totally wrong.' So . . . but I'd say a large number of patients do feel this place is a haven. They come in. They will get three square meals a day. They have a bed. There are authorities here who will act somewhat like parents, tell them what to do. They pretty much have as much free time as they need. For instance, I was sort of—it was sort of nice for me—I was able to take piano lessons, and I never was able to take them before. I could—I just went around to many different rooms—the business machine room—I sat down and boned up on my typing. I would get to try out all the instruments in the music room. I went to the print shop and saw how the printing press was worked. And pretty much got to talk to as many people as I wanted to. A lot of the patients are dissatisfied because they don't have enough to do.

Well, in my spare time I'd read the Bible rather than sit and watch the TV or just bullshit—play cards—so I view the experience as a learning experience. I pretty much feel that I will get out. So I have used the experience to read the Bible, to think, to get my thoughts together, and experience new experiences.

Summary

The diversity of thought, behavior, and moods evidenced by the individuals presented in this chapter, particularly when observed in a variety of contexts, may help the student to better understand the complexity of the issues surrounding contemporary attempts to define and understand schizophrenia. Most of the individuals interviewed expressed thoughts and views of themselves and the world that would be judged deviant or "crazy" by most of "us." Paul is the only possible exception to this observation. But what is it about their thoughts, behavior, or emotions that is different? How are such differences affected by years of hospitalization, medication, the role of mental patient, and awareness of the harsh reality of social attitudes toward chronic mental patients? Can we define one or more characteristics shared by these individuals but rarely observed in the "non-schizophrenic" population? These important questions are yet to be answered.

These case histories illustrate the everyday reality of unreliable psychiatric diagnoses, medication juggling, custodial care, and intellectual confusion disguised by an emphasis on professional jargon that characterize a large proportion of contemporary psychiatric treatment of schizophrenic patients. The state of our knowledge, as it is applied on a day to day basis in mental hospitals across the country, clearly does not approach the idealized version frequently described in the brochures of the local mental health association. The understanding and treatment of persons labeled schizophrenic is often governed as much by cultural biases, economic ideologies, political realities, professional hegemony, and personal frailty as it is by a concern with existing knowledge.

Chapter Five

Dialectics and Schizophrenia

Theories which have been proposed to explain the cause of schizophrenia during this century include a multitude of anatomical, biochemical, constitutional, and genetic hypotheses, as well as a wide range of environmental factors, including: masturbation, birth trauma, social mobility, prenatal stress, social deviance, culture conflict, social change, social isolation, and disturbed patterns of family interaction. There is substantial disagreement in the professional literature about the definition and description of this category, its nature, cause(s), and outcome. Scientists disagree about whether schizophrenia is a single disease, several unrelated diseases, or not a disease at all. After more than eighty years of study, there is disagreement over whether the term refers primarily to disturbances of behavior, ego, meaning, perception, thought, or the ability to assume an accepted social role; whether schizophrenia is present in all cultures or specific to westernized societies; whether it is transmitted genetically or socially; whether an acute schizophrenic attack signals the onset of progressive deteriorative illness, a temporary loss of ego control, or potential breakthrough to a higher level of consciousness.

There is the central question of whether schizophrenia can usefully be differentiated into several qualitatively distinct syndromes, or whether it forms a unity of a more generic character (Dunham, 1976). The social science perspective tends to view schizophrenia as a quantitative variation along a continuum from normal to disturbed (Menninger, 1957). These investigators question the utility of diagnosis into separate categories, and deny that there is any reliable evidence of qualitative differences between schizophrenics and normals. The current psychiatric diagnostic system is representative of the contrasting perspective which views the schizophrenic as essentially qualitatively different from the non-schizophrenic.

The following statements, excerpts from the writings of a cross-section of prominent clinicians and scientists, illustrate the extent of contemporary disagreement about schizophrenia.

> There is abundant genetic and clinical evidence that the disease entity of schizophrenia, as well as other psychotic disturbances, is genuine. The difficulty of the psychiatric community stems from the lack of a simple physical indicator of the disease. (Solomon Snyder, 1974)

> ... the concepts of mental illness in general—and schizophrenia in particular—are not neutral, value free, scientifically precise terms but, for the most part, the leading edge of an ideology embedded in the historical and cultural present of the white middle class of Western societies. ... Schizophrenia ... is a broad gloss. ... (Thomas Scheff, 1970)

> Diabetes mellitus is analogous to schizophrenia in many ways. Both are symptom clusters or syndromes, one described by somatic and biochemical abnormalities, the other by psychological. Each may have many etiologies and show a range of intensity from severe and debilitating to latent or borderline. There is also evidence that genetic and environmental influences operate in the development of both. The medical model seems to be quite as appropriate for the one as for the other. (Seymour Kety, 1974)

> It is clear that many terms—some diagnostic, like schizophrenia—function as panchrestons. In other words, "schizophrenia" is supposed to "explain" so-called insane behavior in much the same way as "protoplasm" explained the nature of life, and "ether" the manner in which energy travels through space. ... (Thomas Szasz, 1957)

> Overwhelming and rigorous evidence exists to show that many forms of mental illness, including schizophrenia and depression, are biologically determined ... in a manner analogous to the link between viruses and cancer. (Solomon Snyder, 1975)

> The term schizophrenia has no particular meaning, does not denote a disease, nor does it even characterize adequately a group of patients. Indeed, as a clinician I find this diagnostic label not only meaningless, but an actual barrier to therapy. (Loren Mosher, 1974)

> Environmental disturbance can cause visible disturbance in schizophrenic

patients, but it does not cause the schizophrenia itself: schizophrenia makes patients more vulnerable to disturbance. (David Hawkins, 1973)

The term "schizophrenic" is not a description but a category on which one relies in establishing a belief in certain essences that are either manifest or not and, if not, that are latently present. . . . One might say about diagnosing schizophrenia that there is a primary metarule to which all such diagnoses conform: past data are reorganized to suit present attributions of essences. . . . There is no "thing" that is schizophrenia. There is only a linguistic convenience that is potentially subject to both viable use or gross social abuse. (Judith Greenberg, 1975)

What Is Schizophrenia?

The concept of schizophrenia has not generated a well-ordered set of observations that fit readily into existing theories and interpretations of the natural world. Schizophrenia refers to a complex set of phenomena associated with the overall situation of the individual in the world; phenomena which can be viewed and understood at different levels: the physical (people as object), biological (people as animal), and the human (people as meaning-creating, intentional). Rather than a specific genetic, biochemical, instinctual, or psychological essence, schizophrenia may be viewed as referring to an overall reaction of the individual taken in his or her totality.

The various levels of scientific analysis and theory may be described as in dialectical relationship to the other, each with its own dynamic form and structure, each higher one a repetition and new structuration of the lower (Merleau-Ponty, 1962). The human, for example, is neither reducible to nor can it be completely understood in terms of the physical level of analysis. Failure to appreciate the fact that separate levels of theoretical understanding complement rather than contradict, and represent completely separate, new structurings has resulted in much unnecessary and futile debate. Each level of analysis lends itself to a separate definition of the phenomena to be studied and focuses on different aspects of the processes to be explained. The usefulness of a specific theory must be measured not by whether or not it is "true," but by its ability to explain and solve the particular questions for which it was created (Millon, 1969). Each level has a legitimate and potentially valuable contribution to make to the study of schizophrenia. Failure to recognize the implications of the existence of different levels of scientific observation and conceptualization has resulted in confusion and useless argument about the "true nature of schizophrenia." Contributing factors include the peculiar difficulty we have in separating ourselves and our emotions from the problems of psychopathology, and failure to recognize that scientists must of necessity concentrate selectively on relatively narrow aspects of the phenomena to be studied. No single level of observation and conceptualization is adequate to include all of the diverse phenomena associated with the diagnosis of schizophrenia. Alternative approaches observe different aspects of the same phenomena, which are variously described and conceptualized within their respective cognitive schema as the result of either genetic predisposition, biochemical imbalance, maladaptive conditioning, ego dissolution, the transformation of self, or complex social forces. Schizophrenia is, in large part, defined according to the level of analysis and theory employed. Thus, the conflicting statements quoted earlier in this chapter may be understood as resulting from a general confusion about the manner in which scientific theories are evaluated and the dialectic nature of different levels of theoretical analysis. Each level of focus attempts to conceptualize different sources of data. The following statements about schizophrenia, grouped according to level of theoretical focus, illustrate the close relationship between level of focus and definition (model) of schizophrenia.

the biophysical level

Theories which focus upon the biophysical level assume that factors such as constitution, genes, neurology, and biochemical errors are the primary causes of the behavioral symptoms of schizophrenia. The model of schizophrenia as physical disease assumes, following the systems of Kraepelin and Bleuler, that descriptive symptoms are merely surface reflections or compensatory adaptations to an underlying physiological deficit, and are not ultimately necessary to the definition and description of the disorder. From this perspective, there are no controversies or issues concerning the reality or usefulness of the diagnostic category schizophrenia viewed as an illness. The requirements of the future are simply to derive more objective and reliable diagnostic indicators of the disorder to facilitate research on biophysical causes.

> Behavioral modifications, brought about in the patient by milieu therapy, operant conditioning, psychotherapeutic technique, or cultural pressures, can bring about external behavioral improvement and modify verbal productions toward the normal range. Although these changes are considered valuable by society, they do not provide an adequate means by which to determine intrinsic changes of the (schizophrenic) disease process itself. (David Hawkins, 1973)

the behavioral level

The behavioral model assumes that disturbed behavior differs from normal behavior only in frequency, magnitude, and social adaptiveness. Most behaviorists assume that schizophrenic behavior is learned according to the same laws as those determining the development of normal behavior. There is, therefore, no theoretical basis for a diagnostic category based on the assumption of a qualitative difference between schizophrenics and non-schizophrenics.

> Learning theory does not postulate any underlying causes, but regards . . . symptoms as simple learned habits. . . . Get rid of the symptom and you have eliminated the . . . disorder. (L. Ullman and L. Krasner, 1965)

the social level

Social theorists view schizophrenia as a form of deviation from culturally accepted values and standards of behavior; a failure to fulfill certain social norm and role requirements that is assumed to result from social conditions such as family disturbance, economic stress, anomie, and the assimilation of deviant social values and role models. This approach inquires into the social aspects of human existence and its interrelationship with the environment. From the social perspective, schizophrenia is not meaningful as a category of mental or physical illness, but is a term used to control, define, or exclude from the social horizon those individuals who are unable or unwilling to abide by the predominant cultural values and norms of western culture.

> It appears . . . that many of the major reasons for psychiatric hospitalization . . . have to do with disruption of the social ties of individuals . . . these disruptions are not initially under the control of, or in any way due to, the behavior of the individuals in question. (Harvey Brenner, 1973)

> . . . The broadness and vagueness of the concept of schizophrenia suggest that it may serve as the residue of residues . . . a conventionalized name for the residual rule breaking . . . the schizophrenic explores not only "inner space" but also the normative boundaries of his society. (Thomas Scheff, 1970)

the intrapsychic level

Intrapsychic theorists view schizophrenia as a meaningful and legitimate category of mental disorder, a disorder of ego function. They propose that psychological factors such as instinctual drives, frustration, fixation, unconscious processes, and ego regression, are the causes of schizophrenic disturbance. Like the biophysical theorists, psychoanalysts assume that the descriptive signs of schizophrenia are caused by, or are compensatory adaptations to, an underlying impairment—in this case a psychic rather than a physical one.

> Schizophrenia . . . must be understood as the final common path of a number of conditions which may lead to and manifest themselves in a severe disturbance of the ego. . . . The characteristics of severe ego disturbance are identical with the formal signs and symptoms of schizophrenia as described by Kraepelin and Bleuler. (Leopold Bellak, 1958)

the phenomenological level

Phenomenological theorists reject all causal analyses, including those psychological theories associated with the assumption of unconscious motivation. Phenomenology attempts to comprehend the consciousness of the schizophrenic individual, to see the world through his or her eyes. Phenomenology does not seek an objective truth, but the truth of intersubjectivity based on the spatial, temporal, bodily, and interpersonal analyses of schizophrenic consciousness. Phenomenological analysis rejects the *a priori* distinction between normal and schizophrenic, for the validity of phenomenological descriptions is not limited by such judgments. This approach attempts to understand the structure of schizophrenic consciousness rather than its "cause."

> ... the conception of schizophrenia which in fact prevails in modern psychiatry evolved from the very process against which phenomenology revolted. The view of socially deviant behavior, mood, and thought as a manifestation of 'disease' came about partly in a rational-scientific effort . . . this approach implied that cause-effect sequences could, or would, be found for each condition and, once discovered, would allow the development of appropriate treatments . . . Phenomenology addresses attention to the individual as a unique whole person and makes possible an "openness" to the patient's experience as valid and potentially useful. (Loren Mosher and Jon Meyer, 1970)

It should be clear from the preceding pages that assumptions about the "nature" of human phenomena implicit in a particular theoretical system determine one's understanding of the concept schizophrenia. Each system attempts to illuminate a different facet of the puzzle called schizophrenia. Most theorists do not deny that there are frequently real and debilitating behaviors and experiences associated with the application of this label. Some do reject the view that this term refers to a diagnostic category or group of individuals affected by an illness (physical or mental, literal or metaphorical), or to a group which is qualitatively different from non-schizophrenics.

The Possibility of an Integrative Model of Schizophrenia as Disorder

Several authors working within the biophysical and intra-psychic traditions (Bellak, 1958; Handlon, 1960) have suggested that schizophrenia as presently conceptualized either refers to multiple disorders or represents the "final common path" of the inter-action of biological, familial, psychological, and social factors. This approach also suggests that multiple causal theoretical models are necessary for a complete understanding of the syndrome or group of disorders called schizophrenia. Handlon (1960) has proposed the following framework:

> Schizophrenia is a class with several members, each member having single or multiple causes which are not necessarily unique to that member.

His model is schematized in Figure 5-1.

According to Handlon's model, several distinct groups may presently be confused within the current concept of schizophrenia. Categories such as hebephrenic and paranoid, acute reaction and simple, or process and reactive have been proposed as examples of distinct sub-groups currently merged together into the confused "final common pathway" of the schizophrenic syndrome. Each group may be best understood in the context of the study of separate causal factors. Simple "schizophrenia," for example, may result from a single inherited mutant gene which causes an inborn error of metabolism which is responsible for the appearance of schizophrenia; process "schizophrenia" may result from a polygenic predisposition, which in combination with a general pattern of life experience may result in a failure of normally adaptive stress-response systems (Rosenthal, 1963); paranoid "schizophrenia" may represent a mixed group in which genetic and psychogenic factors each play a causal role that varies in relative importance from case to case; finally, acute-reactive "schizophrenia" may be the result of psychogenic factors alone.

The difficulty with the implementation of Handlon's model

Figure 5-1. *A Schematic Drawing of Handlon's Framework for Understanding Schizophrenia.*

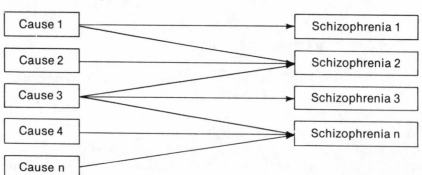

stems from the fact that each hypothesis (and level of focus) creates its own format and experience (Kuhn, 1970). In other words, we rationalize the world through the cognitive schema developed by our particular scientific paradigm. Scientific theories do not describe "objective" reality, but a world created by the paradigm. The task of integrating the various theories into one comprehensive model to explain schizophrenia remains to be done.

REFERENCES

BELLAK, L. (Ed.). *Schizophrenia: A Review of the Syndrome.* New York: Logos Press, 1958.

BRENNER, M. H. *Mental Illness and the Economy.* New Haven: Yale University Press, 1973.

DUNHAM, H. W. Society, culture and mental disorder. *Archives of General Psychiatry, 33,* 1976, 147–156.

GREENBERG, J. Schizophrenia: heretical notes on a diagnostic category. *Schizophrenia Bulletin, 12,* 1975, 10–14.

HANDLON, J. H. A meta-theoretical view of the assumptions regarding the etiology of schizophrenia. *Archives of General Psychiatry, 2,* 1960, 43–60.

HAWKINS, D. The orthomolecular approach to the diagnosis of schizophrenia. In *Orthomolecular Psychiatry,* edited by A. Hoffer and L. Pauling, p. 617. San Francisco: W. H. Freeman, 1973.

KETY, S. From rationalization to reason. *American Journal of Psychiatry, 131,* 1974, 957–963.

KUHN, T. S. *The Structure of Scientific Revolutions.* Chicago: University of Chicago Press, 1970.

MENNINGER, K. Psychiatric Diagnosis. *Bulletin of the Menninger Clinic, 23,* 1959, 226–240.

MERLEAU-PONTY, M. *Phenomenology of Perception.* New York: Routledge and Kegan Paul, 1962.

MILLON, T. *Modern Psychopathology.* Philadelphia: Saunders, 1959.

MOSHER, L. Schizophrenia. *Psychiatric News,* January 3, 1973.

MOSHER, L. and J. MEYER. Phenomenology in perspective: is there schizophrenia? *Schizophrenia Bulletin, 2,* 1970, 11–14.

PAGE, J. *Psychopathology: The Science of Understanding Deviance.* Chicago: Aldine, 1975.

ROSENTHAL, D. *The Genain Quadruplets.* New York: Basic Books, 1963.

SCHEFF, T. J. Schizophrenia as ideology. *Schizophrenia Bulletin, 2,* 1970, 15–19.

SNYDER, S. *Madness and the Brain.* New York: McGraw Hill, 1974.

————. A demonology of dope. *Psychology Today,* February 1975, p. 88.

SZASZ, T. The problem of psychiatric nosology: a contribution to a situational analysis of psychiatric operations. *American Journal of Psychiatry, 114,* 1957, 405–413.

ULLMAN, L. and L. KRASNER. *Cases Studies in Behavior Modification.* New York: Holt, Rinehart & Winston, 1965.

Part Two

Theories of Schizophrenia

Chapter Six

Genetic and Biochemical Models

Genetic Models

Theories which focus on biophysical variables can for convenience, be divided into two groups, those based on the assumption of genetic inheritance, and those based on the assumption that schizophrenia is the result of neurophysiological dysfunction.

genetic transmission

If we consider the ways in which hereditary factors influence behavior, we must be impressed by their diversity. Each of us began as a single cell. The genes in that cell recur in all the cells in the adult body that develops from it, and provide continuity between that cell and the adult. The individual begins when a *sperm* cell from the male penetrates the wall of an *ovum* from the female and fertilizes it. Sperm and ova develop from germ cells. Each germ cell has twenty-three pairs of chromosomes—the normal number of chromosomes found in all human cells. At full maturity, each germ cell divides in two: half the chromosomes go to one sperm or ovum, and half to the other. This division of chromosome pairs is random. Since there are twenty-three different pairs of chromosomes, the number of genetically different sperm or ova that a single human can produce is 2^{23}, or eight million.

When the sperm penetrates the ovum, the resulting *zygote* has a full complement of twenty-three pairs of chromosomes, one of each pair coming from the male and the other from the female. In a single mating, any one of eight million chromosome patterns of the sperm might combine with any of the eight million different chromosome patterns of the ovum to form a single zygote—one of the sixty trillion possibilities.

Chromosomes bear many sets of DNA (deoxyribo nucleic acid) molecules called *genes*. Genes are the determiners of all inherited characteristics—eye color, hair texture, hair color, gender, and so on. This does not imply, however, that one gene is necessarily responsible for each trait. Each gene can produce multiple effects, and each trait is the result of the interaction of many effects from different genes.

Dominant and Recessive Genes.   Every gene has its corresponding partner in a paired chromosome. The two members of any pair may, however, have opposite influences in determining a particular trait. In the case of eye color, for example, one of the sets of genes that plays an important part in determining the color of the eyes may be found in the following pairs: *AA, aa,* or *Aa* (*A* = brown eyes, *a* = blue eyes). In the first case, *AA*, both genes are for brown eyes. The person is *homozygous* for brown eyes, will have brown eyes, and so will his or her children. In the second case, *aa,* the individual is homozygous for blue eyes. If the mate is similarly homozygous, all their children will have blue eyes. The third individual, *Aa,* is *heterozygous;* since *A* is dominant (it suppresses the expression of *a*), the person will have brown eyes but carry a recessive gene for blue eyes.

Psychological traits appear to involve multiple determination by many sets of genes, and rarely exhibit straightforward dominant-recessive properties. A gene is a chemical unit that has only one primary action. Nevertheless, each step of the biochemical processes in which it is involved may have multiple effects. The effects of the action of one gene are likely to be influenced by the actions of other genes so that it is unlikely that there are many instances in which a single gene is solely responsible for the development of a given trait. Furthermore, as soon as the individual is conceived, he or she is subject to environmental effects which alter the phenotypic expression of the genotype.

In spite of the complexities of genetic inheritance of psychological traits, many people have proposed that schizophrenia is caused by a gene—either dominant or recessive. Rosenthal (1971) has considered the genotypes that would occur in the children of different matings if schizophrenia were caused by a dominant or a recessive gene. In the case of a dominant gene, S, a mating between two normal people would be $ss \times ss$. Since the recessive gene s is designated normal, in this instance all children would be ss and normal. If a schizophrenic married a normal person, the pairing would be $SS \times ss$. Thus, each child has an equal chance of getting the dominant or recessive gene from his schizophrenic parent. The child, therefore, will be either Ss (schizophrenic) or ss (normal). The offspring of such marriages would have a fifty-fifty chance of being schizophrenic. If two schizophrenics married ($Ss \times Ss$), one-fourth of their children would be SS (schizophrenic), one-half would be Ss (schizophrenic), and one-fourth would be ss (normal).

If schizophrenia were caused by a recessive gene, s, some marriages between normal persons would be $SS \times Ss$. One-half the children would be SS (normal), and half would be Ss (also normal). A smaller number of marriages would be $Ss \times Ss$. One-fourth of the children of such pairings would be SS (normal), one-half Ss (normal), and one-fourth ss (schizophrenic). Marriages between a schizophrenic and a normal could be of two types: (1) $ss \times SS$ would result in all Ss children (normal); and (2) $ss \times Ss$ where half the children would be Ss (normal), and half ss (schizophrenic). Marriages between schizophrenics, $ss \times ss$, would produce children who are all ss (schizophrenic). Many people believe that schizophrenia is caused by a recessive gene that predisposes the individual to a disorder of nonvoluntary attention, emotional lability, or disruption of cognitive processes by anxiety.

genetic research and theory

Modern genetic research on schizophrenia is based on empirical "risk" figures rather than modern molecular or chromosomal genetics, since the diagnosis of schizophrenia is based on highly complex and variable phenotypic behaviors which cannot at this time be objectified or tied to somatic indicators. From the point of genetic research, schizophrenic behavior is not an identifying characteristic in the "true sense" (Zerbin-Rudin, 1973), but an abnormal pattern of behavior of multiple etiology; the end result of a process that has passed through multiple stages. Genetic research has been plagued with the problems of diagnostic unreliability associated with such etiological diversity. Diagnostic ambiguities result in considerable variability among populations of schizophrenic patients from hospital to hospital and country to country. Such diagnostic variability must inevitably affect the genetic concordance rate observed between studies. Indeed, Tienari (1968) has observed that different concordance rates (6–36 percent) can be obtained from the same subject population by applying different diagnostic criteria. Such variability in diagnostic practice accounts for some of the variance in concordance rates observed (6–73 percent for monozygotic and 2–13 percent for dyzygotic twins), particularly between older and more recent studies, and remains a major methodological problem for genetic researchers. The partisan flavor of early genetic studies in schizophrenia, a consequence of Cartesian dualism which reifies the distinction between mental and physical, is passing from the contemporary scene; genetic studies no longer read as if the importance of life experience is ignored or ruled out. Most contemporary genetic studies reflect a viewpoint which recognizes the importance of both genetic and environmental factors.

sources of evidence for the role of genetics

Family Morbidity Risk Studies. The first body of evidence is derived from two sources of data: studies of the incidence of schizophrenia in the immediate families of schizophrenics as compared to the incidence in the general population; and studies of the incidence of schizophrenia in the relatives of schizophrenics grouped according to the closeness of the blood relationship to index cases.

The incidence of schizophrenia among the general population is widely estimated to be around 0.8 percent (Shields, 1967). Estimates of risk rates vary according to geographic area, and may rise to as high as 2.9 percent, the prevalence among the general population reported for Geneva (Gerrone, 1962). Interpretation of overall risk figures is further complicated by evidence that risk figures for relatives of schizophrenics vary according to diagnostic sub-groups. The risk incurred by relatives of paranoid patients, for example, is reported to be approximately half that incurred by relatives of hebephrenic and catatonic patients (Kallman, 1938; Hallgren and Sjogren, 1959).

Zerbin-Rudin (1972) has compiled an average estimated morbidity risk for schizophrenia among relatives from the available literature. Estimates indicate risk figures of 9–16 percent for children of schizophrenic parents, 8–14 percent for siblings, 1–4 percent for nieces and nephews, and 3–5 percent for parents (Stromgren, 1938). This evidence indicates that the incidence of schizophrenia is higher in first-order relatives (siblings, children, and parents) of schizophrenic patients than in second-order relatives (aunts, nephews), which is in turn higher than the incidence in the general population.

A clear correlation between degree of blood relationship and incidence of schizophrenia in relatives has apparently been demonstrated, but family risk studies have been criticized on two grounds (Rosenthal, 1970). First, most investigators setting out to prove genetic cause have been aware of the diagnosis of the index case during the screening and diagnosis of relatives. Second, psychologically oriented theorists argue that consanguinity studies can just as easily be interpreted as evidence for the effects of psychological variables such as child-parent identification and the difficulties that arise from dealing with a family member who is schizophrenic.

Twin Studies. A second body of genetic evidence comes from twin studies. Concordance rates for schizophrenia are calculated for monozygotic (identical) and dizygotic (fraternal) twin pairs. Kringlen (1966) has summarized concordance studies completed over the past fifty years. Estimated concordance rates vary considerably for both monozygotic (0–76 percent) and dizygotic (0–17 percent) pairs, but most recent studies show a fairly limited range: 25–42 percent for monozygotic and 5–16 percent for dizygotic twins. The large variation in observed concordance rates among studies has been attributed to differences in sampling procedures, diagnostic methods, methods of determining zygosity, and geographic differences (Rosenthal, 1971). A second source of variation in concordance rates is associated with the observation that severity of schizophrenic disorder is positively associated with the rate of concordance; a sample of chronic patients should show selectively high concordance rates in comparison with newly admitted hospital patients.

The proper interpretation of concordance studies has also been the subject of controversy between geneticists and environmentally oriented theorists. Environmental theorists have argued that the higher concordance rate for monozygotic pairs might be attributable to the fact that identical twins develop a unique identification bond. This bond may result in a similar pattern of disturbed behavior in the co-twin following onset of schizophrenic disturbance in the index case. The fact that concordance rates are higher for dizygotic twins than siblings in the same families, even though dizygotic twins and non-twin siblings have about half their genes in common, is also cited as evidence for the importance of common rearing experiences in determining concordance rates. Many would argue that data derived from both consanguinity and twin studies can be interpreted as supporting either genetic or environmental theories.

Adoption Studies: An Attempt to Separate Genetic and Environmental Variables. A third body of evidence is derived from studies in which children have been given up for nonfamilial adoption at an early age. Several investigations have been completed that have attempted to determine the incidence of schizophrenic disorder in these children and their biological families (Heston, 1966; Wender et al., 1968; Karlsson, 1966; Kety et al., 1968; Rosenthal, 1971). This approach appears to be the most effective method for separating possible genetic from parent-child interaction factors. The results of these studies are attenuated by the fact that prenatal factors are not excluded, and because the separation from the mother did not always take place immediately after birth. Nevertheless, all adoption studies have reported a higher incidence of schizophrenic disorder among the biological relatives of schizophrenics than among relatives who were not biologically related but with whom the subjects shared rearing experiences. In one adoption study, Rosenthal (1971) selected adult index (one biological parent was schizophrenic) cases who had been adopted during the first four years of life. Index cases were compared to a matched control group of adoptees whose biological parents had never had a psychiatric hospitalization. A psychiatrist who did not know if the subject was an index or control case interviewed each subject. Among the index cases, three were diagnosed as schizophrenic, only one of whom had been hospitalized. None of the controls were so diagnosed. When diagnoses were expanded to include "schizophrenic spectrum" diagnoses, the rate was almost twice as high in the index cases as in the controls.

Kety and his colleagues (1974) have conducted one of the most extensive adoption studies available. A sample of over five thousand adults who had been adopted early in life by persons not biologically related to them was surveyed. Of this group, thirty-three had been admitted to mental hospitals and could be reliably diagnosed as schizophrenic: severe and chronic, mild and latent, and acute schizophrenic reaction. Matching control subjects were then picked for each schizophrenic index patient from adopted individuals who had never been admitted to a mental hospital. A total of 512 biological and adoptive relatives were identified. Exhaustive psychiatric interviews were conducted with 90 percent of the available relatives. The interviewer was unaware of the relationship of any subject to a proband. Summaries of these interviews were then read independently by three experienced clinicians who rated for all possible psychiatric diagnoses, from no disorder to chronic schizophrenia. Of 365 interviews, twenty-four individuals (7 percent) were rated by all three as having diagnoses within the schizophrenia spectrum. There was a significant concentration of schizophrenia spectrum disorders in the biological relatives of index cases, in contrast to persons not genetically related to the schizophrenic. The prevalence of diagnoses of schizophrenic illness in those genetically related to the schizophrenic index cases was 13.9 percent, compared with 2.7 percent in adoptive relatives, and 3.8 percent in all subjects not genetically related to the index case. Significant differences between index and control groups, as in Rosenthal's study, were observed for "Schizophrenic spectrum" disorders *rather* than clinical schizophrenia. For example, there was one case of chronic or process schizophrenia among 150 biological relatives of the index cases and one among the 156 biologic relatives of the controls, but with regard to all spectrum disorders, thirteen occurred in relatives of index cases as compared with three in controls.

Rosenthal (1973) has indicated several methodological issues which may confound the results of available adoptive studies. In Heston's study, for example, the biologic mothers were actively schizophrenic, hospitalized, and treated with pharmacotherapy during pregnancy. Furthermore, most adoptive families knew about the schizophrenic mother, so the possible effects of prenatal factors and the effects of negative expectations of the adoptive families cannot be ruled out. Karlsson reported an incidence rate for separated index cases twice as high as the highest rates reported for siblings reared together. This artificially high incidence raises questions about the diagnostic methods used in this study. The number of subjects in the Wender study was small, and the examiner was aware of the relationship between parents and proband group prior to making diagnostic judgments; the possibility of experimenter bias in determining differential rates of schizophrenic disorders between index and control cases cannot be ruled out. Kety and his associates found no significant difference between index and control subjects with regard to clear-cut schizophrenia. Biological relatives of index and control subjects were significantly different only when the concept of schizophrenia was broadened to include the controversial concept of a schizophrenic "spectrum" of genetically related disorders. In Rosenthal's study, not one of the adopted offspring of thirty process schizophrenics was hospitalized for schizophrenia, as compared with 16.6 percent reported by Heston, and a median rate of 10 percent for offspring of schizophrenics. Rosenthal (1973) has suggested that one possible interpretation of this finding is that being raised in an adoptive home may protect children of a schizophrenic parent from developing the disorder themselves.

Kety has suggested that the above evidence speaks for the role of genetic factors in schizophrenia but that it is admittedly not conclusive. Methodological problems, and possible environmental factors such as prenatal influences, birth trauma, and early mothering experiences have not been adequately ruled out. Kety and his colleagues have attempted to rule out environmental influences by studying a group of 127 biological paternal half-siblings among the relatives of the subject sample. This was possible because the paternal half-siblings shared the same father but did not share the same mother, neonatal mothering experience, or postnatal environment with their adopted half-siblings. The number of paternal half-siblings was almost the same for index cases and controls, but the number of schizophrenia spectrum diagnoses was markedly different for the two groups: fourteen of the half-siblings of index cases compared with two for the control group. Kety and his colleagues regard this as compelling evidence that genetic factors operate significantly in the transmission of schizophrenia.

summary of genetic evidence

The consistency of findings of evidence for the role of genetic factors in the transmission of schizophrenia suggests that degree of blood relationship to a schizophrenic is the best available predictor of which persons are likely to become schizophrenic. It is the view of most genetic researchers that the case for a role for hereditary factors in the etiology of schizophrenia has been adequately demonstrated. On the other hand, the mode of genetic transmission is unknown, and there is reason to question the assumption of genetic unity of the wide variety of behavior disorders currently referred to as schizophrenia. Categories such as simple, latent, atypical, reactive, schizophreniform, schizoid, schizoaffective, childhood schizophrenia, and infantile autism are widely considered to be variants of schizophrenia. Some question the likelihood of such diverse variants being genetically related. In response to these questions, Rosenthal (1973) has suggested the interesting hypothesis that reactive (good premorbid) schizophrenics who recover relatively quickly probably do not share the genetic background implicated in other categories of schizophrenia. He also suggests that many disorders not usually placed in the schizophrenia spectrum—severe obsessive-compulsive, depersonalization neurosis, prison psychosis, and some other forms of psychopathy—may be genetically related to schizophrenia.

theories of the mode of genetic transmission

Several models for the genetic mode of transmission in schizophrenia have been developed during this century. Rosenthal (1963) has suggested that all genetic theories can be grouped into two main categories: monogenic-biochemical and diathesis-stress theories.

Monogenic-Biochemical Theories. The theories in this category assume that a single pathological gene is sufficient to produce schizophrenia. The schizophrenic phenotype may be dominant (requiring a single gene from one parent), or recessive (requiring one predisposing gene from each parent). The genotype is believed responsible for a specific metabolic error that produces the disturbed patterns of behavior which define the schizophrenic phenotype. Rosenthal (1973) maintains that theories which invoke two single major genes in the etiology of schizophrenia also belong in the monogenic-biochemical group, because they assume that the combination of two genes produces a particular biochemical abnormality that in turn produces the disorder.

Monogenic theories provide the theoretical base for attempts to determine *the* underlying metabolic error and biochemical aberration in schizophrenia. They have generally not fit the data as comfortably as polygenic theories, and consequently have lost support in recent years. There is a clear correlation between the degree of blood relationship and the incidence of schizophrenia in relatives, but the ratios do not correspond to any known Mendelian pattern. Furthermore, monogenic theories which invoke a recessive gene are difficult to support, since siblings are not affected more often than children. Slater (1958) and Elston and Campbell (1970) have proposed monogenic theories which invoke a dominant gene. Such theories are compatible with the search for a simply inherited biochemical error underlying all cases. These theories do not, however, adequately account for the problem of how the abnormal gene has maintained itself in the general population in view of the low fertility rate of schizophrenics (Gottesman and Shields, 1972).

Diathesis-Stress Theories. Diathesis-stress theories also posit an inherited predisposition to develop schizophrenia, but the nature of the predisposition is usually formulated in terms of personality characteristics evidenced early in life, such as high anxiety level, self-preoccupation, social avoidance behavior, or a deficit in pleasure capacity (Rosenthal, 1973). These theories postulate some hereditary deviation which results in a structural neural integrative defect (Minsky, 1969), rather than a specific metabolic error, as the constitutional aberration that leads to schizophrenic disorders. In contrast to monogenic theories, in which the role of environmental factors is considered minimal, diathesis-stress theories invoke models of heredity and environment interaction. The diathesis (inherited predisposition) is usually assumed to involve a large number of genes, called schizophrenic polygenes (Rosenthal, 1973), whose combined effect is additive. Thus, the more polygenes the individual harbors the more vulnerable he or she is to those environmental stresses that trigger schizophrenic disorders. The polygenic view is currently the most widely accepted genetic model. It allows for both heredity-environment interaction and for a spectrum of schizophrenic disorders, ranging quantitatively along a single dimension, rather than the either-or concept associated with monogenic theories. Furthermore, the modal concordance rates for monozygotic twins obtained in the twin studies of the sixties was approximately forty percent compared with the seventy percent rate obtained in earlier studies (Rosenthal, 1969). This figure would require a penetrance rate (the proportion of individuals with a particular genotype in whom the associated phenotype is expressed) of less than fifty percent, a rate too low to substantiate any single gene theory. Polygenic theory also allows for greater flexibility. It can, for example, account for variations in the severity of schizophrenic disorders (hebephrenic versus paranoid, for example) by postulating that the severe cases have more of the pathological polygenes than do mild cases (Rosenthal, 1969).

Polygenic concepts also imply a movement away from the Kraepelinian view of the various psychiatric diagnoses as separate disease entities, each with a distinct etiology. Rosenthal and Kety (1968) have suggested that a core diathesis underlies an extended spectrum of disorders tentatively believed to include borderline schizophrenia, inadequate personality, character disorder, psychopathy, criminality, and suicide. Kringlen (1967) goes even further and argues for a weakly inherited, non-specific tendency (for example, introversion or anxiety threshold) to mental illness in general, which is precipitated primarily by the social environment. Polygenic theory can also readily account for the question of how "schizophrenic" genes maintain themselves in the population when the fertility of schizophrenics is low. Polygenes are viewed as normal variants circulating widely in the population and associated with many traits besides schizophrenia.

Rosenthal (1971) has presented further evidence for a model of polygenic determination of diathesis. In simple polygenic inheritance the incidence of schizophrenia in first-degree relatives of an index case should approximate the square root of the trait's incidence in the general population; the results of seven of nine studies are consistent with expected values. The incidence rate observed between relatives has been found, as predicted by polygenic theory, to be approximately equal to the proportion of genes they share in common.

Theories of Genetic Heterogeneity. Genetic heterogeneity theories are difficult to place in either of Rosenthal's categories. These theories predict that there may be several major single genes which are not alleles (alternative forms of a gene) of one another, each of which may result in a different type of schizophrenia. The concept of genetic heterogeneity, while highly speculative, is an attractive model for explaining the wide range of behaviors associated with the diagnosis of schizophrenia. This model in effect posits a different gene for each clinical subtype, a hypothesis that is very difficult to test. Supportive evidence has been reported by Vartanyan and Gindilis (1971) who have presented data which suggest that chronic, deteriorating forms and periodic, acute-remitting forms are two genetically different types of schizophrenia.

At present, variations of all theories (monogenic, polygenic, and heterogeneity) provide models which are adequate to interpret most available evidence. The preference for a particular genetic model is based as much on one's theoretical perspective as on solid empirical evidence.

Meehl's Model of Diathesis-Stress Interaction. Meehl (1962) has proposed an influential model in which diathesis (*schizotaxia*) must interact with social learning to produce a *schizotype*. The schizotype, if subjected to certain environmental stresses (such as the schizophrenogenic family), develops into schizophrenia. Meehl postulates that the statistical relation between schizotaxia, schizotype, and schizophrenia is class inclusion: all schizotaxics become, on all social learning regimes, schizotypic in personality organization, but most remain compensated. A minority, who have the additional disadvantages of other constitutional weaknesses and environmental stresses, develop schizophrenia. Meehl postulates that schizotaxia is etiologically specific and necessary; that a non-schizotaxic individual, whatever his other genetic makeup and learning history, would not become a schizotype, and so could never manifest its decompensated form, schizophrenia. This theoretical model postulates a two-stage process that allows for possible identification and measurement of the schizotype. Diathesis, for example, may result in a high anxiety level that is further activated by a schizophrenogenic mother, and increased anxiety in a spiraling effect which eventually results in the core characteristics of schizophrenia in Meehl's system: cognitive slippage, anhedonia, interpersonal aversiveness, and ambivalence. Meehl suggests that the wide range of emotional and cognitive disturbances evidenced by schizophrenics cannot be explained in terms of single function defects; the diversity and extent of these dysfunctions suggests the operation of a more diffuse integrative deficiency. He speculates that the major schizotaxic dysfunction in schizophrenia may lie either in a malfunction of the mutual control system between cognitive-perceptual centers and the limbic motivation-emotion system, or in a synaptic inhibitory defect between the positive and negative reinforcement centers of the limbic system.

High Risk Studies.   Diathesis-stress theories have stimulated a new research approach—"high risk" studies—which attempts to identify the constitutional and life experience factors associated with the development of schizophrenic disorders. High risk investigations focus on individuals who, for various reasons (one or both biological parents were schizophrenic, for example) are considered more vulnerable to breakdown. Many studies are currently underway in which high risk and control populations are studied from earliest childhood in order to identify possible biochemical, physiological, psychological, and life history characteristics which distinguish these groups.

Mednick and Schulsinger (1968) reported a pioneering study of 207 high risk (offspring of schizophrenic mothers) and 104 control children. They compared a group of 20 risk children who had developed severe psychiatric disturbances with a matched group from the risk sample who showed no signs of mental disorder. Comparison of these groups implicated hyperlabile and hypersensitive autonomic functioning, complications of pregnancy or childbirth, early maternal loss, and disturbed associative behavior as precursors of psychiatric breakdown. Following these findings of early physiological differences in the offspring of schizophrenic mothers, Schacter has studied the physiological functioning of newborn offspring of schizophrenic mothers. His preliminary results indicate that the heart rate of these infants is more variable than the heart rate of neonates of normal mothers. Gunderson and others (1973) have summarized the preliminary findings of ongoing high risk studies. They present the following characteristics which seem to distinguish high risk from low risk children:

1. inattention, withdrawal, and lack of positive affect in the preschool age
2. psychiatric referral
3. unsocialized aggression among boys and overinhibited hyperconformity among girls
4. absence of intimate peer relationships in early adolescence
5. evidence of neuropathology under age eleven
6. frequent ill health during childhood
7. disorganized, disrupted families, including parental loss

Mosher and his colleagues conclude that high risk studies provide the following approximate picture of the individual likely to become schizophrenic. Prenatal development and birth process are likely to have been disturbed, and as an infant he or she may have shown some neurological abnormalities and evidence of unusual stimulus responsivity. By preschool age he or she probably seemed withdrawn and inattentive, and feelings seemed overly inhibited or poorly controlled. The child was not likely to have been a serious behavior problem in school, but may have been overly aggressive (boy) or inhibited (girl). The child was probably guarded in his or her interaction with peers, and complained of being an outsider. Difficulties with peers may have grown more severe by adolescence; the person will have complained often of loneliness and lack of friendships.

Cross-sectional studies of high risk populations are also underway. Garmezy (1970) and his associates are attempting to isolate the age-specific behavioral indicants of high "vulnerability-invulnerability" to schizophrenia using cross-sectional comparisons of high risk and control groups of children of different ages through adolescence. Garmezy (1971) has pointed to the wide variability of outcome and unpredictability of the effects of exposure to presumed pathologic influences—about half of Mednick's and Schulsinger's (1973) and Heston's (1966) "high risk" subjects were functioning adequately, and in many cases were rated as more spontaneous, creative, and colorful than their controls—to emphasize the need for including indicators of competence in order to determine age-specific indicators of vulnerability and invulnerability. The six competence criteria considered most relevant during middle childhood and adolescence by Garmezy and his colleagues are as follows:

1. Effectiveness in work, play and love; satisfactory education and occupational progress; peer regard and friendships.
2. Healthy expectancies and the belief that "good outcomes" will follow from the imposition of effort and initiative; an orientation to success rather than the anticipation of failure in performing tasks; a realistic level of aspiration unclouded by unrealistically high or low goal setting behavior.
3. Self-esteem, feelings of personal worthiness, a proper evaluative set toward self, and a sense that one can control events in one's environment rather than being a passive victim of them (internal versus external locus of control).
4. Self-discipline, as revealed by the ability to delay gratification and to maintain a future orientation.
5. Control and regulation of impulsive drives; the ability to adopt a reflective as opposed to an impulsive style in coping with problem situations.
6. The ability to think abstractly; to approach new situations flexibly and to be able to attempt alternate solutions to a problem.

The Present Status of High Risk Studies. Ongoing high risk studies have added new descriptive details to the still vague picture of the variables associated with the development of schizophrenic disorders, but *no* etiologic factors (constitutional or environmental) have been definitely established. Available evidence suggests that the schizophrenic mother is more likely than the normal mother to produce a child who will suffer later disorder. The precise source(s) of this relationship are unclear. Sameroff and Zax (1973) suggest that stress and anxiety associated with pregnancy may cause schizophrenic mothers to be more likely to have delivery complications and to produce infants who are autonomically more reactive. They may also be more deviant and inconsistent in their child rearing practices because of their psychopathology. The combination of these factors in transactional relationship may substantially increase the likelihood of later disorders. Adoptive studies have convincingly demonstrated that adopted offspring of schizophrenic patients carry with them constitutional predisposing factors provided by their schizophrenic parents. Sameroff and Zax believe that evidence of high levels of mental disorders among such children can

be explained by the transaction between these constitutional characteristics and an adoptive mother sensitive to the particular nature of
the child and beset by the complex emotional needs and conflicts
associated with the adoptive process.

The specific factors, genetic and environmental, which contribute to the development of schizophrenia in some high risk
adopted children are presently unknown. These authors argue that
it is not necessary to appeal to a specific schizophrenic genotype,
such as Meehl's concept of schizotaxia, to explain the incidence of
constitutional factors, since available evidence suggests that the
range of possible outcomes for infants with the same constitutional
characteristics appears to be limited only by the quality of their
environmental transactions.

Biochemical Models

brain biochemistry

Neurotransmitters. The fundamental unit of the brain is a
specialized cell called a *neuron.* Neurons are extremely excitable
cells which carry nerve impulses along their extensions at a very
rapid rate. Impulses are carried by a flow of metal ions, such as
sodium or potassium, generated when the resting potential of the
cell membrane is disturbed. Neurons may intercommunicate with
many other neurons across their *synapses* (gaps between the nerve
ending of one neuron and the dendrites or cell body of another).
Most synaptic transmission requires the release of a special
chemical, the *neurotransmitter.* As many as ten or more neurotransmitters may operate in the brain; each may act differently in
different regions of the brain—that is, either excite or inhibit the
firing of a neighboring neuron. Each neuron, however, uses only
one neurotransmitter.

The *catecholamines* are the group of neurotransmitters of particular interest to psychopathologists because they appear to be
closely associated with emotional function. Norepinephrine and
dopamine are catecholamines of special interest. Dopamine has
been identified as the neurotransmitter present in those neural tracts
having to do with the coordination of movements, the regulation of

eating and drinking, the releasing effects of the hypothalamus on the pituitary gland, the expression of emotions. Norepinephrine appears to be the primary neurotransmitter in "reward" or "pleasure" areas of the hypothalamus and limbic system. Evidence suggests that norepinephrine pathways are involved in the regulation of pleasurable feelings (elation, euphoria) and with feelings of depression. These neurotransmitters are implicated in most contemporary biochemical theories of schizophrenia.

Biochemical Hypotheses

The critical assumption of biochemical theories is that schizophrenia is caused by aberrant enzymatic or metabolic processes. Genetic and biochemical theories often seem to overlap, but biochemical defects do not necessarily imply genetic sources. Biochemical aberrations may also result from such nongenetic factors as environmental stress, trauma, or infections. Biochemical studies have variously indicated that schizophrenics show aberrations in levels of plasma protein, indole amines and catecholamines, abnormal antibodies, disturbed hemolytic plasma factors, deviant carbohydrate metabolism, aberrant hormonal levels, the presence of abnormal levels of inorganic ions, and vitamin deficiencies (Frohman and Gottlieb, 1973). There is at present, however, no convincing evidence to support any theory of a specific biochemical cause of schizophrenia. The strongest argument for a biochemical etiology of schizophrenia is, as Kety (1969) has pointed out, the evidence for the operation of genetic factors in the transmission of schizophrenia. In spite of the large number of abnormal chemical findings that have been reported in schizophrenic patients, few have been independently confirmed, and there is no general agreement on the significance of any particular finding. The current confusion of competing biochemical research and theories may be attributed to the absence of any overall theoretical framework for the various empirical observations; and to the inordinate number of variables, and possible sources of artifact, associated with clinical studies of schizophrenia. Kety (1969) has listed the following common sources of error and artifact in biochemical research: (1) Despite phenomenologic similarities, there is no evidence that the heterogeneous forms of schizophrenia have a common etiology. Findings from one small sample may not be confirmed by another. (2) Most biochemical research has been conducted on patients with a long history of hospitalization in overcrowded institutions of questionable hygienic standards. (3) The quality and variety of the diet of institutionalized schizophrenics is rarely comparable to that of control groups. (4) Prolonged emotional stress, indolence, and lack of stimulation or exercise may alter many metabolic and physiological functions. (5) Exposure to a long list of therapies, including convulsive therapies and ataractic drugs may affect metabolic function long after the therapies have been withdrawn.

Few biochemical hypotheses have attempted to account for the full clinical picture in schizophrenia; fewer still have attempted account for the characteristics of vulnerability (Kety, 1972). Four prominent biochemical hypotheses are described below.

The Transmethylation Hypothesis. The transmethylation hypothesis was suggested by Osmond and Smythies (1952) over twenty years ago. These investigators pointed out some similarities between mescaline-induced experiences and schizophrenia, and between the chemical structure of mescaline and epinephrine. They cited evidence that the administration of large doses of niacin and nicotinamide (methyl acceptors) to schizophrenics relieved their symptoms. Evidence of the transmethylation of the catecholamine norepinephrine to epinephrine, and the O-methylation of both as an important step in their normal metabolism, led Hoffer (1957) and his associates to maintain that pathological transmethylation may occur in schizophrenia.

Hoffer (1967) continues to assert that nicotinamide diverts the methylating processes and constitutes an effective treatment for schizophrenia, but a substantial number of controlled studies have failed to confirm his claims (Ban and Lehman, 1971). This evidence does not refute the transmethylation hypothesis (it does counter Hoffer's therapeutic claims), since nicotinamide has since been determined not to constitute an appropriate test of the hypothesis (Baldessarini, 1966). Further support for the hypothesis that pathologic transmethylation may occur in schizophrenia comes from the discovery that a number of psychotomimetic (hallucinogenic) drugs, in addition to mescaline, are methylated congeners of normal body metabolites (Kety, 1969). Pollin and others (1961) found that administration of L-methionine (an essential precursor of S-adeno-sylmethionine, the active substance which transfers its methyl group to acceptor compounds in the process of transmethylation) to chronic schizophrenic patients resulted in an aggravation of symptoms in some patients. This exacerbation of symptoms in between twenty and fifty percent of schizophrenics has been confirmed by other investigators (Alexander et al., 1963; Brune and Himwich, 1962). It is not clear whether the exacerbation of symptoms is an intensification of the schizophrenic process, or a toxic psychosis induced by the administration of large doses of amino acid. Furthermore, there is no indisputable evidence than an increase in transmethylation follows the administration of methionine.

Biochemical studies suggest that methionine could favor methylation of normal metabolites to hallucinogenic substances (Baldessarini, 1966) catalyzed by an enzymatic activity in the brain (Morgan and Mandell, 1969). Friedhoff and Van Winkle (1962) have reported a dimethylated catecholamine (DMPEA) characteristically excreted by some schizophrenics, but independent investigators (Creveling and Daly, 1967) have not been able to confirm this finding. Transmethylation theory is at present a viable but unconfirmed hypothesis.

the dopamine system

A number of investigators have cited evidence that the dopaminergic synapses are involved in schizophrenic disorders (Snyder, 1974; Matthysse, 1974). This hypothesis was originally derived from two sources: the involvement of the dopamine system in toxic amphetamine psychosis, which closely resembles some forms of schizophrenia; and the possible involvement of dopaminergic synapses in the action of the major tranquilizing drugs.

The fact that the toxic psychosis induced by amphetamines closely resembles some aspects of acute paranoid schizophrenia, and the possible relation of amphetamine to naturally occurring catecholamines, has increased interest in the site of action of this drug. Snyder has presented evidence that both the dextro- and levo-isomers of amphetamine act on dopamine receptors. The dextro-amphetamine form also appears to act on norepinephrine receptors.

Cole and Davis (1968) maintain, along with many others, that tranquilizers do not just control secondary symptoms, but that they actually treat the fundamental schizophrenic disorder. According to Matthysse (1974), evidence suggests that the actual mode of therapeutic action of these groups of antipsychotic drugs (phenothiazines and butyrophenones) is an inhibitory action on dopamine receptors in the brain. These tranquilizing agents also tend to produce Parkinsonian symptoms (involving dopaminergic synapses). Thus, evidence from toxic amphetamine psychoses, and the apparent site of pharmacologic action of the major tranquilizers, suggest that the adrenergic systems may be involved in schizophrenia. A growing body of literature has implicated the adrenergic system (the catecholamines dopamine and norepinephrine) in a wide variety of functions—including arousal, attention, motivation, hunger, mood, and pleasure (Kety, 1970). Kety (1973) has speculated that an overactivity of dopamine, an insufficiency of norepinephrine, or an imbalance between the two at appropriate central synapses could be part of the biochemical vulnerability to schizophrenia. There is not yet evidence to support specific hypotheses.

Snyder's Theory.   Solomon Snyder (1974) has formulated a theory which implicates dopamine in the origin of schizophrenic symptoms. He postulates that the "antischizophrenic" potency of the major tranquilizers is a function of the ability of these drugs to block dopamine receptor sites in certain areas (limbic and midbrain) of the brain. Snyder speculates that phenothiazines act as effective tranquilizers by blocking specific dopamine systems in the brain, and that amphetamines produce model psychoses by activating the same systems. Snyder has linked these observations with recent evidence from animal research that link dopamine neurons in the brain with the integration of sensory perception and internal mental states such as hunger, thirst, and tactile stimulation. He postulates that phenothiazines protect schizophrenics from being "overwhelmed by the world" by blocking dopamine receptors, which decreases the activity of dopamine systems and separates sensory perceptions from the internal feelings and memories on which they normally impinge. This model explains the effectiveness of phenothiazines in making the environment more bearable without causing sensory deprivation or putting the patient to sleep as sedatives do. Amphetamines, in contrast, stimulate these dopamine systems and expose the internal states of the patient to his noxious environment.

Snyder's theory is based on secondary biochemical evidence which suggests that amphetamines elicit psychosis via dopamine systems, and that phenothiazines relieve the symptoms of schizophrenia and of amphetamine psychosis by altering the same systems. Direct validation of the theory awaits new breakthroughs in biochemical and neurophysiological research techniques.

The Stein-Wise Theory. Stein and Wise (1971) have proposed that schizophrenia may be related to the genetically determined endogenous production of a neurotoxin 6-OHDA (6-hydroxydopamine) within the noradrenergic neurons of the medial forebrain bundle. The toxin is thought to lead to the destruction of these neurons, implicated in the ability of rats to mediate goal-directed behavior and to experience pleasure (self-reinforcement). Deficits in both capacities are said to be characteristic of schizophrenias. Stein and Wise have proposed that 6-OHDA may be formed endogenously from dopamine in the synaptic cleft by enzymatic action or auto-oxidation. This theory postulates a genetically determined enzymatic error which results in biochemical aberrations, and destruction of selected brain tissue in the reward-pleasure centers of the brain. Difficulties with replication of results, criticisms of biochemical assay methods, and small subject samples suggest that at the present time there is little firm evidence to support the Stein-Wise theory.

Orthomolecular Theory. Hoffer (1967) has claimed that ingestion of large doses of niacin results in dramatic improvement in schizophrenic patients. His work has led to the popularity of megavitamin therapy for schizophrenia. Linus Pauling (1968) has studied the claims for vitamin C and niacin in schizophrenia, and proposed a broad theory of molecular psychiatry. Pauling postulates that each individual has a different requirement for various vitamins, and that by adequately satisfying this requirement many psychiatric illnesses, including schizophrenia, can be treated. Megavitamin therapy involves specialized diets and the administration of massive amounts of a number of vitamins for long periods of time. Hoffer's reports of consistently positive results using megavitamin therapy for schizophrenia have not been confirmed by independent investigators (Ban, 1969). In fact, niacin treatment has been reported to exacerbate symptoms in some schizophrenic patients (Heninger and

Bowers, 1968). Oken (1968) has sharply criticized Pauling's claims for megavitamin therapy, asserting that they are based on little more than remote plausibility and unsubstantiated opinion. Oken has criticized the published reports cited by Pauling on the grounds that they show inappropriate sampling, inadequacy of controls for extraneous intake and for activity or the effects of hospitalization, loose diagnostic criteria, and opportunities for experimenter bias. After an extensive review of the literature, Frohman and Gottlieb (1973) have concluded that much more positive data must be presented before vitamins can be shown to play a role in the schizophrenic process.

biophysical therapy

The major tranquilizers were introduced during the latter half of the 1950's. These drugs have proved to be effective agents for reducing the individual's reactivity to external and internal stimuli, for blunting levels of emotional arousal, and for decreasing overall levels of perceptual input (Lehman, 1975). There is no definitive theoretical explanation of the effects of these drugs available, but it is generally believed that tranquilizers effectively diminish the overall arousal level of the central nervous system without seriously impairing higher cortical function. Tranquilizers are considered to be effective agents for reducing the intensity of the following categories of symptoms of schizophrenia (Lehman, 1975): *arousal symptoms*—hyperexcitement, irritability, aggressiveness, and insomnia; *affective symptoms*—anxiety, depression, and withdrawal; and *cognitive-perceptual symptoms*—delusions and hallucinations.

Attitudes towards the overall effectiveness of pharmacological treatment vary according to the theoretical orientation of the therapist. Biologically oriented clinicians view major tranquilizing medication as the most effective means of "curing" schizophrenia. Psychologically oriented theorists usually consider tranquilizers as a means of controlling arousal level which must be supplemented by intrapsychic and/or environmental changes for long-lasting improvement.

Research on the effectiveness of drug treatment has generally supported claims of the efficacy of tranquilizers in increasing the likelihood that a patient will be discharged and remain out of the hospital. May and others (1968) conducted a one-to-five year follow-up investigation of 228 schizophrenic patients. Each patient received one of five treatments: milieu therapy, electroconvulsive therapy, drugs, drugs and individual psychotherapy, and individual psychotherapy alone. Results indicated that patients receiving drug treatment were released from the hospital significantly more quickly than patients in the other three experimental groups. Patients receiving drugs with psychotherapy were not significantly different from those receiving drugs alone. Three-year follow-up found that patients from drug and from electroconvulsive therapy groups spent less total time in hospitals than did patients from milieu and from psychotherapy groups. Follow-up studies indicated that electroconvulsive therapy appeared to be roughly comparable to drug therapy at both short-term and long-term follow-up (May and Tuma, 1976).

Results of recent studies (Keith et al., 1976) suggest that drugs alone are the single most effective and economical means of stabilizing schizophrenic patients to a point where they can live outside of the hospital. Most studies do not provide adequate long-term follow-up data, however, and the advantages of one treatment approach over another have been found to diminish with time (Pasamanick et al., 1967). Furthermore, marked differences exist in the outcome criteria used in available studies in terms of types of patients, types of therapy, experience level and theoretical orientation of therapists, and measures or indices of the effects of therapies. These methodological differences make any conclusions about the relative long-term effects of any two approaches to therapeutic intervention premature.

Recent research (Goldstein, 1970) indicates that different groups of schizophrenic patients respond to drugs quite differently. Goldstein's research suggests that tranquilizing drugs are most effective with paranoid and/or premorbid patients, and appear to adversely affect (make them worse according to ward ratings) good premorbid-nonparanoid schizophrenic patients. Rappaport and others (1976) completed a three-year follow-up of patients assigned to drug or placebo treatment on a special intensive milieu ward. On follow-up, placebo-treated patients appeared significantly better in overall functioning than their drug-treated counterparts. These studies, while suggestive rather than definitive, indicate that the effects of tranquilizing drugs must be evaluated in terms of the particular group of patients and set of outcome criteria selected.

Critique and Evaluation of Biochemical Theories.   The biophysical approach has produced a large number of empirical studies. The apparent simplicity of biophysical hypotheses, and their potential for verification through relatively straightforward empirical tests, has led many to assume that this approach is somehow more objective—and, therefore, more valid—than theories which focus on other levels of analysis. Recent publicity given to the therapeutic claims of some biochemical theorists, and to the findings of some genetic studies, has led many professionals and nonprofessionals to conclude prematurely that schizophrenia can be understood as a biochemical disorder. The highly publicized claims for the discovery of biochemical etiological agents, or the therapeutic effects of megavitamin therapy, have not been confirmed when subjected to rigorous scientific testing by independent investigators. Poor experimental design, placebo effects, experimenter bias, and the difficulties of separating the effects of prolonged institutionalization, emotional turmoil, and physical therapeutics, such as drugs, from the properties of the disorder itself render the verification of biophysical hypotheses far more difficult than many researchers have assumed. Furthermore, since schizophrenic patients are identified only after they break down and are institutionalized, discoveries of reliable biochemical differences between schizophrenics and non-schizophrenics may be interpreted in one of several ways: 1) factor y caused the schizophrenic disorder; 2) differences between groups on factor y resulted from the "treatment" of the disorder; 3) group differences on factor y were caused by the disorder.

The complex issues surrounding the derivation of acceptable and reliable diagnostic criteria have been largely ignored by biochemical theorists. Schizophrenic patients are routinely treated as a homogeneous group, and few attempts are made to control for even the most salient confounding variables—gender, socioeconomic class, ethnic group, and length of time in an institution, for example. Biochemical hypotheses focus on single links in complex and poorly understood chains of biochemical events within the brain; they are then tested on populations of schizophrenic patients which are notoriously heterogenous. It is not surprising that most widely publicized biochemical "discoveries" of the "cause" or "cure" of schizophrenia are not replicated and are soon forgotten. Even the most viable contemporary biochemical hypotheses are based on the assumption of causal parallelism among questionably related phenomena. The transmethylation hypothesis, for example, is based on the assumption that the experience induced by hallucinogenic drugs closely resembles that of acute schizophrenia. According to the logic of this hypothesis, these assumed similarities suggest that the underlying biochemical changes must also be similar. The hypothesis that the dopamine system is involved in schizophrenia is also based on two questionable assumptions: that amphetamine psychoses resemble some forms of acute paranoid schizophrenia, and that major tranquilizers do more than simply control symptoms, that they directly treat and cure schizophrenia. Both sets of assumptions are controversial, yet they provide the basis for our most widely accepted biochemical theories.

Contemporary evidence indicates that there can be little question that genetic factors play a role in the origin of some schizophrenic phenomena. This evidence also demonstrates that genetic factors in and of themselves *are not sufficient* to elicit schizophrenia. Heredity, in those instances in which it is a relevant etiological factor, appears to serve as a predispositional base that makes the individual more likely to develop a wide range of problems in living. Contemporary genetic research suggests, however, that most genetically predisposed individuals *do not* become schizophrenic. Genetic factors must be supplemented by environmental variables in order to explain the results of recent studies. The concordance rate for monozygotic twins, for example, is approximately thirty-five times greater than that expected for the general population. In two-thirds of the cases in which one twin is schizophrenic, the genetically identical twin does not and will not develop the disorder. Concordance studies provide impressive evidence for the importance of both genetic predisposition and life experience factors in the origin of schizophrenia.

The contributions of the biochemical approach must be considered from the perspective of the separate dialectic levels of scientific analysis described in Chapter 5. Whatever assumptions of causal priority are espoused by the proponents of one level of analysis, each level is complementary, not prior, to another. Biophysical research and theory can help elucidate the organic variables associated with some schizophrenic disorders, but this approach has nothing to say about the meaning of delusional systems. Nor can this approach contribute to the understanding of the role of each individual meaning structure in reducing both existential and situational anxiety. Biochemical and genetic theories focus on human beings as biological organisms. Other models are required to deal with issues such as the significance of personal meaning, intentionality, and responsibility in the formation of schizophrenic "symptoms."

REFERENCES

ALEXANDER, F., G. CURTIS, H. SPRINCE, and A. CROSLEY. L-methionine and L-trytophan feedings in nonpsychotic and schizophrenic patients with and without tranylcypromine. *Journal of Nervous and Mental Disease, 137,* 1963, 135–142.

BAN, T. A. On-going national collaborative studies in Canada: niacin in the treatment of schizophrenics. *Psychopharmacology Bulletin, 5,* 1969, 5–20.

BAN, T. A., and H. E. LEHMANN. Nicotinic acid in the treatment of schizophrenics. In *Progress Report 1, Canadian Mental Health Association Study.* Toronto: Canadian Mental Health Association, 1971.

BRUNE, G., and H. HIMWICH. Effects of methionine loading on the behavior of schizophrenic patients. *Journal of Nervous and Mental Disease, 134,* 1962, 447–450.

COLE, J. O., and J. M. DAVIS. Clinical efficacy of the phenothiazines as antipsychotic drugs. In *Psychopharmacology: A Review of Progress, 1957–1967,* edited by D. H. Efron, p. 1057. Washington, D.C.: U.S. Public Health Service Publication, 1973.

CREVELING, C., and J. DALY. Identification of 3, 4-dimethoxyphenethylamine from schizophrenic urine by mass spectometry. *Nature, 216,* 1967, 190.

ELSTON, R. C., and M. A. CAMPBELL. Schizophrenia: evidence for the major gene hypothesis. *Behavior Genetics, 1,* 1970, 3–10.

FRIEDHOFF, A., and E. VAN WINKLE. Characteristics of an amine found in urine of schizophrenic patients. *Journal of Nervous and Mental Disease, 32,* 1962, 135–550.

FROHMAN, C. E., and J. S. GOTTLIEB. The biochemistry of schizophrenia. In *American Handbook of Psychiatry,* edited by S. Arieti. New York: Basic Books, 1973.

GARMEZY, N. Vulnerable children: implications derived from studies of an internalizing-externalizing symptom dimension. In *Psychopathology of Adolescence,* edited by J. Zubin and A. Freedman. New York: Grune and Stratton, 1970.

_____. Vulnerability research and the issue of primary prevention. *American Journal of Orthopsychiatry,* 41, 1971, 101–116.

GARRONE, G. Etude statistique et génétique de la schizophrénie à Genève de 1901 à 1950. *Journal Genet. Luminse 11,* 1962, 89–219.

GOLDSTEIN, M. J. Premorbid adjustment, paranoid status, and patterns of response to phenothiazine in acute schizophrenia. *Schizophrenia Bulletin, 1,* 1970, 24–37.

GUNDERSON, J., J. AUTRY, L. MOSHER, and S. BUCHSBAUM. Special report: schizophrenia, 1974. *Schizophrenia Bulletin, 9,* 1974, 16–54.

HALLGREN, B., and T. SYROGEN. A clinical and genetic-statistical study of schizophrenia and low-grade mental deficiency in a large swedish rural population. *Acta Psychiatrica, Suppl. 140,* 1959.

HEATH, R. G., and I. M. KRUPP. Schizophrenia as an immunologic disorder demonstration of antibrain globulins by fluorescent antibody techniques. *Archives of General Psychiatry,* 1967, 1–9.

HENINGER, G. R., and M. B. BOUEERS. Adverse effects of niacin in emergent psychosis. *Journal of the American Medical Association, 204,* 1968, 1010–1011.

HESTON, L. L. Psychiatric disorders in foster home reared children of schizophrenic mothers. *British Journal of Psychiatry, 112,* 1966, 819–825.

HOFFER, A. Treatment of schizophrenia with a therapeutic program based upon nicotinic acid as the main variable. In *Molecular Basis of Some Aspects of Mental Activity,* Volume 2, edited by O. Walass. New York: Academic Press, 1967.

HOFFER, A., H. OSMOND, and J. SMYTHIES. Schizophrenia: new approach; result of year's research. *Journal of Mental Science, 100,* 1954, 29.

KALLMAN, F. J. *The Genetics of Schizophrenia.* New York: Augustin, 1938.

KARLSSON, J. L. *The Biologic Basis of Schizophrenia.* Springfield, Ill.: Charles C Thomas, 1966.

KEITH, S. J., J. G. GUNDERSON, A. REIFMAN, S. BUCHSBAUM, and L. R. MOSHER. Special report: schizophrenia 1976. *Schizophrenia Bulletin, 28,* 1976, 509–565.

KETY, S. S. Biochemical hypotheses and studies. In *The Schizophrenic Syndrome,* edited by L. Bellak and L. Loeb. New York: Grune and Stratton, 1969.

_____. The biogenic amines in the central nervous system: their possible roles in arousal, emotion, and learning. In *The Neurosciences: Second Study Program,* edited by F. Schmitt. New York: Rockefeller University Press, 1970.

————. From rationalization to reason. *American Journal of Psychiatry, 131,* 1974, 959–963.

————. Toward hypotheses for a biochemical component in the vulnerability to schizophrenia. In *Seminars in Psychiatry, 4,* 1972, 233–238.

KETY, S. S., D. ROSENTHAL, P. WENDER, and F. SCHULSINGER. The types and prevalence of mental illness in the biological and adoptive families of adopted schizophrenics. In *The Transmission of Schizophrenia,* edited by D. Rosenthal and S. S. Kety. New York: Pergamon Press, 1968.

KRINGLEN, E. Schizophrenia in twins: an epidemiological-clinical study. *Psychiatry, 29,* 1967, 172–184.

SAMEROFF, A., and M. ZAX. Schizotaxia revisited: model issues in the etiology of schizophrenia. *American Journal of Orthopsychiatry, 43,* 1973, 744–754.

SCHACHTER, J. Reactivity of neonates of schizophrenic patients. Pittsburgh: Pittsburgh Child Guidance Center, University of Pittsburgh School of Medicine, 1972.

SHIELDS, J. The genetics of schizophrenia in historical context. In *Recent Developments in Schizophrenia,* edited by A. Walk and A. Coppen. *British Journal of Psychology,* Special Publication, no. 1, 1967.

SLATER, E. The monogenic theory of schizophrenia. *Acta Genetica et Statistica Medica* (Basel), *8,* 1958, 50056.

SNYDER, S. Catecholamines in the brain as mediators of amphetamine psychosis. In *Prospects for Research in Schizophrenia,* edited by S. Matthysse and S. Kety, *Neurosciences Research Program Bulletin,* 1974.

————. *Madness and the Brain.* New York: McGraw-Hill, 1974.

STEIN, L., and C. D. WISE. Possible etiology of schizophrenia: progressive damage to the noradrenergic reward system by 6-hydroxydopamine. *Science, 121,* 1971, 1032–1036.

STROMGREN, E. *Beitrage sur Psychiatricschen Erblehre.* Copenhagen: Munksguard, 1938.

TIENARI, P. Schizophrenia in monozygotic male twins. In *Transmission of Schizophrenia,* edited by D. Rosenthal and S. Kety. New York: Pergamon, 1968.

VARTANYAN, M., and V. GUNDILIS. The role of chromosomal aberrations in the clinical polymorphism of schizophrenia. In *Genetics and Mental Disorders,* edited by L. Erlenmeyer-Kimbling. *International Journal of Mental Health, 1,* 1971, 93–106.

WENDER, P., D. ROSENTHAL, and S. KETY. A psychiatric assessment of the adoptive parents of schizophrenics. In *The Transmission of Schizophrenia,* edited by D. Rosenthal and S. Kety. New York: Pergamon, 1968.

WHITTINGHAM, S., I. MACKAY, L. JONES, and B. DAVIES. Absence of brain antibodies in patients with schizophrenia. *British Medical Journal, 1,* 1968, 347–348.

ZERBIN-RUDIN, E. Genetic research and the theory of schizophrenia. *International Journal of Mental Health, 3,* 1972, 46–72.

Chapter Seven

Behavioral, Motivational, and Cognitive Theories

The theoretical concepts and models presented in this chapter have at least one thing in common: they focus on and are closely tied to empirical observations of behavior. These models are based on a particular philosophy of science, the rules and assumptions of which include: (1) *physicalism,* the requirement that only statements about physical events which are capable of verification are admissible as meaningful scientific statements. All psychological concepts and laws must be derived from descriptions of the observed behavior of humans and animals; and (2) *operationalism,* which asserts that all theoretical constructs must be tied as closely as possible to descriptions of concrete operations involving the manipulation of empirical events. In other words, the meaning of any scientific statement must be tied explicitly to its method of verification. A statement made about the emotional state of another person, that he or she is angry, for example, can mean only that that person is behaving in a particular way, in response to certain stimuli, and that his or her nervous system is in a given state. Strict interpretation of these principles does not allow for the claim that over and above these facts there is an inner experience or state of anger which is apart from them and which has causal significance (Malcolm, 1964). Such rules of evidence for psychological science inevitably shape the subject matter of psychology and the characteristics of its theories.

Behavioral Models

Behavioral psychology attempts to limit its subject matter to the observable activity of the organism. The most radical of behavioral theorists, B. F. Skinner, considers psychology to be that branch of natural science which concerns itself solely with the investigation of the relation between behavior and environment. Skinner (1971) contends that, apart from genetic factors, human behavior is controlled solely by environmental contingencies: "A person does not act upon the world, the world acts upon him." He argues that constructs which refer to inner "mental" events and experiences are inefficient and misleading ways of representing outer events, and that they incorrectly represent information about a stimulating field and obstruct accurate scientific description.

A schematic drawing of a simple behavioral model is presented in Figure 7-1. From this perspective, schizophrenic behavior, like all behavior, is understandable as part of the world of observable events, for which the methods of the natural sciences are completely adequate. Bandura (1974), among others, has attempted to broaden the model of contemporary behavioral psychology beyond the radical view that human behavior can be understood adequately by a model which recognizes only the role of proximate external contingencies. He agrees with the assertion that behavior is regulated by its consequences, but argues that environmental contingencies are partly of the person's own making, that behavior creates environment and environment influences behavior in a reciprocal fashion. This interpretation of the behavioral model to include the role of personal determinants such as inherited potential and acquired skills has broadened the observational bases of contemporary behavioral concepts of learning and deviance.

Behaviorism and Schizophrenia.   Schizophrenia is not considered an entity or disease by behavioral psychologists; it is viewed, at

Figure 7-1.   *Schematic Drawing of a Simple Behavioral Model.*

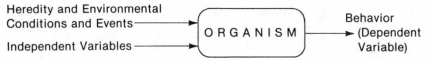

best, as a misleading summary term used to refer to a pattern of learned behaviors. The behavioral model assumes that the principles which govern behavior do not differ for schizophrenic and normal behaviors. The designation of particular patterns of behavior as schizophrenic is understood to be based on the degree to which the behavior in question deviates from social norms.

Behavioral theorists are critical of the use of the medical model in psychiatry, and propose the learning model as an alternative to assumptions of illness. Ullman and Krasner (1965), for example, maintain that patterns of maladaptive behavior are better understood through such concepts as deviance, social roles, and role reinforcement, rather than illness. The following passage is representative of behaviorist attitudes.

> Maladaptive behaviors are learned behaviors, and the development and maintenance of a maladaptive behavior is no different from the development and maintenance of any other behavior. There is no discontinuity between desirable and undesirable behavior. The first major implication of this view is the question of how a behavior is to be identified as desirable or undesirable, adaptive or maladaptive. The general answer we propose is that because there are no disease entities involved in the majority of subjects displaying maladaptive behavior, the designation of a behavior as pathological or not is dependent upon the individual's society . . . The person whose behavior is maladaptive does not fully live up to the expectations for one in his role, does not respond to all the stimuli actually present, and does not obtain typical or maximum forms of reinforcement available to one of his status . . . Maladaptive behavior is behavior that is considered inappropriate by those key people in a person's life who control reinforcers (Ullman and Krasner, 1965, p. 120).

Behaviorists have not developed a specific theory of schizophrenia, since general learning theory is considered adequate to account for all patterns of behavior, deviant and normal. The most notable efforts of this group have been directed to the application of learning principles to modify the behavior of "schizophrenic" patients.

Behavior Therapy. The studies of Ayllon (1965) and his colleagues are among the most prominent early applications of behavior therapy to institutionalized schizophrenic patients. Ayllon has published several reports on the application of operant conditioning procedures to reduce bizarre behaviors in schizophrenics. His studies indicate that "schizophrenic symptoms" such as overeating, hoarding, and wearing of excessive clothing can be reduced or eliminated through the application of learning principles. Reinforcement contingencies have also been used to develop such adaptive behaviors as social interaction, self care, and participation in housekeeping activities; to reinstate verbal behavior in mute, chronic schizophrenic patients (Isaacs et al., 1966); to control self-destructive behavior (Wolf et al., 1966); to increase cooperative respones in early childhood schizophrenics (Hingtgen et al., 1966); to teach mute and echolalic autistic children to use socially functional speech (Lovaas, 1967); to reduce the frequency of bizarre verbalizations (Liberman et al., 1973); and to increase sensorimotor attentiveness (Meichenbaum and Cameron, 1973).

Reinforcement techniques have been applied on a large scale basis in "Token Economy Programs" to increase adaptive behaviors in institutionalized populations. Group reinforcement practices have proved effective in fostering self care, cooperation, social interaction, the acquisition of educational and vocational skills, job performance, and increased knowledge of events occurring outside of the hospital in chronic institutionalized populations (Kazdin and Bootsin, 1972; Shean and Zeidberg, 1971).

A Case Study. In one of Ayllon's studies (1966), a forty-seven-year-old woman, hospitalized for over nine years and diagnosed as *chronic schizophrenic,* was observed to occupy a disproportionate amount of nursing staff energy in attempts to cope with her "symptom" of wearing excessive clothing—a half-dozen dresses, multiple pairs of stockings, sheets and towels wrapped around her body, and a turban-like headdress made up of several towels. In addition, the patient carried two to three cups in one hand while holding a bundle of miscellaneous clothing and a large purse in the other. Daily observations for a two-week period indicated that clothing and hand-carried articles averaged twenty-five pounds over body weight. Body weight plus twenty-four pounds was designated as the initial weight limit with gradual reductions as each limit was successfully met. Failure to meet the required weight resulted in the patient missing the meal at which she was being weighed. In such instances the nurse was instructed to state matter of factly, "Sorry, you weigh too much, you'll have to weigh less." Whenever the patient discarded more clothing than required, the weight requirement was adjusted to correspond to this new limit.

The patient gradually shed her clothing to meet the increasingly demanding weight requirement, until she dressed normally. At the end of approximately eleven weeks the weight of her clothes averaged three pounds. At the start of the experiment, the patient "showed some emotional behavior," crying, shouting, and throwing chairs around. The nursing staff was instructed to withhold social reinforcement by ignoring this emotional behavior. The patient initially missed several meals because of the weight requirement, but she soon learned to discard her superfluous clothing. First, she discarded assorted items she carried in her arms. Next, she removed her elaborate headgear and assorted capes and shawls. Eventually, she began to shed the eighteen pairs of stockings she customarily wore. Finally, after fourteen weeks of treatment, the patient began dressing normally and started to participate in small social events in the hospital.

Shortly thereafter the patient's parents came to visit, and insisted on taking her home for a visit for the first time during nine years of hospitalization. They remarked that they had not wanted to take her out previously because her excessive clothing made her look like a "circus freak."

evaluation of the behaviorist approach

The behaviorist approach to the modification of schizophrenic behavior has several positive features. First, it is related to a systematic and explicit set of theoretical propositions derived from established theories of learning. Second, the close ties of all constructs to observable behavior has encouraged empirical research. Finally, the basic theoretical constructs of learning theory are supported by a sizeable number of empirical studies. This approach has generated important contributions to schizophrenia research, theory, and treatment and is likely to continue to do so in the future. Many of the most difficult to "treat" chronic patients, previously considered to be hopelessly "ill," have been able to return to live in the community as a direct result of the application of behavior modification techniques. The behaviorist approach has introduced a highly pragmatic, functional concern with the effects of immediate environmental contingencies on behavior. In contrast to the biophysical view, which leads to a singular concern with chemical and physical modes of intervention, or the psychodynamic model, which also fosters a relative indifference to the immediate environmental consequences of behavior, the behaviorist emphasis has resulted in many positive changes in therapeutic and institutional practices. Furthermore, the positive behavioral changes effected by reinforcement techniques have often resulted in indirect and unanticipated changes which can have a progressive effect on the overall adjustment of patients—a patient who no longer dresses in a bizarre manner or has temper tantrums may be more readily accepted by other patients, staff, family, and community.

Despite many reports of positive results from the application of learning principles, several theorists have questioned the adequacy of the behavioral model and its associated treatment techniques. Scheff (1966), for example, has observed that the target for most behavior modification techniques is the individual rather than the social system. Scheff questions the possibility of the behavior therapist bringing about significant changes through the individualized application of learning principles when the technique used constitutes only a small portion of all environmental stimulation and social contingencies to which the patient is exposed.

Psychodynamic theorists object to the behavioral approach because it limits its concepts to observable behavior-environment interactions, and fails to allow for the role of intrapsychic constructs. These theorists predict that symptomatic changes produced by behavior modification techniques will be superficial, temporary, and subject to symptom substitution unless underlying personality dynamics are also changed.

Existential psychologists argue that humans have the capacity to anticipate and know the consequences of their actions, and thus to choose to influence or alter how they will relate to their "fate." Existentialists consider all deterministic models incomplete because they ignore those qualities which most clearly distinguish human beings from things and animals—consciousness and intentionality.

Despite the general success of reinforcement practices in modifying the behavior of schizophrenic patients, the results have not been uniformly positive. Some patients appear to be unresponsive to group reinforcement contingencies (Kazdin, 1973). In addition, there is no reliable evidence that the positive changes induced by reinforcement practices generalize to situations off the ward or outside of the hospital (Kazdin and Bootzin, 1972).

Reinforcement therapies have been criticized for focusing on reversing the undesirable effects of institutional life rather than on teaching and maintaining generalizable, socially adaptive behaviors (Magaro, 1976). Behaviorists tend to apply their techniques to those motor behaviors most compatible with their model (self-care behavior, housekeeping activities, the quantity of words verbalized in a specific social context) and to ignore those problems which do not fit readily.

The case of Harvey, presented in Chapter 4, illustrates the basis for this criticism. Harvey resided on a token economy ward for eight years. He earned the maximum number of tokens each day, was neat, clean, and cooperative, cheerfully made his bed and cleaned his living area each morning, spoke appropriately in reality-oriented group sessions, and visited town each week to shop. He worked four hours each weekday for three years as an employee of the hospital janitorial staff, and was prudent in the expenditure of his money. Yet, Harvey was *very* delusional for over fifteen years. He did not discuss his delusions with most people, because Harvey's conversations with staff and patients seldom progressed beyond the level of "weather talk." It was possible to devise an individualized reinforcement program to help Harvey broaden the content and scope of his "weather talk," and perhaps keep his grandiose ideas to himself more often. But the reinforcements apparently lacked the power to induce Harvey to significantly alter the structure of his delusional system.

This may not be of major concern if one assumes that Harvey *is* his behavior. Since Harvey may no longer engage in bizarre verbal behavior, at least when he is in the presence of his behavior therapist, he is (in a naive sense), by definition, no longer schizophrenic. But long-term participants in behavior modification programs, like Harvey, remain in the hospital because their problems often seem more complex and refractory than this model would lead one to expect. And many patients stay because they are afraid to leave, because they become very upset whenever they attempt to assume minimal responsibilities, because they do not have any close relationships with other human beings, no matter how many groups they attend, because even minor changes in their life circumstances increase their anxiety to unendurable levels, because they lose control, act in a bizarre fashion, become overtly confused and delusional.

Harvey tried, with considerable staff encouragement, to visit home on the bus for a weekend several years ago. He was removed from the bus by the police before he got home, and returned in an acutely disturbed state which lasted for several weeks. Perhaps Harvey would also benefit from the application of counter-conditioning and extinction procedures to his anxieties about leaving the hospital. The general lack of success of these techniques suggests, however, that these patients have established lifestyles within the protected environment of the mental hospital that are compatible with their intuitive sense of their own psychological strengths and weaknesses. They become upset when this equilibrium is disrupted.

Counterconditioning procedures and reinforcement practices can help build social skills (Hersen and Bellack, 1976), decrease situation-specific anxieties (Wolpe et al., 1974), and increase the likelihood that some long-term patients may leave the hospital. Nevertheless, we understand very little about the variables associated with the success and failure of these techniques. An approach which focuses on the manipulation of contemporary environmental events to change observable behaviors provides a set of highly useful but limited therapeutic techniques. These techniques may foster a more socially acceptable pattern of mechanical existence in the institution without, in effect, penetrating beyond the regulation or control of stereotyped motor behavior.

motivational models

Thought Disorder. Interest in thought disorder as the primary symptom of schizophrenia originated with Bleuler's formulation of schizophrenia as a disturbance of associative processes. Thought disorder has since been used to refer to different aspects of schizophrenic function. Psychodynamically oriented theorists, for example, use it to refer to the presence of bizarre content and delusions (secondary symptoms in Bleuler's system) in schizophrenic patients. Schizophrenic thought disturbance, as evidenced in delusions, is viewed as a manifestation of a general withdrawal from reality and from seeking gratification through interpersonal relationships.

Experimental models, in contrast, tend to follow Bleuler's suggestion that there is a specific defect in the cognitive function of schizophrenics. These theories attempt to specify and explain, using objective laboratory measures, the manner in which schizophrenic thought differs in form or structure from that of normal thought. A number of research studies and theoretical models have been generated to define and explain "formal" thought disorder in schizophrenia, only a few of which can be presented here.

Response Strength Ceiling.   Broen and Storms (1961, 1966) have presented a theoretical explanation of some schizophrenic behaviors based on Hull-Spence learning theory. These theorists attempt to account for cognitive disorganization in schizophrenics by assuming that as drive (arousal) mounts, an increasing number of responses are brought to a ceiling, and thereby acquire equal response probabilities. High drive levels are assumed to destroy response hierarchies and result in cognitive confusion and disorganization. A variety of schizophrenic symptoms, including delusions, hallucinations, regression, and formal thought disturbance, are explained by this model by postulating that response strength is a multiplicative function of drive (arousal) and habit strength, and that there is a ceiling for optimal response strength. Thought disturbances are said to be produced by response tendencies that relate to appropriate responses, that are, in effect, thrown into the pot of equally available responses once drive is above optimal strength, and are picked out at random.

Broen (1968) has suggested that schizophrenics are characterized by higher drive than normal subjects, by lower ceiling on response strength, or by both higher drive and lower ceiling. If any one of these conditions are present, schizophrenics should reach ceiling more than normal subjects and should evidence a subsequent breakdown in the hierarchical order of responses. Response disorganization occurs, in other words, when weaker, inappropriate responses come to have strength equal to that of the stronger, appropriate response(s).

This formulation accounts reasonably well for delusions and regression. Delusions occur, in theory, when inappropriate thoughts are raised to the same ceiling as appropriate thoughts. Delusions tend initially to be fragmented and disorganized because of the random occurrence of equally probable thoughts. Certain thoughts that are most effective in reducing anxiety gradually become stabilized, and a fixed delusional system develops. The concept of regression assumes that the patient has returned to a response that was dominant at an earlier stage. The effects of higher drive and/or lowered ceiling render the childhood response equivalent to the strength of the dominant response.

evaluation

Broen and Storms have constructed a limited theory of schizophrenic disturbance with a few basic concepts, but there are several problems with it. It is impossible, for example, to specify response ceiling independently or to justify the existence of a ceiling for response strength but not for arousal. Since the location of ceiling is inferred from data it is used to explain, the theory is *post hoc* and lacks predictive power. In addition, some data presented by Broen and Storms (1964) in support of their theory can be explained using simpler hypotheses. They report, for example, that increased muscular tension markedly increases discrimination errors in schizophrenic subjects, but does not affect normals. A simpler explanation of these results than that of a hypothetical lowered ceiling for response strength in schizophrenics is that the technique of inducing arousal (squeezing a hand dynanometer) introduced distracting proprioceptive stimuli rather than heightened drive. Boland and Chapman (1971) have tested one of the few definitive predictions derived from this theory, that the rank order of strengths of responses is the same for schizophrenic and normal subjects. The results of this investigation were not consistent with this hypothesis. The theory is also contradicted by clinical evidence. Schizophrenic behaviors such as compulsions, stereotyped movements, and fixed delusions tend to increase under mounting stress rather than being replaced, as predicted, by randomized behavior.

input dysfunction

Peter Venables (1964) has postulated that schizophrenics suffer from an "input dysfunction." The hypothesis is that chronic nonparanoid schizophrenics have heightened cortical arousal, which leads to greater sensitivity and resulting restriction of the attentional field. Acute schizophrenics, in contrast, are believed to have subnormal arousal levels, are less sensitive to stimulation, and are consequently unable to restrict their attentional processes. Venables' model which emphasizes the inability to focus attention in acute schizophrenics is consistent with reports by acute patients of being flooded by stimulation (McGhie and Chapman, 1961). Venables bases his assumption of a relationship between arousal and attention (the higher the arousal level of the central nervous system the narrower the attention) on limited evidence that arousal in normals is related to breadth of attention (Kinsey et al., 1953).

Venables supports his view that acute schizophrenics are hypoaroused and chronic schizophrenics are hyperaroused (despite the fact that these formulations appear contradictory to clinical behavioral observations) with evidence of differential group threshold responses to depressant and activating drugs (Fulcher et al., 1957; Lindemann, 1932; Stevens and Derbyshire, 1958) and studies of differential levels of autonomic activity (Malmo et al., 1951; Williams, 1953).

Venables has based his ideas concerning the presumed relationship between attention and arousal largely on the work of Callaway (1959), whose studies suggest that heightened arousal induced in normals by stress, or the administration of sympathetic excitants, resulted in a breakdown in perceptual size constancy (objects are perceived correctly, regardless of the effect of distance on the retinal image). Venables has concluded that chronic schizophrenics are overconstant, that they are therefore also overaroused. Recent reviews of the literature on size constancy and schizophrenia do not consistently support Venables' conclusions (Chapman and Chapman, 1973).

Evidence supporting Venables' arguments has been reviewed by several authors (Buss, 1966; Maher, 1966). They indicate that different measures of arousal have low correlations, but conclude that most evidence supports Venables' formulation that chronic schizophrenics tend to be more aroused than normals; thereby more sensitive to stimulation. The evidence is less clear for acute patients. Possible error is introduced, however, by Venables' distinguishing between acute and chronic states on the basis of length of hospitalization, which fails to exclude the influence of other factors correlated with length of hospitalization. Additional possibilities for error are introduced by Venables' comparisons between studies of chronic patients in one hospital using a specific procedure and measure with acute schizophrenics in another hospital using a different procedure and measure. Such differences between studies make the interpretation of results difficult and equivocal. Finally, Venables has stressed the importance of narrowing of attention as the basic input dysfunction in chronic schizophrenia without providing a means of predicting the stimulus to which the subject narrows (Chapman and Chapman, 1973). His theory is largely *post hoc,* because of this lack of predictive specificity.

evaluation

Venables has presented a sophisticated and specific theory of input dysfunction in schizophrenia, has proposed important differences between schizophrenic subtypes, and has provided *post hoc* scales for measuring such variables as arousal, reactivity, and stimulus input dysfunction. Future research will determine whether these differential predictions between subtypes can be cross-validated. This limited theory emphasizes the perceptual and motivational aspects of schizophrenic symptoms, but contributes little to the understanding of the origins of other symptoms.

Cognitive Theories

excessive yielding to normal biases

Chapman and Chapman (1973) have suggested that schizophrenic thought disorder may result from the accentuated expression of normal associative response biases. This principle is derived from a series of word association studies, which suggest that a single principle may subsume the variety of cognitive phenomena observed in groups of schizophrenic patients, such as concreteness, loss of response set, disturbances in concept formation, and errors in syllogistic reasoning. Specifically, Chapman and Chapman have hypothesized that schizophrenics rely excessively on normal preferred word meanings, rather than weighing the several different aspects of word meaning before responding to a statement. This hypothesis is derived from studies that indicate that schizophrenics neglect to use weak aspects of meaning on some tasks even though they can demonstrate their knowledge of those meanings on other tasks. In other words, schizophrenic subjects tend to interpret a word as if it has only the single aspect of meaning preferred by normal subjects, and fail to use appropriate nonpreferred meaning responses.

Normal associates with "water" are "drink," "ocean," "wet," and "rain." An associate is any word called to mind by a stimulus when the subject is instructed to relax judgment as to the appropriateness of his or her responses. Normals produce predictable associates when instructed to say whatever comes to mind, but are able to limit and direct their associations to remote meaning connections in the context of goal-directed discourse. Schizophrenics appear to substitute normal associates for goal-appropriate responses on a variety of measures, including spontaneous writings (Maher et al., 1966), conceptual sorting (Chapman, 1958), and in naming things essential to a concept (Craig, 1967). In like manner, normal subjects respond with normal associates when they do not know the correct answer. Chapman and Chapman contend that schizophrenics show an intrusion of normal associative responses which cannot be attributed to a generalized deficit. In other words, schizophrenic patients have learned the same associative word meanings as normals, but they tend to interpret a word as if it has only that single meaning aspect preferred by normal subjects, rather than weighing the different aspects of meaning and choosing that aspect (perhaps low in associative strength) appropriate to the question or context.

Chapman (1958) asked schizophrenics and normals to sort cards bearing the name of one object with one of three cards that named something belonging to the same conceptual class. On one item the subject was asked to sort *gold*, choosing from among *steel* (correct), *fish* (associate), and *typewriter* (irrelevant). Schizophrenics significantly exceeded normal subjects in their choice of associative alternatives. Chapman and Chapman (1974) have summarized a number of studies which indicate that schizophrenics fail to use context-appropriate low strength meaning responses, but have not lost access to nonpreferred meaning responses any more than to preferred meaning responses.

A number of theories have been proposed to provide explanations for the behavior described by Chapman and Chapman. Cromwell and Dokecki (1968) have suggested that schizophrenics' excessive yielding to normal biases results from an inability to disattend from strong stimuli. This is viewed as an information-processing defect manifested in an inability to disattend from a strong stimulus and to scan all available stimuli (of lesser strength) for purposes of screening potential responses to them. Broen and Storms (1966) have suggested that schizophrenics' elevated drive levels result in a narrowing of attention so as to exclude some contextual cues from awareness. Sullivan (1944) has set forth a clinical theory which suggests that schizophrenic patients have given up the attempt to communicate meaningfully in or out of the experimental laboratory because they have lost hope of gaining satisfaction in relationships with other people.

evaluation

The descriptive principle articulated by Chapman and Chapman (1974) appears to account for a large body of evidence derived from studies designed to compare schizophrenics and normals on such measures as conceptual performance (Gonen, 1970), response bias (Miller and Chapman, 1968), judgments of synonymity (Chapman and Chapman, 1965) and the misinterpretation of words in context (Chapman et al., 1964). These studies provide an impressive array of experimental support for the descriptive principle set forth by Chapman and Chapman. The principle must be supplemented by corollary hypotheses, however, for it does not explain why schizophrenics fail to screen out inappropriate responses. Nor does such a limited principle seem adequate to account for the wide range of clinical phenomena and diagnostic subcategories associated with the label *schizophrenia*.

bannister's construct theory

Donald Bannister (1962) has attempted to describe normal and schizophrenic thought within the unified framework of his modification of personal construct theory. He claims that the only conclusion that can be drawn from the diversity of clinical descriptions of schizophrenic thought disorder is that schizophrenic communications are often incomprehensible to the listener. Construct theory next raises the question of the degree of *meaning* versus *noise* (incomprehensible nonsense) in schizophrenic communications, and offers a method of answering this question through the application of repertory grids. These measures are designed to show relationships between a subject's responses and to provide a system of revealing organization, or lack of it, without reference to content.

Bannister and his colleagues have published a series of experiments (Bannister, 1962; Bannister and Fransella, 1966; Foulds et al., 1967) that indicate that thought-disordered schizophrenics evidence a gross loosening of construing—the mathematical relationships between constructs are low, and the patterns of relationships between constructs are temporally unstable. Additional research (Bannister and Salmon, 1966) suggests that schizophrenics may be selectively, rather than globally, thought disordered. Results of the comparison grids for persons and objects of normals, other clinical groups, and schizophrenics indicate that the greatest difference between groups was the discrepancy between "object" and "people" construing. Schizophrenic patients were only slightly worse than normals in their construing of objects, but they were substantially less stable in their construing of people. This evidence suggests that schizophrenic thought disorder is not a nonspecific trait, as postulated by Bleuler, but may be particularly related to interpersonal construing.

Bannister has hypothesized that the relatively low consistency scores of thought-disordered schizophrenics may be the result of a history of early and/or repeated invalidations of predictions about people. He postulates that repeated invalidation of predictions leads to a loosening of links among constructs. Thought-disordered schizophrenics, it is argued, have been driven to *loosen* these links beyond the point at which there are an adequate number of workable lines of implication among constructs for the patient to re-tighten his system. He or she is thus protected against further invalidation, but it is also impossible for the patient to make clear-cut or stable predictions about interpersonal events. Bannister (1965) has presented experimental evidence that serial invalidation of the interpersonal constructs of normal subjects produces movement toward the gross loosening found in thought-disordered schizophrenics, which gives additional support to his hypothesis.

Construct theory also implies that many interpersonal events have no meaning to thought-disordered schizophrenics because they have no means of making sense of the experiences. This conclusion suggests that one important therapeutic strategy with schizophrenics would involve the implementation of training procedures in which the minimal interpersonal conceptual structures of schizophrenic patients are tightened and expanded through repeated validation experiences. Bannister has attempted to differentiate between subgroups of diagnosed schizophrenics by postulating that thought disorder may be the fate of the person whose construct system had never developed beyond a relatively primitive system, while the acute paranoid reaction may be the result of pressures on a system that was largely workable until certain interpersonal difficulties were encountered (Bannister et al., 1971).

evaluation

Bannister's theoretical predictions have been generally well supported by research evidence, although more extensive studies—by independent investigators—of the serial invalidation hypothesis with diverse clinical populations must be done for adequate validation.

The serial invalidation hypothesis is a particularly interesting experimental model because it can be related to a number of clinical descriptive concepts and theories of the etiological significance of the schizophrenic family, including the "double-bind" hypothesis of Bateson and others (1956), the learning of confused and distorted meanings (Lidz, 1964), and the process of "mystification" (Laing and Esterson, 1964).

Bannister's hypothesis does not attempt to account for the great variety of motor and affective symptoms that are associated with this diagnosis, nor does it seem adequate to account for the many subtypes of schizophrenia. It emphasizes the role of environmental (parent-child interactions) factors in the origin of schizophrenic thought disorder, but it is also possible to posit an inherited predisposition to conceptual disorganization as a supplement to the invalidation hypothesis.

A Review of the Failures and Successes

Research on formal thought disorder in schizophrenia has not yet resulted in substantial clarification of the questions and issues raised by Bleuler's initial introduction of this concept. We still cannot state with any strong conviction whether thought disturbance is a primary symptom of schizophrenia or an expression of severe emotional disturbance in general. Nor has it been consistently demonstrated that the thought processes of many schizophrenic patients are less influenced by the principles of logic, grammar, and syntax than are those of normals.

It appears that there are several patterns of cognitive disorder or deviance, including disturbances of content, meaning, and the formal and structural aspects of cognitive function associated with the diagnosis of schizophrenia. Many reactive patients form highly logical delusional systems and do not evidence signs of formal thought disturbance on measures of cognitive function following the acute stage of the disorder (De Wolfe, 1974; Gilfoil, 1976; Sanford, 1976). It may be that the concept of formal thought disturbance applies to selected categories of schizophrenic patients, such as hebephrenic, process-chronic, and simple, but does not describe the cognitive functions of other categories, such as acute-reactive, catatonic, and paranoid patients. Results of attempts to define and measure the formal aspects of thought disorder suggest that the cognitive aspects of some of the most debilitated patients may eventually be understood not as cognitive disturbances but as sensory deficits, perceptual aberrations, or communication problems (Chapman and Chapman, 1973).

The theoretical models reviewed in this chapter are to be commended for their clarity, simplicity, and verifiability of their predictions. It is these very qualities that lead to their limited clinical application. It is also difficult to understand how some delusional systems (consider Winston) can be understood in the context of contemporary theories of response disorganization, perceptual vigilance, or information-processing deficits.

Cognitive and motivational theories have been closely tied to laboratory research, and have not generated any therapeutic efforts of consequence. Behavior modification techniques, on the other hand, based on learning principles, have been extensively applied in the rehabilitation of schizophrenic patients. As stated previously, behavior therapists do not attempt to "treat" schizophrenia; rather, they attempt to help individuals to develop more effective behaviors and/or to reduce the frequency of occurrence of maladaptive behaviors. Behaviorists maintain that whatever the level of adaptation of the individual prior to hospitalization, the deprived social environment of the mental hospital functions to condition patients to be compliant, passive, and incompetent. Ambitions and social and vocational skills are effectively extinguished by the lack of any support provided in the quasi-medical environment of the mental hospital.

Individualized reinforcement programs and token economy ward systems have been designed to reverse these adverse consequences of institutionalization through the systematic manipulation of the consequences of patient behaviors. Hospital wards are used to reinforce approximations of socially appropriate and adaptive behaviors, and to extinguish those behaviors associated with long-term institutionalization and invalidism. Patients are taught specific social skills necessary to adjust to life outside the hospital (how to be assertive, how to express warm feelings, how to act in a job interview, and so on) through the application of learning techniques and the principles of modeling, role playing, social reinforcement, and transfer of training (Goldstein et al., 1976). Behaviorally oriented psychologists have demonstrated that many so-called chronic schizophrenic patients can be taught effective social skills and can learn to form cohesive social groups which provide social support and new, meaningful social statuses. It has been demonstrated that these group programs can function as effective alternative social systems which enable many chronic patients to live productive lives in the community, and to avoid rehospitalization (Sanders, 1972; Shean, 1973).

Behavior therapists have accomplished a great deal in designing highly pragmatic reinforcement and training programs for institutionalized individuals. Their focus on specific behavioral targets, their emphasis on concrete reinforcement, training and educational techniques, and their dedication to empirical evaluation of the results of programs have unquestionably resulted in some reforms in mental institutions, and have directly benefitted many patients. Behaviorists tend to focus on goals appropriate to their procedures rather than on nonspecific indices of change, such as insight, the cessation of delusional thinking, or alteration of personality structure. Their goals often seem overspecific and mundane, but are of obvious importance in getting the patients to attend classes, to care for themselves, and to work and/or live in the community.

REFERENCES

AYLLON, T. Some behavioral problems associated with eating in chronic schizophrenic patients. In *Case Studies in Behavior Modification,* edited by L. Ullmann and L. Krasner. New York: Holt, Rinehart and Winston, 1956.

BANNISTER, D. The nature and measurement of schizophrenic thought disorder. *Journal of Mental Science, 108,* 1962, 825–842.

BANNISTER, D., and F. FRANSELLA. A grid test of schizophrenic thought disorder. *British Journal of Social and Clinical Psychology, 5,* 1966, 95–102.

BANNISTER, D., F. FRANSELLA, and J. AGNEW. Characteristics and validity of the grid test of thought disorder. *British Journal of Social and Clinical Psychology, 10,* 1971, 144–151.

BANNISTER, D., and P. SALMON. Schizophrenic thought disorder: specific or diffuse? *British Journal of Medical Psychology, 39,* 1966, 215–219.

BATESON, G., D. JACKSON, J. HALEY, and J. WEAKLAND. Towards a theory of schizophrenia. *Behavioral Science, 4,* 1956, 251–264.

BOLAND, T. B., and L. J. CHAPMAN. Conflicting predictions from Broen's and Chapman's theories of schizophrenic thought disorder. *Journal of Abnormal Psychology, 78,* 1971, 52–58.

BROEN, W. E., JR. *Schizophrenia Research and Theory.* New York: Academic Press, 1968.

BROEN, W. E., JR. and L. H. STORMS. A reaction potential ceiling and response decrements in complex situations. *Psychological Review, 68,* 1961, 405–415.

————. The differential effect of induced muscular tension (drive) on discrimination in schizophrenics and normals. *Journal of Abnormal and Social Psychology, 68,* 1964, 349–353.

————. Lawful disorganization: the process underlying a schizophrenic syndrome. *Psychological Review, 73,* 1966, 265–279.

BUSS, A. H. Stimulus generalization and schizophrenia. *Journal of Abnormal Psychology, 72,* 1967, 50–53.

CHAPMAN, L. J. Intrusion of associative responses into schizophrenic conceptual performance. *Journal of Abnormal and Social Psychology, 56,* 1958, 374–379.

CHAPMAN, L. J., and J. P. CHAPMAN. The interpretation of words in schizophrenia. *Journal of Personality and Social Psychology, 1,* 1965, 135–146.

————. *Disordered Thought in Schizophrenia.* New York: Appleton-Century-Crofts, 1973.

CHAPMAN, L. J., J. CHAPMAN, and G. MILLER. A theory of verbal behavior in schizophrenia. In *Progress in Experimental Personality Research,* Volume 1, edited by B. Maher. New York: Academic Press, 1974.

CRAIG, W. J. Breadth of association in psychiatric patients. *Journal of Clinical Psychology, 23,* 1967, 11–15.

CROMWELL, R. L., and P. R. DOKECKI. Schizophrenic language: a disattention interpretation. In *Developments in Applied Psycholinguistics Research,* edited by S. Rosenberg and J. Koplin. New York: Macmillan, 1968.

DEWOLFE, A. S. Are there two kinds of thinking in process and reactive schizophrenics? *Journal of Abnormal Psychology, 83,* 1944, 285–290.

FOULDS, G. A., K. HOPE, F. M. MCPHERSON, and P. R. MAYO. Cognitive disorder among the schizophrenias. 1: The validity of some tests of thought-process disorder. *British Journal of Psychiatry, 113,* 1967, 1361–1368.

FULCHER, J. H., W. J. GALLAGHER, and C. C. PFEIFFER. Comparative lucid intervals after amobarbital CO_2 and arecoline in chronic schizophrenics. *Archives of Neurology and Psychiatry, 78,* 1957, 392.

GILFOIL, D. *Overinclusiveness and schizophrenic subtypes.* Unpublished master's thesis, College of William and Mary, 1976.

GOLDSTEIN, A. P., R. P. SPRAFKIN, and N. J. GERSHAW. *Skill Training for Community Living: Applying Structured Learning Therapy.* New York: Pergamon, 1976.

GONEN, J. Y. Associative interference in schizophrenia as a function of paranoid status and premorbid adjustment. *Journal of Consulting and Clinical Psychology, 34,* 1970, 221–225.

HERSEN, M., and A. S. BELLACK. Social skills training for chronic psychiatric patients: rationale, research findings, and future directions. *Comprehensive Psychiatry, 17,* 1976, 559–580.

HINGTGEN, J., B. SANDERS, and M. DEMYER. Shaping cooperative responses in early childhood schizophrenics. In *Case Studies in Behavior*

Modification, edited by L. Ullman and L. Krasner. New York: Holt, Rinehart and Winston, 1965.

ISAACS, W., J. THOMAS and I. GOLDIAMOND. Application of operant conditioning to reinstate verbal behavior in psychotics. In *Case Studies in Behavior Modification,* edited by L. Ullman and L. Krasner. New York: Holt, Rinehart and Winston, 1965.

KAZDIN, A. E. The failure of some patients to respond to token programs. *Journal of Behavior Therapy and Experimental Psychiatry, 4,* 1973, 7–14.

KAZDIN, A. E., and R. R. BOOTZIN. The token economy: an evaluative review. *Journal of Applied Behavior Analysis, 5,* 1972, 343–372.

KEY, R. J. Effects of lysergic acid diethylamide on potentials evoked in the specific sensory pathways. *British Medical Bulletin, 21,* 1965, 30–35.

KINSEY, A. C., W. B. POMEROY, C. E. MARTIN, and P. H. GEBBARD. *Sexual Behavior of the Human Female.* Philadelphia: Saunders, 1953.

LAING, R. D., and A. ESTERSON. *Sanity, Madness and the Family.* London: Tavistock, 1964.

LIBERMAN, R. P., J. TEIGEN, R. PATTERSON, and V. BAKER. Reducing delusional speech in chronic paranoid schizophrenics. *Journal of Applied Behavior Analysis, 6,* 1973, 57–64.

LIDZ, T. *The Family and Human Adaptation.* New York: International Universities Press, 1963.

LINDEMANN, E. Psychological changes in normal and abnormal individuals under the influence of sodium amytal. *American Journal of Psychiatry, 11,* 1932, 1083.

LOVAAS, O. I. A behavior therapy approach to the treatment of childhood schizophrenia. In *Minnesota Symposia on Child Psychology* Volume 1, edited by J. P. Hill. Minneapolis: University of Minnesota Press, 1967.

MAGARO, P. *The Production of Madness.* New York: Pergamon, 1976.

MAHER, B. A., K. O. MCLEAN, and B. MCLAUGHLIN. Studies in psychotic language. In *The General Inquirer: A Computer Approach to Content Analysis,* edited by P. J. Stone, D. Dunphy, M. Smith, and D. Ogilvie. Cambridge, Mass.: The MIT Press, 1966.

MALCOLM, N. Behaviorism as a philosophy of psychology. In *Behaviorism and Phenomenology,* edited by T. W. Wann. Evanston, Ill.: University of Chicago Press, 1964.

MALMO, R. B., C. SHAGASS, and A. A. SMITH. Responsiveness in chronic schizophrenia. *Journal of Personality, 19,* 1951, 359.

McGHIE, A., and J. S. CHAPMAN. Disorders of attention and perception in early schizophrenia. *British Journal of Medical Psychology, 34,* 1961, 103.

MEICHENBAUM, D., and R. CAMERON. Training schizophrenics to talk to themselves: a means of developing attentional controls. *Behavior Therapy, 4,* 1973, 515–534.

MILLER, G., and L. CHAPMAN. Response bias and schizophrenic beliefs. In L. Chapman and J. Chapman, *Disordered Thought in Schizophrenia.* New York: Appleton-Century-Crofts, 1973.

SANDERS, D. H. Innovative environments in the community: a life for the chronic patient. *Schizophrenia Bulletin, 6,* 1972, 49–59.

SANFORD, L. *Information processing and thought disorder in schizophrenia.* Unpublished doctoral dissertation, College of William and Mary, 1976.

SCHEFF, T. *Being Mentally Ill: A Sociological Theory.* Chicago: Aldine, 1966.

SHEAN, G. D. An effective and self-supporting program of community living for chronic patients. *Hospital and Community Psychiatry, 24,* 1973, 97–99.

SHEAN, G. D., and A. ZEIDBERG. Token reinforcement therapy: a comparison of matched groups. *Journal of Behavior Therapy and Experimental Psychiatry, 2,* 1971, 95–105.

SKINNER, B. F. *Beyond Freedom and Dignity.* New York: Alfred A. Knopf, 1971.

————. The steep and thorny way to a science of behavior. *American Psychologist, 30,* 1975, 42–49.

STEVENS, J. M., and A. J. DERBYSHIRE. Shifts among the alert-repose continuum during remission of catatonic stupor with amorbarbital. *Psychosomatic Medicine, 20,* 1958, 99.

SULLIVAN, H. S. The language of schizophrenia. In *Language and Thought in Schizophrenia,* edited by J. S. Kasanin. New York: W. W. Norton, 1944.

ULLMAN, L., and L. KRASNER. *Case Studies in Behavior Modification.* New York: Holt, Rinehart and Winston, 1965.

VENABLES, P. H. Performance and level of activation in schizophrenics and normals. *British Journal of Psychology, 55,* 1964, 207–218.

WILLIAMS, M. Psychophysiological responsiveness to psychological stress in early chronic schizophrenic reactions. *Psychosomatic Medicine, 15,* 1953, 456.

WOLF, M., T. RISLEY, and H. MEES. Application of operant conditioning procedures to the behavior problems of an autistic child. In *Case Studies in Behavior Modification,* edited by L. Ullman and L. Krasner. New York: Holt, Rinehart and Winston, 1965.

WOLPE, J., J. BRADY, M. SERBER, W. S. AGRAS, and R. P. SILVER-MAN. The current status of systematic desensitization. *American Journal of Psychiatry, 130,* 1973, 961–965.

Chapter Eight

Sociopsychological Theories

The Social Context of Schizophrenia

Sociological theories are based on group observations, such as cultural values, demographic variables, economic conditions, role expectations, migration patterns, and socioeconomic class. This approach attempts to understand the phenomena called schizophrenia in terms of the effects of social variables on the organization of individual and group function. In this context schizophrenia is viewed as a social phenomenon rather than a disease, an intrapsychic process, or a personal experience. The causes of schizophrenia are to be found at the interface of the person's behavior and the moral judgments that others make about that behavior. On this basis, some theorists (Sarbin, 1972) argue that "diagnosis" or the labeling of certain culturally disapproved behaviors as irrational, mad, insane, or schizophrenic is a moral enterprise, *not* a medical one.

The findings of social ecologists have articulated the complex role of the social context in which the diagnosis of schizophrenia occurs in determining incidence rates. Cross-cultural research, for example, indicates that incidence rates vary substantially 'from culture to culture (Kramer, 1969) and that patients from different cultural backgrounds can present widely different symptom pictures. Such evidence, as well as evidence of variations of rates within cultures, cannot readily be explained by contemporary biologic or intrapsychic models. Faris and Dunham (1939) published the first major study of the social ecology of the incidence of schizophrenic diagnoses in two large American cities. Evidence indicated that first admission rates varied substantially in different areas of cities, ranging between one hundred and one thousand per one hundred thousand population. The highest rates of schizophrenia were observed in the central city areas of lowest socioeconomic status and highest population density, particularly among unskilled workers, immigrants, and single persons. Isolation, poverty, the breakdown of a stable social structure, and social disintegration have been cited as possible explanations of these findings (Faris, 1955).

Socioeconomic class has also been related to the incidence of schizophrenic diagnosis. Hollingshead and Redlich (1958) first reported evidence that the highest rates of diagnosed mental disorder, particularly schizophrenia, are concentrated in the lowest socioeconomic sections of large metropolitan areas. This relationship between social class and the incidence of schizophrenic diagnoses is perhaps the most firmly established empirical data available on the topic of schizophrenia (Kohn, 1968).

It is now accepted that geographical mobility, social isolation, and low socioeconomic class affect the distribution, prevalence, and course of schizophrenia. The role of these factors as the "causes" of schizophrenia, however, remains in dispute. Two hypotheses have been suggested to explain the inverse relationship between the incidence of mental disorder and socioeconomic status. The *life-stress model* suggests that more stressful life circumstances associated with lower socioeconomic levels of society result in higher rates of mental disturbance. The contrasting *drift* hypothesis suggests that schizophrenics tend to "drift" into lower status areas of the city because of a drop in social position which results from either the schizophrenic disturbance or general social incompetence. Evidence suggests that more schizophrenics than normals have been downwardly mobile (Kohn, 1968). This downward mobility does not seem to result, in most cases, from a loss of achieved occupational position, but reflects a failure to achieve as high an occupational level as do most individuals of similar social class origins.

Kohn argues that such evidence suggests that a simple drift hypothesis must be replaced by a more sophisticated model which states that pre-schizophrenics show some effects of inadequacy and deviance at least as early as the time of their first jobs, and are never able to achieve the occupational levels that might be expected of them. In other words, the downward drift appears to begin long before the initial psychiatric hospitalization. Turner and Wagonfeld

(1967) have reported evidence to support both the life-stress proposition that lower class origins are conducive to schizophrenia, and the drift hypothesis that most lower class schizophrenics come from higher socioeconomic origins. Thus, both hypotheses may be partially correct, i.e., most diagnosed schizophrenics show a downward drift from their original socioeconomic class, but a large proportion of schizophrenic patients are also originally from the lower socioeconomic strata of society. Kohn has suggested several additional aspects of life at the lowest social strata that may contribute to an overall reduced ability to cope with stress. Occupational conditions, cultural values, and limited educational opportunities may encourage the lower classes to focus on the concrete and the habitual aspects of life. Inexperience in dealing with abstract issues and ambiguities may result in a general impairment of the ability to deal with the stresses of cultural ambiguity, uncertainty, and economic unpredictability.

economic conditions and schizophrenia

Brenner (1973) has reported evidence which may help to clarify some aspects of the drift-stress controversy. He has published evidence which indicates that instabilities in the national economy have been the single most important source of fluctuation in mental hospital admission rates during the past 127 years. Brenner maintains that large scale economic changes, *not* personal incompetence, are responsible for downward mobility among mental patients. Economic instability is also much more likely to disrupt (life-stress) the lives of those in lower socioeconomic groups, who are most likely to hold marginal jobs. These individuals, for this reason, show the highest rates of mental hospitalization.

In similar fashion, marginally adjusted workers, or those with a history of psychiatric disturbance, may also become the first victims of economic downturn. Brenner argues that economic evidence suggests that many of the major reasons for psychiatric hospitalization have to do with disruption of the social ties of individuals—disruptions not initially under the control of, or in any way due to, the behavior of the individuals in question. He suggests that schizophrenic diagnoses and psychiatric intervention and hospitalization most often function to compound the overall economic and social disruption brought about by economic stress, and that economic stress is the most important cause of psychiatric (schizophrenic) symptoms.

Investigators have presented startling supporting evidence for the role of social and economic conditions in the incidence of schizophrenic diagnoses. These theorists have not, however, formulated viable explanations of the origins of particular patterns of disturbed behavior (paranoid vs. catatonic, for example), the personal significance of "symptoms," or the fact that only a small proportion of any social class, geographic region, or of those who suffer severe economic setbacks ever enter a mental hospital. These data indicate that social variables must be incorporated into any "final" theory of schizophrenia, but does not in and of itself appear to provide an adequate basis for the formulation of such a model.

Sociopsychological Approaches

The observations and theoretical models presented in this section represent a selection of contemporary attempts to apply the concepts and methods of social science to the understanding of schizophrenic phenomena. These works typically do not attempt or claim to provide systematic or complete models for understanding these phenomena; they do, however, demonstrate the heuristic value of this perspective and the limitations of traditional psychiatric approaches.

the moral career of the mental patient

Goffman (1962) has published a series of essays on the application of social role analysis to understanding the "career" of mental illness. Goffman has based his theoretical analyses on extensive field observations gathered while he was a recreational aide in a large mental hospital. He suggests that schizophrenia may be understood in the context of career analysis, particularly the *moral* aspects of social careers. The moral aspects of a career refer to the sequence of changes that a particular career works in the person's self and in his or her framework of imagery for judging self and others. The moral career of each person is understood to involve a standard sequence of changes in the manner of conceiving of selves, including one's own. Moral careers are viewed as residing within the context of institutional systems; thus, the self is viewed as *something* that resides in the arrangements prevailing in a social system for its members, rather than as a property of the person to whom it is attributed (this perspective represents a radical departure from traditional psychological use of the term to refer to an enduring inner personality construct). In this model, the self is constituted by the pattern of social control that is exerted in connection with that person. The moral career of the mental patient is of particular interest in this context, for in Goffman's view psychiatric hospitalization is among the most rapid and complete disinvestitures of the old self, and the development of a new career (self) that is sanctioned by contemporary society.

Goffman began his studies with the assumption that any group of persons, including mental patients, develops a life of its own that becomes meaningful, reasonable, and normal once the observer's social distance from the situation the patient is in is reduced. This perspective fosters the corollary assumption that so-called "sick" or "schizophrenic" behavior is not primarily a product of mental illness, but of the social context of psychiatric procedures and the mental hospital.

In Goffman's view, most acute "symptoms" of schizophrenia are situationally induced and transitory, no matter how terrifying to the person at the time they are experienced. The perception that one is losing one's mind during such experiences is understood to come from socially ingrained beliefs about the significance of these experiences. These stereotypes lead to a disintegrative re-evaluation of the self, which may lead both to increased anxiety and to efforts to conceal one's feelings which serve to confirm the cultural stereotype of mental illness. Patients may enter the hospital willingly or unwillingly, but Goffman maintains that, once embarked on the social career of mental patient, each is helplessly caught in the web of the psychiatric social structure and is no longer regarded, by society or self, as a responsible participant in society. Goffman does not concern himself with the types of offenses which lead to hospitalization, but argues that schizophrenia may be viewed as a social career, that patients suffer not from mental illness but career contingencies. He has described the myriad forms of betrayal, mortification, stripping of previous career identities, and the processes of identity transformation to which entering mental patients are subjected. Terms such as "degradation ceremony" and "betrayal funnel" are introduced to denote events associated with contemporary psychiatric practices, including psychiatric examinations and the testimony of "experts" before mental health commissions. Such practices are re-interpreted as methods of altering or reducing an individual's social status to that of mental patient and of confirming and affirming the assumption that the labelled person must indeed be "sick." This transformation process is particularly compelling, according to Goffman, because institutional psychiatry claims to treat the "whole" person, and recognizes no limits to the discretionary power exerted over the personal life and civil rights of the patient.

Goffman maintains that pre-schizophrenics can be distinguished from normals only by the fact that they represent a group of individuals who have caused the kind of trouble on the outside that led someone close to them to take psychiatric action against them. This trouble is often associated with improprieties of some kind. Symptoms of mental illness are often culturally defined as misconduct. This conveys a moral rejection by the communities, establishments, and individuals to which one is attached. Society answers such offenses against propriety with stigmatization of the offender as mentally ill, and institutional confinement. Once the person is embarked on the social career of mental patient, signs of alienation (insolence, silence, uncooperativeness, angry protests, destruction of property) are interpreted as symptoms by mental health personnel. In this context, "signs of disaffiliation are read as signs of their maker's proper affiliation." Psychiatric doctrine outmaneuvers the patient, and robs him or her of the expressions commonly used to resist the intrusions of organizations by defining alienative acts as psychotic ones.

Goffman maintains that redefinition of an individual as a mental patient effectively transforms him or her into the kind of subject on whom various psychiatric treatments can be justifiably performed. All aspects of the patient's life are reinterpreted in the context of the mental illness model; thus, the patient's presence in the hospital is taken as *prima facie* evidence that he or she is mentally ill; institutional regimentation is viewed as providing the requisite structured, safe, predictable environment; cooperation is viewed as improvement and rewarded with promotion to "good" wards, and routine activities and assignments are redefined as therapies: gym becomes recreational therapy; folding linens, industrial therapy; crafts, occupational therapy, and so on. The central effect of mental institutions, according to Goffman, is that a medical-like service is being provided by the staff.

Goffman has observed that mental hospitals, like prisons and other "total institutions," are characterized by a proliferate under-life among the inmates. This underlife of *secondary adjustments* allows chronic patients to preserve a sense of autonomy and self-hood beyond the influences of the institutional context. On this basis, Goffman has revised the "simple" sociological view of the individual self of the mental patient (as constituted solely in terms of what the patient's place in the social organization defines him or her to be) to include the concept of a self with conflicting dedications.

One important strategy by which mental patients are to maintain this sense of self-autonomy, despite their lack of status in the hierarchical power structure of the mental hospital, is referred to as the counterpower technique of *impression management* (a form of role playing in which individuals manage their expressive behavior in order to control the impressions others form of them). This concept was introduced to refer to counterpower techniques, such as exaggeration of symptoms and rule-breaking, employed by hospitalized patients both to attain desired goals (remain on a preferred ward, obtain a holiday pass, gain access to recreational facilities, avoid unwanted release or undesirable treatment techniques) and to preserve some sense of autonomy. Goffman maintains that many of the "symptoms" of schizophrenia can be understood as meaningful and reasonable responses to the social context and contingencies associated with entrance into and the assumption of the social role of mental patient.

schizophrenia as residual rule-breaking

The sociologist Thomas Scheff (1966) has attempted to formulate a theoretical model which supplements and expands on Goffman's observations. Scheff's theory views the "symptoms" of schizophrenia as labeled violations of social norms, and the "illness" schizophrenia as a social role. The two basic assumptions of this approach are: that mental illness is a social role; and that societal reaction is the most important determinant of entry into that role. Scheff asserts that schizophrenia is a social status rather than a disease, and that the definition of behaviors "symptomatic" of schizophrenia is dependent on social rather than medical contingencies. The quasi-medical language of psychiatry (symptoms, diagnoses, therapies) functions to (mis)lead us into focusing on disturbances (organic or psychic) assumed to exist within the individual, and to ignore the important role of the social system in the establishment and maintenance of these role behaviors.

Scheff suggests two concepts that allow for the translation of the notion of psychiatric "symptoms" and illness into a sociological framework: *rule-breaking* and *deviance.* Rule-breaking is defined as behavior which is in clear violation of group rules (social norms). The particular norm violations categorized as psychiatric symptoms are referred to as residual rule-breaking. In Scheff's theory, psychiatric symptoms are viewed as instances of residual rule-breaking, and diagnostic syndromes are understood as patterns of residual deviance. Thus, symptoms such as withdrawal, hallucinations, muttering to oneself, odd dress, posturing, and so on, are categorized as violations of *residual rules,* social norms so taken for granted that they are not explicitly verbalized. Scheff suggests that these rules are often associated with what a particular culture defines as "real" or "decent." Each culture tends to assume that its own definitions of reality and decency are "truth," so violations of these cultural norms seem strange, puzzling, and unthinkable to most members. Since residual rule violations are "unthinkable," cultures do not provide effective mechanisms for routine handling of these violations, and such unamenable transgressions are characteristically lumped together into a *residual* category—witchcraft or mental illness, for example.

Scheff also places great emphasis on the social context in which the rule violation occurs. He cites Goffman's (1964) observations as evidence for the view that residual rule violations such as occult involvements, religious visions, and loitering, do not elicit censure unless performed by socially unqualified persons, or in inappropriate contexts.

Scheff maintains that residual rule-breaking is caused by diverse factors (physical, psychological, and social) and that the incidence of residual rule-breaking is extremely high relative to the incidence of diagnosed mental illness. He believes this is the case because most rule-breaking is denied and is of transitory significance. Scheff suggests that the most important single factor in the prolongation of transitory residual rule-breaking into the fixed social role of mental illness is the societal reaction to the rule-breaking behavior. Thus, rule-breaking may be stabilized into a deviant status (such as schizophrenia) only under the following conditions: the rule-breaking is exaggerated and defined as mental illness; the rule breaker is assigned a deviant status; and he or she is induced to assume the role of the mentally ill.

Scheff does not suggest that schizophrenics are merely pretending, role-playing or malingering. In his view, the traditional stereotypes of mental illness are learned early in childhood and are continuously reaffirmed in various contexts including social discourse ("you're driving me out of my mind," "running like mad," "chattering like crazy"), jokes, newspapers ("an escaped mental patient"), and the mass media. These stereotypes are widely shared in the culture and form the basis for a complex set of expectations about appropriate social behavior, particularly regarding attitudes about reality and the culturally shared view of decent behavior. Violations of these rules lead, under certain circumstances, to the labeling of the rule breaker as deviant (schizophrenic). At this point, social agents may seek outer signs of abnormality in the deviant's life history to demonstrate (the "degradation ceremony") to all concerned that he or she was always essentially a deviant.

In Scheff's model, the severity of societal reaction to residual rule-breaking, and the likelihood that such deviance will be labeled mental illness, are functions of: the degree, amount, and visibility of the rule-breaking; the power and social distance of the rule breaker in relation to the agents of social control; the tolerance level of the community; and the availability of alternative non-deviant roles within the community. The traumatic circumstances of psychiatric labeling, in which high status societal agents and persons previously intimately involved in the daily life of the deviant react to him or her uniformly in terms of the cultural stereotypes of insanity, result in the crystallization of transient and unstructured rule-breaking behavior into conformity to social role expectations for the mentally ill. In this manner the labeled deviant becomes similar to other deviants referred to as mentally ill, and these processes become increasingly uniform and stable until the imagery of mental illness is finally assimilated as an integral part of the deviant's (self) orientation for governing his or her own behavior. Mental patients are *not* viewed as individuals who have chosen the role or career of mental illness, but as those who are induced by the contingencies of the labeling process to assume a career of residual deviance and to internalize the uniform cultural stereotypes of mental illness as their self-image.

In Scheff's theory, schizophrenia is understood as a social role which complements and reflects the status of the insane in the social structure. Scheff suggests that several aspects of our cultural reaction to and treatment of the "mentally ill" foster acceptance of the deviant role. First, labeled deviants are rewarded for playing their role—for example, psychiatric staff and fellow patients reward patients who display "insight" and "accept their illness" with praise and access to desirable privileges (Balint, 1957; Goffman, 1962). Second, labeled deviants are punished when they attempt to return to conventional or previous roles. Finally, Scheff suggests that the crisis associated with public recognition and labeling of rule-breaking may induce a state of anxiety, confusion, and shame in which the deviant is highly suggestible and likely to accept the proferred role of mental patient. Once the rule breaker views himself or herself within the stereotype of mental illness and that view is validated by prestigious, trusted others, the patient will embark on a career of chronic deviance.

Acceptance and internalization of the social role of schizophrenia is illustrated in the following excerpts from an interview with a chronic patient.

I: You have been in the hospital for over twelve years now and you still have no idea why you were brought here?

P: Well, I've never understood the purpose of it, but if it's mental illness then I feel that it has a purpose. So I feel that it has ended rather happily . . . and basically I don't have much to do with it, I just let them (the staff) go on with their work while I go on with mine.

I: I'm not clear how the idea of mental illness helps you to understand the purpose . . .

P: Well, mental illness I think is a nice thing to do. Actually I'm kind of vague on it but basically I feel that it is a nice career, as nice as any other.

I: So you've come to view your mental illness as a career or vocation. Have you chosen that career?

P: Well, I've come here. I've chosen it because I'm doing it. I mean I could have done something else but with mental illness I really don't think I can . . . I've finally realized that mental illness is the only job I can really do. . . . I'm relieved to know this and stop worrying about starting new jobs. . . . Mental illness has been a real improvement for me.

I: In what sense?

P: Well, because I have a job, and one that I like, and one that I can do competently in the hospital. I really don't think the hospital wants me to act wild or dangerous. As a patient in a mental hospital my job is to be mentally ill.

I: How do you go about your job of being mentally ill?

P: Well, mainly I have persecution and other symptoms like inferiority, superiority, Oedipus and castration complexes. Mostly I do persecution complexes. I don't know much about the others, although I must have them since I am a mental patient. Oedipus and castration complexes, I don't know what I could do with them or what the required activities would be, especially since I don't like sex . . .

Scheff (1966) has conducted a series of studies which provide indirect support for some aspects of his theory. For example, his investigations of psychiatric screening procedures in mental health commissions suggest that approximately seventy percent of all judicial hearings failed to establish that committed mental patients were in fact insane according to legal criteria, i.e., risk to self or others. Scheff maintains that the medical perspective leads psychiatrists to presume illness, and thus to accept and provide treatment to all comers. This predisposition is particularly noticeable in hospital admission units where practically all new patients are treated in a uniform manner which includes: administrative processing, admission, interview, transfer to locked observation unit, medication, diagnosis, confinement, and disposition.

Scheff's investigations also suggest that social and situational variables, rather than the patient's psychiatric condition, are crucial in release decisions. He concludes that mental patients may be compared with other disadvantaged persons of low social status; that the concept of insanity can be viewed as constituting a "status line" between the culturally positive status ideal, sanity, and the negative status ideal, insanity. Each social position is comprised of a set of rights, duties, and role expectations recognized as legitimate by members of society. Cultural stereotypes such as those associated with the status of mental illness may be understood as means of maintaining the predominant social order by providing a negative contrast to the positive model, a contrast which serves to reaffirm the assumptions of the culturally accepted world view.

Rosenhan (1973) has presented evidence which supports Scheff's view that schizophrenia may be a product of the social context of institutional psychiatry rather than the result of underlying disease processes. He maintains that psychiatric diagnoses exist primarily in the minds of the diagnosticians, and are not valid summaries of characteristics displayed by the "patient." He cites evidence obtained from a study of the experiences of eight normal volunteers, admitted to twelve different mental hospitals after stating matter of factly that they heard voices, to support his claim. Seven of the eight pseudo-patients (all were instructed to act naturally immediately after admission) were diagnosed schizophrenic, factual personal histories were interpreted as indicative of serious personal and familial pathology, and over 2,100 tranquilizing pills were administered to the participants during their hospital stay. Pseudo-patients were discharged as "improved," or "in remission" after an average hospital stay of approximately three weeks. Rosenhan suggests, on the basis of this evidence, that many patients might be "sane" outside the psychiatric hospital but seem insane in it because they are responding to a bizarre setting.

schizophrenia as a social refuge

The predominant view in western culture is that schizophrenia is a catastrophic illness over which its victims have no control. The standard social prescription (despite widespread public cynicism) is "treatment" in a mental hospital. There is a growing body of evidence, however, to indicate that many schizophrenic patients *want* to be in the hospital, and view mental institutions as refuges where adequate housing, food, medical care, and recreational facilities are provided (Farina, 1976). This evidence supports a theoretical model that treats "symptomatic" behaviors as forms of social communication—as patterns of behavior that are used to control outcomes in social situations—rather than as disease syndromes. Schizophrenia is considered a misleading label (mis)applied to the large proportion of "patients" who enter the hospital as a refuge from the world in which they are reluctant or unable to be effective social participants. Proponents of this model do not argue that schizophrenia refers to nothing more than a group of social outcasts and failures seeking a haven, but do maintain that a large proportion of long-term patients act on the basis of comprehensible motives and goals that have more to do with such variables as socioeconomic class, economic downturns, and other social circumstances than with traditional intrapersonal concepts such as ego-strength, personality disorganization, or biochemical aberrations.

The social psychologists Braginsky, Braginsky, and Ring (1969) have formulated the most systematic and radical presentation of this perspective. They maintain that for many people hospitalization may be the only alternative to debilitating social conditions and economic privation, and that in these cases the concept of chronic schizophrenia merely reifies as biological disease the social conditions of poverty, discrimination, and powerlessness. They claim, in contrast to Rosenhan's (1973) account of the dehumanizing aspects of institutional psychiatric practice, that for many people hospitalization is less dehumanizing than the social conditions they leave behind.

Braginsky and his colleagues have observed that many hospital patients are highly motivated and successful at managing impressions in order to control their hospital fate, and have conducted a number of studies which provide empirical support for this observation. In one study (Braginsky et al., 1966), hospitalized patients were divided into two groups, "old-timers" (most had been in the hospital over three years) and "short-timers" (their first hospitalization, for less than three months). Fewer than twenty percent of the old-timers were discharged during any one year, as compared to a discharge rate of eighty percent for short-timers within the first three months of hospitalization. The authors assumed that short-timers would be anxious to leave the hospital and that old-timers would be motivated to remain in the hospital and that both groups would effectively use counterpower tactics to control the impressions the staff forms of them. The authors predicted that short-timers would, if given a test purported to measure degree of psychopathology, attempt to answer the items in such a way as to appear disturbed. The authors constructed a test of thirty items of "neutral" content. The test was described to half the old-timers and half the short-timers as a "Mental Illness Test." Instructions were that the more items answered *true,* the higher the mental illness score and the greater the likelihood that they would remain in the hospital a long time. Items answered *false* were described as indicative of health, and a short hospital stay. The test was described to the remaining half of the old-timers and short-timers as a "Self-Insight Test." Patients were told that items marked *true* were indicative of self-insight, psychological health, and probable early discharge. Items marked *false,* on the other hand, indicated illness and a long hospital stay. Results showed that old-timers answered two-thirds of the items as *true* when they believed *true* answers were indicative of mental illness, and only one-third of the items as *true* when they believed that a *true* response would indicate mental health. Short-timers showed the opposite pattern of responses. The authors cite this study as evidence that patients can use impression management in a deliberate fashion to control their hospital fate.

Braginsky and others (1969) have conducted demographic studies of admissions which suggest that a relatively large proportion of hospital admissions are acquaintances and neighbors who apparently decide to enter the hospital together. They believe this evidence substantiates their belief that people entering mental hospitals are not all helpless victims of disease, and that many want to be in the hospital and are quite capable of attaining their goal. Social living conditions are cited as the primary reason many "mental patients" seek hospitalization. Braginsky maintains that some individuals learn how they must behave to gain admission by talking to friends who have previously been there.

One of the most impressive studies of the use of impression management techniques (Braginsky et al., 1969) used long-term, open ward schizophrenic patients. The experimenters predicted that old-timers would be motivated and use impression management tactics effectively to stay in the hospital and to maintain open ward privileges. Each patient was escorted to an interview with a staff psychologist. On the way there an assistant informed the patients, in a confidential manner, that the purpose of the interview was: (1) to see if the patient was ready for discharge, or (2) to see if the patient should be transferred to a closed ward, or (3) to determine the patient's mental condition.

The interviews were tape recorded and three staff psychiatrists independently rated each tape both for severity of psychopathology and amount of hospital control required. Results indicated that patients in the closed ward condition were consistently rated as showing significantly less pathology and needing less hospital control than patients in the other groups. Discharge and mental status groups did not differ significantly from each other. The researchers interpreted these findings as evidence that the closed ward subjects feared loss of open ward privileges, and presented themselves as healthy. The other groups thought they were being considered for discharge, and so presented themselves as mentally ill. Analyses of the tapes indicated that simple positive and negative self-references ("I feel good" or "I feel bad") were most significantly related to psychiatric ratings, and that half of the discharge and mental status patients reported hallucinations or delusions, while not one subject in the closed ward condition reported such experiences. Braginsky and his colleagues cite this study as further evidence that "pathological" behaviors are often voluntary, and are comprehensible in terms of the patient's living conditions, goals, and social alternatives.

Studies of the styles of institutional adaptation established by patients (Braginsky et al., 1969) suggest that some long-term patients learn a great deal about hospital recreational facilities (the location of the canteen, theater, gymnasium) and very little about therapeutic facilities, access to therapy, the names of psychiatrists, and so on. Others, usually short-term patients, learn about therapeutic facilities rather than recreational ones. Each style of adaptation has been demonstrated to lead to different hospital outcomes: patients using the former tend to remain in the hospital, while those using the latter are likely to be discharged. These outcomes are independent of ratings of the severity of psychopathology. This evidence suggests that some patients enter the hospital to gain access to therapeutic facilities, but that many others consider the hospital a social haven. These patients manifest a lack of therapeutic involvement, maintain attitudes that stress striving for a comfortable, nondemanding hospital existence, do not perceive themselves as mentally ill, and acquire more information about the recreational aspects of the institution than about hospital staff and therapeutic facilities.

Braginsky and his colleagues conclude that in most cases schizophrenia is not a medical problem at all, but one which is produced by a patient's relationships with others and with society as a whole. Evidence that many patients exploit the hospital environment in a goal-oriented and effective manner is cited as indicative of the need for introducing a new paradigm. The authors propose that the term schizophrenia and correlative expressions (e.g., hospital, patient, therapy) be abandoned as misconstructions which serve to obscure reality. They propose a new social paradigm which recognizes that the demands of social careers in an increasingly complex and technically demanding society create a growing proportion of people who do not fit into that society; those who for one reason or another give up, fail, withdraw, and cease to function as accepted, productive members of society.

Today's chronic schizophrenics are viewed as social descendants of the nineteenth century poor, a group both rootless and rejected. Life in a mental institution has some obvious advantages for this group. The institution provides shelter, bed, board, protection, stability, access to leisure activities, freedom from responsibility, freedom to determine one's fate, opportunities for friendship, and a social role. (Veterans hospitals provide the very best public facilities, along with disability benefits which often amount to more than the patient can earn on the outside. The patient is simply required to remain "ill" to continue to maintain the disability rating.) The mental hospital is viewed not as a medical facility, but as a *haven,* a handy place of escape, for the poor, the disadvantaged, the immature, and those who choose to retire to lead unmolested and uninvolved lives.

The authors suggest a new paradigm for the "treatment" of mental illness. They propose that cooperative retreats should be set up to service individual communities. These retreats would be available to any member of a community, without time limits and without charge. Each retreat would provide facilities for self-enhancement and entertainment. Those who cannot return to society, or do not want to, may choose to remain in the retreat, where they can maintain self-respect by functioning as members of a cooperative community. These retreats, it is argued, will free us from the hypocrisy of the "mental illness myth." "Patients will no longer have to degrade themselves by acting 'crazily'; professional persons will no longer have to intellectually divorce themselves from reality in order to justify their roles; and society will no longer have to misdirect its energies and resources in defense of a myth. . . . Only then will society be able to embark upon appropriate reforms that will enhance and enrich the lives of its citizens" (1969, p. 186).

Social ecological studies suggest that the incidence of schizophrenia will be substantially reduced when those social changes are introduced which reduce the likelihood of severe economic stress, unemployment, social inequality, and alienation. Such an approach leads to a focus on political issues and preventive social engineering, rather than therapy.

evaluation

Social theorists have contributed to the broadening of the context in which we consider and attempt to understand the complex set of phenomena called schizophrenia. Their observations and attempts to explain these phenomena, in terms of the interplay of cultural, economic, career, and class variables, have effectively challenged the traditional view that schizophrenic behavior can be understood solely in terms of intrapersonal constructs. The concept of schizophrenia is understood as defining cultural values regarding acceptable and nonacceptable views of decency, morality and reality, rather than disease or emotional disorder. Human beings are seen as social role players, and the concept of *self* is understood as nothing more than the aggregate of roles an individual has assumed in the social system. Social theorists are "soft" determinists; they view schizophrenics as social rejects or inadvertent residual rule-breakers *caught* in the powerful flow of social forces called mental health services. Signs of emotional distress are considered transient phenomena, elicited by the mortifying rituals which accompany entry into the career of the mental patient.

Evidence for the influence of demographic, economic, and social class variables on the incidence of schizophrenic diagnoses is a reminder that human beings live in a social context, as well as a psyche or soma, but it does not support the assumption that human behavior, schizophrenic or otherwise, can be understood as determined entirely by social forces. Adverse social circumstances must eventually be understood as variables which may compound the effects of constitutional, psychological, and intrafamilial factors, to reduce individual tolerance for the stresses and demands of life within a particular cultural context.

Social theorists appear to overlook the readily observable fact that most people who loaf in public places, espouse radical political views, speak in tongues, believe in poltergeists and clairvoyants, see the devil, spot flying saucers, or often leave their flies unzipped, do not end up in mental hospitals. They ignore the fact that the vast majority of individuals labelled acute or reactive schizophrenic are seriously disturbed, anxious, confused, and delusional *before* the processes of psychiatric "mortification." Most process schizophrenic patients have lengthy histories of personal inadequacy, social rejection, academic underachievement, dependency, confusion, vocational failure, anxiety, extensive fearfulness, and inability to assume responsibility for their own lives long before psychiatric labelling, no matter what their social class, economic circumstances, or ethnic origins.

Social theorists have correctly indicated that psychiatric "diagnosis" and "treatment" procedures are not socially neutral or unequivocally helpful actions, and that the course of emotional disturbances can be significantly altered and adversely affected by the psychiatric model for understanding and treating these problems. They ignore, however, the complex, idiosyncratic meaning structures created by individual schizophrenic patients. Attempts to understand the complex delusional systems of the individuals described in Chapter 4 in terms of such concepts as "impression management" seem hopelessly inadequate. Delusions may be used as counter-power techniques, but this does not imply that they can be understood, in any complete sense, within this framework.

The empirical evidence cited by social theorists to support their theoretical systems is inadequate. Goffman, for example, jotted notes over the course of a year whenever he observed some aspect of institutional routine that confirmed his assumptions about what mental illness "really" is and how mental hospitals "actually" operate. Psychoanalytic theories, in contrast, are based on the observations of countless highly trained individuals who have studied individual cases intensively for many years, yet are sometimes criticized as metaphysical and unempirical by social psychologists while Goffman's views are widely cited and accepted. Scheff cites little more than limited evidence of the arbitrary nature of psychiatric testimony during legal commitment proceedings, and the variations in release rates between institutions, as evidence in support of his theory. Braginsky and others (1969) have based their conclusions on studies using samples of as few as ten subjects per group, and have concluded that friends and acquaintances decide jointly to seek out the resort potentials of the mental hospital on the basis of one limited demographic study of a "grand" total of 118 admissions to a single mental hospital. Rosenhan (1973) has suggested that mental patients are "sane" residents of "insane places" on the basis of his studies of the experiences of a sample of eight pseudo-patients who were instructed to feign auditory hallucinations upon admission.

Research does indicate consistently that schizophrenics, like most human beings, are capable of varying degrees of impression management (Kelly et al., 1971). This evidence does not, however, indicate that the behavioral and cognitive deficits of schizophrenics are necessarily the result of these tactics. In fact, research suggests that psychiatric patients are less adept than others, and that process schizophrenics are particularly inept in this regard (Chapman, 1969; Price, 1973; Watson, 1973). Recent research suggests that the role of impression management in the origin and maintenance of schizophrenic "symptoms" has been exaggerated, and that, where it does appear, it is more frequent in milder disorders than in long-term schizophrenic patients (Price, 1972; Watson, 1973, 1975).

Evidence that schizophrenic patients are capable of accurate social perception of adaptations to institutional life, and of occasional attempts to present an impression that will most likely further their personal goals, does not contradict any theory of schizophrenia. No biological or psychological model implies that schizophrenic patients are necessarily lacking in social awareness or in the ability to adapt to their surroundings. Traditional models have largely ignored the debilitating effects of institutionalization that are superimposed on the existing difficulties of labelled schizophrenics.

Long-term schizophrenic residents of mental hospitals are characteristically anxiety-ridden, have difficulties in concentration and communication, are fearful of new situations, are capable of only limited and stereotyped forms of social participation, and characteristically express concrete, simplistic views of the world. It is also clear that institutionalization and psychiatric diagnosis can compound such problems (Wing and Brown, 1970), but the behavior itself is not produced by career contingencies, by labelling, or by psychiatric "initiation rites."

REFERENCES

BALINT, M. *The Doctor, His Patient, and the Illness.* New York: International Universities Press, 1957.

BRAGINSKY, B., and D. BRAGINSKY. Schizophrenic patients in the psychiatric interview: an experimental study of their effectiveness at manipulation. *Journal of Consulting Psychology, 21,* 1967, 543–547.

BRAGINSKY, B., D. BRAGINSKY, and K. RING. *Methods of Madness: The Mental Hospital as a Last Resort.* New York: Holt, Rinehart and Winston, 1969.

BRENNER, M. *Mental Illness and the Economy.* Cambridge, Mass.: Harvard University Press, 1973.

CHAPMAN, L. J. Schizomimetic conditions and schizophrenia. *Journal of Consulting and Clinical Psychology, 33,* 646–650.

FARINA, A. *Abnormal Psychology.* Englewood Cliffs, N.J.: Prentice-Hall, 1976.

FARIS, R. E. *Social Disorganization.* New York: Ronald Press, 1955.

FARIS, R. E., and H. W. DUNHAM. *Mental Disorders in Urban Areas.* Chicago: University of Chicago Press, 1939.

GOFFMAN, E. *Asylums.* New York: Doubleday, 1962.

HOLLINGSHEAD, A., and F. REDLICH. *Social Class and Mental Illness: A Community Study.* New York: John Wiley, 1958.

KELLY, F., A. FARINA, and D. L. MOSHER. Ability of schizophrenic women to create a favorable or unfavorable impression on an interviewer. *Journal of Consulting and Clinical Psychology, 36,* 1971, 404–409.

KOHN, M. L. Social class and schizophrenia: a critical review. In *The Transmission of Schizophrenia,* edited by D. Rosenthal and S. Kety, pp. 155–173. New York: Pergamon Press, 1968.

KRAMER, M. Cross-national study of diagnosis of mental disorders: origin of the problem. *American Journal of Psychiatry, 125,* 1969.

PRICE, R. H. The case for impression management in schizophrenia: another look. In *The Making of a Mental Patient,* edited by R. Price and B. Denner. New York: Holt, Rinehart and Winston, 1973.

ROSENHAN, D. L. On being sane in insane places. *Science, 179,* 1973, 250–258.

SARBIN, T. R. Schizophrenia is a myth, born of metaphor, meaningless. *Psychology Today,* June 1972, 18–27.

SCHEFF, T. J. *Being Mentally Ill: A Sociological Theory.* Chicago: Aldine, 1966.

TURNER, R. J., and M. O. WAGONFELD. Occupational mobility and schizophrenia, an assessment of the social causation and social selection hypotheses. *American Sociological Review, 32,* 1967, 104–113.

WATSON, C. G. Conspicuous psychotic behavior as a manipulative tool. *Journal of Clinical Psychology, 29,* 1973, 3–7.

———. Impression management ability in psychiatric hospital samples and normals. *Journal of Consulting and Clinical Psychology, 43,* 1975, 540–545.

WING, J., and G. BROWN. *Institutionalism and Schizophrenia.* Cambridge: Cambridge University Press, 1970.

Chapter Nine

Family Interaction Models

The Family as the Source of Disturbance

Clinicians have often observed that the development of schizophrenic disorders appears to be significantly related to disturbances in the familial environment (Sullivan, 1925). During the 1930's, growing interest in psychoanalytic treatment of schizophrenic patients led to increased concern with the systematic study of the role of family relationships in the etiology of schizophrenia. The assumption, widely shared by traditional psychoanalysts, that libidinal fixation in schizophrenia occurred during the earliest phases of the oral stage of psychosexual development, led to a search for evidence of associated disturbances in the mother-child relationship during infancy. Early clinical studies of the mothers of schizophrenic patients seemed to confirm the assumption that the mother-child relationship was often seriously disturbed (Lidz and Lidz, 1949). The concept of the *schizophrenogenic mother* was introduced to refer to this source of schizophrenic disturbance (Arieti, 1955). As more sophisticated family systems models were formulated, during the late 1950's, emphasis was placed on disturbances in the total family system rather than single child-parent relationships.

Attempts to understand the role of the family in the etiology of schizophrenia range from the psychological view of the family as "an environment in which the patient lives," to the psychosocial view of the family as "a set of individuals whose behaviors influence each other," and the sociological view of the family as "a dysfunctional system that supports a sick person" (Waxler, 1975).

176

Descriptions of family interactions and parental traits were, for the most part, derived from the non-systematic observations of individual psychotherapists rather than from controlled observational studies. One consistent observation recorded in the early clinical literature was that family members were often not responsive to each other's existence as separate persons. The mother in particular was described as "impervious" to the personal characteristics and needs of the child, as someone who does not hear or recognize what her child is communicating and does not genuinely accept and attend to his or her needs, but appears to do so while actually responding on the basis of her own needs projected onto the child (Fromm-Reichmann, 1948). A fusion or symbiosis of identities between parent and child, in which the child is responded to and comes to perceive himself or herself largely on the basis of the projected needs, wishes, anxieties, and fantasies of the parental figure, was the observed outcome of this interactional process. Symbiotic relationships (Mahler, 1952) were postulated to be of major etiological significance in the developmental life process that eventually leads to schizophrenic reactions. In this pattern of parent-child relationship, the ego-identity of the child becomes (con)fused with that of the parent, for the child exists as little more than an extension of the parent and as a substitute source of gratification of his or her displaced needs.

Laing (1960) introduced the term *mystification* to emphasize the communicational aspects of symbiotic relationships. In brief, mystification refers to those interactive situations, most commonly observed among families of schizophrenics, in which one person responds to another in terms of his or her own needs but at the same time acts as if he or she is really responding to the needs of the other. Such communications from parent to child are thought to be an essential aspect of the formation of the etiologically significant symbiotic relationship.

Mystifying communications and symbiotic interactive patterns appear, of course, to be present at various times and to varying degrees in practically all social interactions. It is hypothesized that for these conditions to result in psychological deficits so severe as to result in later schizophrenic developments, they must occur very early in life, with exceptional intensity and duration, and focus on particular content areas (e.g., sexual issues).

Families of schizophrenics are also said to be characterized by a marked failure to recognize the child's needs and an unacknowledged indifference to his or her separate existence. The degree to which the child is unconsciously caught up in this process and functions as a substitute source of gratification in the life of the parent is thought to determine, at least in part, the degree to which he or she will develop the capacities necessary to cope with the stresses of maturation and the eventual establishment of a satisfactory independent existence.

The interactive processes described in the preceding paragraphs are illustrated by the following case.

Richard was admitted to a mental hospital for the second time shortly after his twenty-first birthday, following an assault on his mother. Richard's father had returned from work that day to discover him angrily kicking his mother, who had fallen semi-conscious into the bathtub. The parents were frightened by this angry outburst and brought Richard to the hospital on the advice of a private psychiatrist who had been treating Richard for eleven years. The psychiatrist described Richard as "assaultive" and "potentially dangerous," and recommended institutionalization. He described the family as "dysfunctional," the father as "inadequate," a "Walter Mitty" type, and Richard's mother as a "borderline" personality who projected her many anxieties and hypochondriacal concerns onto her son.

Richard was moderately retarded. He had previously been hospitalized for several months at nine years of age and diagnosed schizophrenic, childhood type. An assault on his mother also precipitated this initial hospitalization. At that time, Richard was placed in the children's unit, received chemotherapy, evidenced rapid and marked diminution of signs of emotional disturbance, and was released to outpatient treatment after four months. The psychiatrist in charge of his treatment prescribed heavy dosages of major tranquilizers for Richard during the following eleven years to control his "assaultiveness." He had given up attempts at family therapy as "hopeless" after several unsuccessful attempts. In his view, Richard was a seriously disturbed, chronic undifferentiated schizophrenic, with an extremely poor prognosis.

Richard was agitated during his initial hours on the admissions ward. He screamed continuously in a high-pitched voice, threw chairs across the dayroom, flapped his hands and arms in agitation, and gouged the skin on his arms and body.

Several days after his admission, Richard's mother called and requested a meeting with the staff on his "progress." The family conference rapidly shifted away from the topic of Richard's hospital status and into the area of long-standing parental conflict. The father accused his wife of "babying" Richard and underestimating his son's abilities. He stated that he stayed with his wife only because his religious beliefs did not permit divorce, and that he had not slept with her in over five years. He believed that the psychiatrist gave Richard too much medication, which impaired Richard's ability to function because it made him "sleepy all the time." He claimed that his wife caused Richard's tantrums first by babying him, then by "fussing" after his health all the time. He reported feeling helpless to intervene because his wife was so irrational and his job required frequent travel.

Richard's mother was extremely agitated and at times incoherent during the conference. She accused her husband of ruining her son's health by keeping him out late at night, and of plotting to induce Richard to kill her. She believed that her husband had induced Richard to assault and attempt to kill her on the day of his hospitalization. She demanded that Richard be released to her custody and that her husband take his place in the hospital.

Several days after the family "conference," the hospital received the following letter from Richard's mother.

Dear Doctor (or anyone attending Richard X),

Richard has much trouble with his bowels. His doctor has prescribed 100 mg of *Colace* to be given every morning (I placed two bottles in his suitcase last weekend), along with six ounces of prune juice twice *each* day, an enema, and Dulcolax suppositories (also in his suitcase) to be used every other day, or as needed. I usually start with plain glycerin suppositories, six tablespoons of milk of magnesia, and then the Dulcolax suppositories.

He likes spinach, raisins, and all-bran but won't eat other laxative foods unless I coax him to. Richard is reluctant to have a bowel movement unless he is at home with me, *mostly* because he is afraid of disease and of not getting clean. I usually *finish* the job of cleansing his body with waxy tissue. I know from experience, when he is out with his father, that he will not use a public restroom for this purpose!

Richard has, when on a trip with his father (who is not concerned with Richard's health), withheld bowel movements for 3 or 4 days until he returned home *half-sick* and with his stomach so distended that he looked as if he were *pregnant!* If you see his stomach protruding this way, please give him a strong laxative! There may be a problem, however, because Richard hates to tell anyone but me whether his bowels have moved, because he is *afraid* someone will hurry him out of the bathroom before he gets clean! His stool is so *large* that it often stops up my toilet at home!

His bowels last moved at home two days before he was taken to the hospital. I managed to persuade him to *try* again on the day of our staff conference; he went only after I promised to *wait* and clean his body. The bowel movement was not very large, although he didn't seem constipated either. I would guess that he will need a laxative by the time you receive this letter. His bowels usually move between 2 and 3 p.m. Just prior to this he bends over and holds his stomach, but must be told *several times* to go on and get it over with, otherwise he will not. At this time he becomes very restless and excited and is most inclined to become upset just before going. I don't know exactly why; whether from discomfort, a build-up of medication, his father's influence, or just what. A pharmacist told me that the tranquilizers Richard takes often cause restlessness and agitation in some people. Richard settles down after his bowels have moved, but it is necessary for someone to always watch him for the "blown up" stomach and not to just take his word about whether his bowels have moved or not.

Richard will pour his prune juice and raisins down the drain unless constantly watched and encouraged at the table. I've told him to tell the nurse the truth about his bowel movements, but I doubt that he will.

Sincerely,

P.S. I left a package of raisins, fig newtons, and some cans of prune juice in his suitcase, please see that he gets these each day!

This letter illustrates the confusion of needs, anxieties, and concerns between mother and son which, in this case, have become focused on the highly symbolic area of anal function. Interestingly, the clinical literature suggests that families of schizophrenic patients rarely appear to have been willfully abusive or neglectful of their children; rather, the child's development into a separate, functional, adult human being is most often impaired in the context of loving but overwhelming symbiotic concern.

The following assumptions characterize research on family processes and the development of schizophrenic disorders reviewed in the remainder of this chapter: (1) schizophrenic reactions develop in a family milieu which is seriously though subtly disturbed in a manner distinguishable from patterns associated with most other diagnostic syndromes; (2) these disturbances, particularly in early parent-child relationships and familial communication processes, begin relatively early in the life of the patient; (3) disordered family relationships may be a necessary but not sufficient condition for the development of schizophrenia (Goldstein and Rodnick, 1975; Chodoff and Carpenter, 1975). Theories are presented in order of their relative emphasis on individual rather than social constructs and variables.

schizmatic and skewed family patterns

Theodore Lidz and his colleagues have published a series of intensive studies of the families of schizophrenic patients (Lidz et al., 1965). Working initially from a psychodynamic framework, they define schizophrenia as a disturbance of ego function manifested in aberrant symbolic processes (distortions of perception, meaning, and logic) that occur in the absence of evidence of deterioration of intellectual potential. The obvious importance of the family in the transmission of the techniques, knowledge, and social roles required for adequate ego development and social adjustment led this group to search for family interaction processes that might be associated with the development of schizophrenic disturbances.

Lidz and his colleagues attempted to explore and reconstruct the interactional processes of the families of schizophrenic patients from the time of inception of the primary family unit. Seventeen upper- or upper-middle-class families of schizophrenic patients, in which both parents and at least one sibling were available for prolonged observation, interviews, testing, and family sessions, formed the core sample for this project. Observation indicated that in each case the family of origin was seriously disturbed long before the patient was born. The great majority of marriages upon which the families were based were gravely disturbed, torn by conflict and split into factions. In each family, the parents were unable to maintain appropriate boundaries between generations, so that the child was chosen and felt compelled to complete the life of one or both parents. Each parent openly expressed fear that the child would resemble the other, and at least one parent in each family suffered from serious emotional disturbance. The families evidenced pronounced suspiciousness and distrust of outsiders and frequently did not adhere to culturally accepted ideas of causality and meaning.

Families that tend to produce schizophrenic offspring were divided into two types, *schizmatic* and *skewed* (Lidz et al., 1975). The *skewed* pattern was most commonly observed in families with schizophrenic sons. In this pattern the focus of attention falls upon the mother, who is described as impervious to the needs of other family members as separate individuals, and as extremely intrusive into *her* child's life. The father's inability to provide an adequate role model and to effectively counter the mother's aberrant ways of child-rearing were also of critical importance. The fathers tended to be passive men, frequently behaving more like sons than husbands. Some forfeited their family responsibilities, others were seriously disturbed, alcoholic, or psychotic. Whatever the characteristics of the father, he was ineffectual in the home and held in disdain by his wife, who impressed her son that he must not become like his father.

The mother in the *skewed* family pattern might have had serious difficulties in being close and maternal to her son when he was an infant, but she soon became overprotective, and was unable to believe that the child could exist without her constant supervision and assistance. The mother seemed unable to differentiate her own anxieties, needs, and feelings from those of the child, and sought completion through her son. Having grown up in this dependent relationship, the adolescent or young adult continued to believe that he could not get along without his mother, and feared that any attempt to separate from her would destroy her. Despite her manifest solicitude, the mother opposed any movement toward increased autonomy.

In these families, the mother's and sometimes the father's emotional equilibrium was so tenuous that emotional stability could be maintained only by insisting that events were perceived according to his or her needs. As a consequence, the family atmosphere and worldview seemed strange and unreal, yet the children were required to fit into and accept this distorted view or risk rejection. The world as others come to know it, and the emotions ordinarily elicited by events, were denied as possibilities for the child.

The *schizmatic* family was most commonly associated with the background of *female* patients. In these families there was frequent open conflict, and each spouse actively attempted to undercut the worth of the other to the children. Usually the parents competed for the loyalty of the daughter. The mother was insecure in her maternal role and had little self-esteem; her worth was further undermined by her husband's contempt and derogation. The father, insecure in his masculinity, married a woman he believed would docilely cater to his wishes. Poorly organized and ineffectual, the mother could not hold her own against a husband who often had delusions of grandeur or was overtly paranoid. She was unable to convey any sustained emotional warmth to her daughter, and usually conveyed a sense of the meaninglessness and hopelessness of life.

The father characteristically turned to the daughter, often in a seductive manner, when his unrealistic demands on his wife were unfulfilled. In some instances, the father assumed a mothering role to the daughter because of the mother's antipathy or her inability to be nurturant. To gain her father's affection, the daughter sought to become someone quite different from the mother. A son in such families typically felt incapable of satisfying the expectations of his father, and assumed the primary task of making his mother happy. Any attempt to please one parent, however, meant rejection by the other. Service as a scapegoat or "problem" child in order to mask parental incompatibility and strife resulted in the sacrifice of the child's own developmental needs.

characteristics of the parents

Maternal Characteristics. Lidz (1973) suggests that mothers of schizophrenic sons must be considered separately from mothers of schizophrenic daughters; some traits, however, are common to both groups: 1) imperviousness to what the child seeks to convey; 2) inordinate intrusiveness into the privacy of the child; 3) a tendency to confuse the child's needs with their own needs; 4) disparity between what is expressed verbally and emphatically; 5) failure to recognize ego boundaries between themselves and the child; 6) the need to have the child live out an existence closed to them; 7) undue restrictiveness resulting from obsessive anxieties or, conversely, an inability to set limits. The following general personal difficulties are also common: uncertainty concerning sexual identity, low self-esteem as a woman, projective trends, and chronic distortions of situations to maintain a preconceived notion of self and family.

Lidz's findings suggest the importance of a feedback system of disharmony in the mother-child relationship, created by a combination of the mother's personal difficulties, her husband's difficulties, and serious problems of the marriage.

Paternal Characteristics. The fathers of schizophrenic patients were observed to be insecure in their masculinity, and required undue admiration and attention to bolster their self-esteem. A substantial proportion were paranoid or subject to paralogical or irrational behavior that seriously affected the attitudes of the entire family. The fathers also tended to be impervious to the needs of the child. They frequently interfered with the mother's ability to be mothering even in the first months of the child's life, and later fostered a confusion between the roles of the two generations in the home. Their failure to provide the necessary model of masculine identification interfered with the development of both male and female children. In short, the fathers as well as the mothers were typically so caught up in their own emotional problems that they could rarely satisfactorily fill the essentials of a parental role.

The quality of parental interaction, as well as each parent's personality and the dyadic relationship with the child, was also associated with the development of schizophrenic reactions. Rejection of the child, for example, may reflect a wish to be rid of the marital relationship which the child binds, and anxiety conveyed to the child by the mother may have more to do with the relationship between the parents than that between the mother and the child. Many fathers were passive and felt emasculated by the mother. They provided poor identity models, a distorted image of the role of the man in the family, and were associated with the sons' fear of women, an important factor in the genesis of homosexual concerns common to many schizophrenic patients.

the functions of the family

Lidz and his colleagues were impressed by the extent and complexity of the responsibilities for basic socialization, acculturation, and personality growth which must be assumed by the family to prepare the child for independent life. Their observations served to emphasize the inadequacy of classic clinical and psychoanalytic theories, which imply that normal development occurs in children as a natural outgrowth of physical maturation, unless impeded by serious traumatization or faulty nurturance during infancy. According to Lidz, there are at least four requisites that the family must provide to ensure adequate personality development in the child: (1) Parental *nurturant functions,* including the manner and appropriateness with which the parents meet the child's changing needs from infancy through adolescence. These functions are of crucial importance to the development of the child's sense of emotional security, development of autonomy, emotional reactivity, and the sense of trust in himself or herself and the world. (2) The *family organization* must provide conflict-free and guilt-free opportunities for self-expression and independent growth free of inappropriate or incestuous erotic attachments and faulty gender identifications. (3) The family as a *basic unit of society* must effectively teach the child to understand and value the basic social roles and institutions of society. (4) The family must adequately *transmit the basic instrumental techniques* of the society, including the language and shared systems of meaning.

the failure of family function

Failure of Parental Nurturance.   Nurturance is used by the authors to refer to the parents' abilities to relate appropriately to the child and meet his or her needs during each developmental phase. Disturbances appear to occur in every developmental phase of the child who later becomes schizophrenic. Such behavior cannot be attributed only to frustrations in the oral phase, as it has been by traditional psychoanalysts. Mothers of schizophrenic patients were typically intensely involved with their children; difficulties usually arose because of deficiencies in the mother's own development which led to profound empathic difficulties and insecurities about her ability to adequately care for the child. As the child developed, began to ambulate, interact with peers, and seek greater independence, these anxieties were increased. At some point the mothers typically projected their sense of personal inadequacy onto the child, providing a rationale for the imposition of unusual limitations, concerns, and controls which served to reduce their own anxiety.

Lidz categorized the mothers of schizophrenic offspring into two groups. In one group, the mothers cannot set boundaries, and treat the child as an extension of themselves. These mothers feel terribly inadequate as women and seek to fulfill the fantasy that the child will give completion and meaning to their unhappy lives. This type of relationship was most commonly observed with sons, perhaps because in order to develop normally a boy must differentiate from the mother more completely. Mothers in the second group are unable to involve themselves in the mother-child relationship. They tend to be apathetic toward the infant, and become increasingly withdrawn emotionally as the child grows older. The child is deprived of the basis for personal intimacy, trust, and closeness.

Nurturance deficiencies result in a poor sense of being able to guide one's own life. Boundaries between internal and external, between feelings of self and feelings of others, are never firmly established. Later in life, unacceptable feelings and impulses are projected onto others, and even controls of forbidden impulses are externalized (hallucinated or delusional form). Such individuals are unable to function autonomously, to assume responsibility for themselves, and must find direction through magical interpretations of casual, unrelated events (delusion).

Fathers typically provided little nurturance as they were involved in protecting themselves from their own insecurities, and so provided poor models. A variety of additional deprivations added to the impediment in the child's development: problem-solving through verbal communication was not rewarded; there was interference with peer play; transfer of care to child-teacher relationships was impeded by the mother's anxiety; the mother experienced all movement toward others as a threat of emotional abandonment, and reacted accordingly.

Failure of the Family as a Social Institution. In all families studied, serious disturbances were observed in the organization of the family, which interfered with adequate ego integration. Lidz posits that spouses must form a coalition as parents which maintains the boundaries between generations, and must adhere to their respective gender roles to form a family environment conducive to integrated personality development in their children. A majority of the parents of schizophrenic offspring evidenced a pervasive antagonism in which each parent undercut and competed with the other for the loyalty of the child. In the remainder of the families studied, one spouse, typically the father, abdicated his role as parent to the other, who had eccentric ideas about family life and child-rearing. This failure to develop a parental coalition interferes with the child's transition away from the fantasy of dividing his or her parents. According to psychodynamic theory, each child requires two parents: a parent of the same sex with whom he or she can identify and can use as a model, and a parent of the opposite sex who becomes a basic love object and forms the basis for all later love relationships. Lidz indicates that parents in these families filled neither function effectively for the child, since each was depreciated by the spouse, undercut, or treated as an enemy.

Failures of coalition between parents also led the child to fall into the role of scapegoat or "problem," whose difficulties mask parental discord. The child may invest energy in attempting to bridge the gap between parents, or may feel responsible for satisfying the needs of both parents. The child typically focuses on completing the life of one parent and thereby fails to participate in the experiences necessary to his or her own development.

Security of sexual identity is of utmost importance to psychodynamic theorists in the achievement of stable ego identity; sexual identity confusion was characteristic of almost all schizophrenics. Role reversals in parents, such as a cold, unyielding mother or an ineffectual father, thus distort the child's development and gender identity. Role reversals—ranging from strong homosexual tendencies to paternal passivity and maternal coldness—were common in the families studied. Lidz points out that few if any "normal" families meet all requisites described above. Families of the schizophrenic patients studied, however, met few or none of these requisites. Lidz maintains that although many other factors are involved in the establishment of a firm sense of identity, the basis for a reasonable outcome is established only if the parents form a firm coalition, maintain generational boundaries, and adhere to their respective gender-linked roles.

Defective Transmission of Instrumental Techniques.   In addition to nurturance and an emotional atmosphere and patterns of family interaction that facilitate growth, the family must also acculturate and encourage the child's basic knowledge of social roles and social institutions. Each child must learn his or her culture's system of categorizing experience in order to communicate, share meaning, and think coherently. Parents of schizophrenic offspring were typically unprepared for and lacked tools and techniques necessary for relating to others and directing their own lives; difficulties which extend far beyond problems of language transmission. The families studied were characterized by idiosyncratic use of words, confusion of communicative and personal meanings, impairments in the ability to categorize, and vague, fragmented styles of communication which fostered primary process associations and impeded the child's efforts to learn from experience, to relate, collaborate, and share with others.

According to Lidz and Fleck (1964), extreme early deprivation in all areas of family function is most likely to result in the insidious early development of delusional thought and social inadequacy associated with process schizophrenia. Less severe patterns of disturbance occurring later in life are associated with more adequate family function and ego development in the child. From this perspective, schizophrenia is not so much an illness as a possible mode of adjustment for individuals raised in families that failed to provide the essentials for integrated personality development in the areas outlined above. Lidz concludes that schizophrenia is not a clearly defined entity for which a single cause is likely to be discovered; rather, the behavioral and inferred referents for this concept must be understood in the context of the sources of alteration of developmental processes which eventually result in the features associated with the label schizophrenic. These features are, according to Lidz, associated with failure to achieve or maintain an adequate workable personality integration; with retreat into asociality; and with partial inability to share in the logic and meaning systems of the culture, which is associated with attempts to resolve conflicts by altering one's inner construction of the world without regard for external reality.

Lidz's emphasis on the importance of disturbances in each basic function in the families of schizophrenic patients illuminates the extensive nature of the disruption of adequate family function observed in the group studied, and broadens the focus of family researchers beyond a narrow emphasis on the early mother-child relationship or specific traumatic incidents. The shortcomings of the families as adequate developmental settings were so extensive in each of the functions listed that Lidz and Fleck (1960) postulated that schizophrenia is basically a deficiency disorder. In their view, the disordered language and thought of most schizophrenic patients does not arise from some metabolic dysfunction, but is a reflection of or reaction to the severely disturbed thought processes and patterns of communication of the parents.

evaluation

Lidz and his colleagues have conducted a series of pioneering studies of the families of young schizophrenic patients. Their concepts and descriptions have been widely accepted by practicing clinicians, and are consistent with more specific concepts proposed by independent investigators, such as symbiosis, mystification, and double-bind communications. This research has contributed substantially to our understanding of the complex task of child-rearing assumed by the nuclear family in our culture, and has provided vivid clinical descriptions of the makeup and pattern of interactions characteristic of families of some schizophrenic patients.

There are, however, a number of deficiencies in the design of this research and its descriptive concepts. First, Lidz and his colleagues conducted observational studies on a very limited sample (approximately forty families) of upper-middle and upper-class families of adolescent or young adult schizophrenic patients. Systematic ratings of premorbid adjustment or subtype were not reported. Furthermore, the investigators were aware of the nature of the child's disorder throughout the study. Research based on such a design (perhaps required by the complexities of the nature of the subject matter and practical reality) must be considered to be exploratory and tentative at best, for Lidz's studies are subject to all the criticisms associated with designs that do not control for the role of experimenter bias and attempt to provide *post hoc* explanations of phenomena. Theoretical concepts derived in this way are informative but do not provide the basis for scientific hypotheses or validating research.

patterns of family communication:
the double-bind hypothesis

Bateson and his colleagues (1956) have focused on communication patterns in families of schizophrenics. The approach adopted by this group is derived from a theoretical model which studies *levels* of communication rather than the content of what is communicated. Communications are divided into *primary* (basic content) and *metacommunications* (a communication about the communication). Metacommunications may be congruent or incongruent with primary communications, e.g., one person greets another with "How are you?" A friendly, interested manner would be congruent with the primary communication, while an angry or indifferent tone would represent an incongruent metacommunication. Bateson maintains that it is the metacommunication which most often affords a definition of the actual nature of the relationship between two parties, be it love, anger, or indifference. The essential concept in this theory is the *double-bind* communication. A double-bind is defined as a special learning context involving metacommunications. Double-bind theory postulates that pre-schizophrenic children are reared in family contexts from which they cannot escape, and in which they are subjected to incongruent messages that require them to deny important aspects of themselves or their experience in order to respond. The double-bind is expressed in an incongruency between the primary (content) and metacommunicative (tone, gesture, context) aspects of the message.

The double-bind occurs when incongruent messages are communicated and the recipient must respond to the message without the opportunity or ability to clarify or label the incongruent messages. It is hypothesized that repeated exposure to incongruent communications, in which the child is prohibited from either escaping or correctly labeling the incongruency, and feels he or she must understand the message to make an appropriate response, results in the child selectively ignoring the meaning of certain communications in order to avoid the punishment which would likely ensue from appropriate response to the metacommunication. This theory suggests that family members maintain stability in their interactions by developing rules governing who says what to whom in particular contexts.

The general characteristics of the double-bind situation are described as follows (Weakland, 1960):

1. An individual is involved in an intense relationship in which it is vitally important that he or she discriminate accurately what sort of message is being communicated in order to respond appropriately.
2. The individual is caught in a situation in which the other person in the relationship is expressing two orders of message, one of which denies the other.
3. The individual is unable to comment on the messages being expressed in order to correct his discrimination of what order message to respond to, and so is unable to make a metacommunicative statement.

The unilateral roles of "binder" and "victim" implicit in the above formulation are considered most likely to occur early in the parent-child relationship. Subsequently, the "victim-child" soon learns reciprocal patterns of communicating incongruent messages, and responds to all communications as if they were incongruent. Weakland (1960) has expanded the double-bind hypothesis to include three-party interactions. He suggests that contradictory messages sent by two senders, in which one may negate the message of the other by communicating at a higher level of abstraction, or two double-bind messages which appear to come from a single unit (coalition), may also be of major etiological significance.

The double-bind situation can be summarized as follows: 1) A person is faced with a significant communication involving a pair of messages, of different logical type, which are related but incongruent with each other. 2) Escape is blocked, usually because of dependence on the person(s) giving the contradictory messages. 3) It is important to respond adequately to the communication, which includes responding to its duality and contradiction. (An adequate response would be one that recognizes and points up the incongruity through overt labeling, giving a dual message in reply or giving a humorous response that exposes the nature of the incongruence.) 4) An adequate response is difficult to formulate because of the concealment (one message masking another), denial (that any contradiction exists), and inhibition (prohibition against recognition of concealed message) inherent in the contradictory messages, all operating within a frame of "authority," "love," "unity," and "benevolence."

Haley (1959) maintains that all human interactions can be viewed as attempts to define relationships through the communication of messages. This is an aspect of every relationship because communications often serve the dual function of reporting something and of asking that certain responses be made. The message, "I feel tired," both reports a subjective state and requests that the listener recognize this state and respond accordingly. In Haley's view, the only way to avoid defining a situation is to communicate in such a way that specific words are negated by qualifications attached to them. This pattern of communication is widely used by persons who wish to avoid defining a situation clearly because of mixed feelings about it. Suppose a husband is asked to prepare the salad for dinner. He doesn't want to but also doesn't want to anger his wife by directly refusing. The husband responds by saying, "I'd like to but my back is aching." He thus refuses to help and at the same time denies that he is refusing. According to Haley, one can avoid defining a relationship through the denial of any one of the four formal characteristics of interpersonal messages: I (speaker) am saying something (content) to you (object) in this context (situation). A person can avoid definition of a relationship, for example, by denying that it is he or she who is speaking, by claiming to speak for an authority, speaking while intoxicated, having amnesia, or adopting a delusional identity.

Haley postulates that schizophrenic communication can be understood as an attempt or strategy which effectively allows the speaker to avoid defining relationships. From this perspective, life in a family in which the child is constantly confronted with contradictory messages leads to the development of equally incongruent patterns of communication which in their extreme form are referred to as schizophrenia.

An example of the denial of several formal characteristics of interpersonal messages is presented in the following interview with a chronic patient.

I: How long have you been in the hospital?

P: I was born 100 years ago . . .

I: You're very old.

P: My mother was a Confederate general.

I: Do you know where you are now?

P: German guard, I'm in the German Guard . . . Stonewall Jackson . . . Spitfires.

I: Are you a soldier?

P: My mother and my sister killed me over the telephone . . . they cut me up and murdered me with their guns, and tubes, and needles.

I: When did this happen?

P: World War II, Civil War battles . . .

I: What is your name?

P: Cigarette, you got a cigarette? . . . Robert E. Lee, Stonewall Jackson, Kaiser Wilhelm . . . Stalin . . . Thalidomide . . .

evaluation

The double-bind hypothesis appears to be one of the most scientifically respectable theories of schizogenic family interaction. First, it is derived from the application of an established theoretical model (communications theory). Second, it is consistent with the observations of a number of independent clinical research groups. Finally, it is stated in a specific and systematic fashion. A number of studies have been conducted to test the hypothesis that schizophrenia is a particular pattern of communication, but there have been difficulties in reaching adequate rater reliability in the identification of double-bind statements, as well as difficulties in meeting the conditions stipulated for etiologically significant double-bind communications in the experimental situation. One conclusion can be derived from available studies, however, i.e., double-bind messages are not specific to the parents of schizophrenics (Hirsch and Leff, 1975). This suggests that double-bind messages in and of themselves cannot be considered to be necessary and sufficient causes of schizophrenia. Perhaps, such communications are one aspect of a complex pattern of parent-child and family interaction frequently associated with the development of schizophrenic disorders.

styles of communication in families of schizophrenics

Wynne, Singer, and their colleagues have focused on the quality and structure of family interactions, emphasizing family roles and norms rather than specific content. Their model attempts to describe acute schizophrenic experiences as the direct result of the ways of thinking, irrationality, confusion, and ambiguities expressed in the shared mechanisms of the total family social organization. This focus leads to the formulation of concepts that treat the entire family rather than individuals or specific role players as the basic unit of analysis. Schizophrenics are defined as persons who seem to handle meaning in unusual ways and do not appear (to varying degrees) to share meanings with others. Wynne and his colleagues have hypothesized that recurrent patterns of family communication contribute to the vulnerability of some individuals to handle meaning in unusual ways. They have attempted to determine the specific types of transactions which are not unique to families of schizophrenic patients, but occur with higher frequency and impact in them. Their research has focused primarily on acute schizophrenic patients in late adolescence or early adulthood.

The concepts derived by Wynne and his colleagues (1958) are based on two assumptions: that striving for relatedness with other human beings is a fundamental aspect of all human existence; and that every human being strives throughout life for a sense of personal identity. Striving for a stable sense of relatedness and identity in the changing and unpredictable world of relationships can have one of three outcomes. In *mutuality,* two people come together as separate identities, learn something about each other's identities, and appreciate each other's potential. In *non-mutuality,* two people interact in minimal ways for a specific purpose, and there is no investment in developing a closer relationship. In a *pseudo-mutual* relationship, the predominant concern is in maintaining a sense of complementarity or fitting together at the expense of the differentiation of the identities of the persons in the relationship. The changes which must inevitably occur with growth and situational changes (non-complementarity) are viewed as threatening to disrupt not just that particular transaction, but as possibly destroying the entire relation. Divergences of interest and identity which inevitably occur with growth cannot be tolerated in pseudo-mutual relationships because they threaten the illusion of unity. In mutual relationships, on the other hand, each person brings his or her own sense of meaningful, positively-valued identity which allows him or her to tolerate, appreciate, and learn from divergence. Pseudo-mutuality involves a fundamental dilemma: divergence is perceived as threatening disruption of the relation, and is therefore to be avoided; but avoiding divergence makes growth in the relation impossible.

Wynne considers pseudo-mutuality a major feature of the particular family setting in which some forms of schizophrenia develop. He hypothesizes that the intense and enduring threat of non-complementarity in relationships within families leads to a pattern of family pseudo-mutuality characterized by a persistent sameness of the role structure of the family, despite all situational changes and despite all changes in the experience of family life; an insistence on the appropriateness of the role structure; intense concern over possible divergence from this role structure; and a marked absence of spontaneity, novelty, humor, and enthusiasm from family enterprises.

A person who grows up in a pseudo-mutual setting is prevented from developing a firm sense of personal identity, inside or outside the family. All communications reflecting divergence from family complementarity are blurred in such a way that the child is seriously handicapped in extrafamilial interactions, so that his or her role within the family becomes all-encompassing.

Wynne and his colleagues (1958) have hypothesized that the intensity of pseudo-mutuality within the families of potential schizophrenics leads to the development of shared family mechanisms by which deviations from the family role structure are excluded from recognition or are delusionally reinterpreted. These mechanisms operate to diffuse, distort, blur, and prevent the articulation of any meanings that might enable an individual family member to differentiate a firm sense of personal identity. The mechanisms identified by Wynne and his colleagues include: the myth that catastrophe will follow divergence from the family role structure; bland approval of the inappropriate or bizarre behavior of a family member; secrecy; focusing on physical ailments; communication through an intermediary. According to Wynne, the family member labeled schizophrenic is often a scapegoat who is excluded from the family system in order to assume an important covert family role in maintaining the appearance of complementarity for the rest of its members.

In the family relations of potential schizophrenics, conscious recognition of divergence is not simply suppressed, as in neurosis. Instead, the perceptions of events that constitute divergence are aborted and blurred. It is hypothesized that these mechanisms mitigate the full impact of confused experience by providing a role structure in which the person can exist (pseudo-mutually) without developing a meaningful sense of personal identity or age-appropriate interests and abilities. According to Wynne, the family of a pre-schizophrenic acts as if it were an enclosed, self-sufficient social system. This metaphorical unstable but continuous boundary surrounding the schizophrenic family is referred to as the "rubber fence" because it appears to stretch to include that which appears complementary to the family role structure, and to shrink to exclude that which appears noncomplementary.

The experiences of the acute schizophrenic episode are explained as the result of an internalization of characteristics of the family social structure which leads to disturbed modes of thinking, perceiving, and communicating and renders it impossible for the person to attach clear meanings to his or her own feelings and experiences. In Wynne's view, the acute schizophrenic episode represents a breakdown of pseudo-mutuality, its attempted restoration, the attainment of a distorted kind of individuation, and the vicarious expression of the need of other family members for individuation. Wynne and his colleagues regard the chronic state that often follows the acute disturbance as a return to pseudo-mutuality at a greater distance, with symptoms that represent a more stable form of compromise.

evaluation

Singer and Wynne (1965) have recently focused their research efforts on attempts to further delineate patterns of handling attention and meaning characteristic of schizophrenic families. They have derived a series of criteria which allow independent judges to correctly predict the diagnoses of offspring from the transcripts of parents' projective test protocols (Wynne, 1968). This research evidence supports, in general, the researchers' hypothesis that there is a relationship between the content and form of parents' communication and the development of abnormal thought patterns in the children.

Wynne (1972) has described two types of transactions believed to have schizophrenogenic impact when they occur with great frequency and high emotional impact: the *injection of meaning* and the *concealment of meaning*. Wynne believes that these transaction patterns have at least two features in common: they tend to undermine the recipient's trust in his or her own capacity to derive meaning from his or her own experience, and they stimulate the escalation of counteractive responses which bind the persons together in the relationship.

Wynne and his associates have adopted a psychosocial view of the family as a group of individuals which must be understood as an integrated unit since each member influences the other. Their observational studies are subject to all of the criticisms of limited sample size and bias previously raised against the research by Lidz. Attempts to validate the model through the use of specialized scoring of psychological test protocols have provided interesting and valuable evidence in support of some constructs, but this evidence is subject to all the qualifications regarding the validity of projective tests, and by the close association of the individual doing the predictions and test scoring with the formulation of the concepts of this model.

madness and the family

R. D. Laing and his colleagues have intensively studied the families of twenty-five young schizophrenic patients for more than five years. These investigators attempted to apply the concepts and methods of dialectical science (Esterson, 1970) to the study of families of schizophrenics. This approach attempts to focus simultaneously on each person in the family, the relations among members of the family, and the family itself as a system.

Jean-Paul Sartre's (1960) concept of a *series* (a group category referring to a stage of minimal group cohesion in which members share a common goal but are not dependent on one another for its achievement) was adopted to refer to a pattern commonly observed in families of schizophrenics. In this pattern, members lack any genuine personal concern for one another, though they may evidence a great display of concern. The motivation for such family interactions is understandable in terms of social expectations: "what they expect," "what the neighbors will say." Sartre's description of a *bonded group* (a band of individuals linked together in activity directed toward a common goal, such as the reduction of fear, guilt, or a concern for mutual protection) served as a basis for Laing's concept of a contrasting family constellation termed a *nexus*. Sartre's distinction between *praxis* and *process* was adopted to distinguish between certain patterns of family interaction. *Praxis* refers to social events that are intelligible as the outcome of definite decisions by motivated people. Laing introduced this term to emphasize his intent to seek intelligibility (or *praxis*) in even the most bizarre "symptoms" and communications. *Process* refers to events that seem just to happen without any specifiable causal agent(s).

Laing and Esterson (1964) have attempted to illustrate the degree to which schizophrenic symptoms are comprehensible in terms of a description of the flux of family praxis. In their view, the apparent irrationality of individuals labelled schizophrenic finds its rationality in the irrationality of the family context.

The creation of the family as an internalized system of operations and relations occurs, according to Laing (1971), during the first years of life. The "family," as an internalized set of relations, is mapped onto one's body (posture, tone, mode of expression), feelings, thoughts, fantasies, dreams, and so on. Laing believes that reciprocal mapping draws the family into a closed system.

Laing and Esterson observed that in each of the families studied, the person labelled schizophrenic was caught in an interactional web of misunderstanding, characterized by ambiguities and contradictions of a highly *"mystifying"* (misidentification of issues) nature, which served to invalidate the patients' attempts to make "sense" out of their experience. Families consistently confused praxis and process in their experience of the diagnosed patient, and saw the patient's acts as if they were the result of process rather than the expression of his or her intentions. The authors present transcripts of interviews with families as evidence for their conclusions. This mode of presentation, it is argued, best illustrates the degree to which the experience and behavior of the patient are understandable as intelligible responses to a confused family praxis.

Laing's observations of schizophrenic families led to the conclusion that the web of mystification may reach back at least three generations (1971). In his view, each generation projects onto the next elements derived from at least one of the following three factors: what was *projected* onto it by prior generations, what was *induced* in it by prior generations, and its *response* to this projection and induction. Each person is induced, without being aware of it, to embody and enact a "shadow play" of previous generations. These attributions may have the function of instructions or injunctions; when this function is denied, we observe a pattern of *mystification.* For example, parents tell a child he is naughty (induction) because he does not do what they tell him to. However, through the attribution, "You are naughty," they effectively tell him *to do* what they ostensibly are telling him not to do.

Laing believes our family of origin gives us its range of distinctions, identities, definitions, rules, roles, attributions, and repertoires. These allow us to identify ourselves as a Christian, a married person, a patriot, a dutiful son, a good soldier, a good mother, a successful businessman, or a schizophrenic, but rarely tell us who we are when we play these parts. In Laing's view, we are all acting parts in a play that we have never read, whose plot we do not know, whose existence we occasionally see, but whose beginning and end are beyond our present imagination.

Laing (1971) argues that we can only begin to understand the experience and worldview of the schizophrenic by suspending judgment of "symptomatic" phenomena in terms of our contemporary view of "reality." He argues that our culturally conditioned beliefs about the dichotomies that appear to exist between inner and outer, body and mind, reason and unreason, and so on, are based on a split induced by the social conditions, competition for scarce commodities, and political relationships which have developed in western societies. This emphasis on the relativity of our concepts of reason and unreason, reality and fantasy, sanity and insanity, is associated, beginning in the late 1960's, with a growing mystical emphasis in Laing's writings. In the *Politics of Experience* (1967), Laing first expressed the view that some schizophrenics have embarked on a voyage back to the "void," the point of primeval oneness, in effect retracing the steps of human social evolution which affords the individual the opportunity—when not "aborted" by contemporary psychiatric practice—to "break through" our culturally shared dichotomies to a "higher" noncategorical present.

evaluation

Laing and his group have adopted a sociological view of the family as a dysfunctional system that supports the behavior of the person labelled schizophrenic. This group has provided valuable case illustrations of their views of the generalized patterns of family interaction characteristic of schizophrenogenic families based on a very small subject sample. Their criticisms of the application of standard scientific research procedures to the evaluation of family research studies have helped clarify the issues surrounding the eventual formulation of a scientific model appropriate to the complexities of human interactions. The initial promise of their descriptive concepts and dialectic approach has not been fulfilled, however, by sustained efforts to gather validating evidence.

experimental studies of interactions in families of schizophrenic patients

Mishler and Waxler (1968) have attempted to test systematically several clinical theories regarding the role of the family in the etiology of schizophrenia. Their research design used an experimental procedure to generate discussions among family members, measurement and coding of interactions during these discussions, and use of control groups (for pre-morbid social adjustment and gender of patients as well as normal control families and the well siblings of patients) for purposes of comparison.

The design of the study included families with schizophrenic children, male and female, with either good or poor pre-morbid social adjustment histories, and families with normal children. Intrafamilial controls were also afforded by the inclusion of a well sibling of the same sex as the schizophrenic patient in a separate experimental session with the parents. Thirty-two families of schizophrenic children and seventeen families of normal children participated.

The method of revealed differences was used as the experimental procedure in this investigation. Parents and one of their children—the patient on one occasion and the well sibling on the other—were asked to respond individually and privately to a questionnaire resembling an attitude inventory. Family members then came together and were asked to discuss a number of items on which they had disagreed privately. Members were asked to try to reach agreement on an answer or answers that would best represent the family decision. Family discussions were tape recorded and transcribed; typescripts were used for analysis and interpretation. A total of eighty-eight experimental sessions were completed by forty-nine families.

The results of this study indicated that the control variables of gender, level of premorbid social adjustment, and a well sibling of the patient were important factors that allowed for more detailed and precise descriptions of family functioning than would otherwise be possible. Significant differences between parents of normal children and the parents of schizophrenic patients occurred even more frequently than between the patients and either their well siblings or normal controls. This evidence strongly supports the recent focus on the possible etiological importance of the family of schizophrenic patients. Specific measures and findings reported in this study are reported in the following sections.

Expressiveness. Clinical observations suggested two hypotheses to guide Mishler and Waxler in their analyses of levels of expressiveness in family interactions. First, levels of expressiveness were expected to be higher in normal families than in the families of schizophrenics, and the affective quality of behavior was expected to be more positive in normal families. Second, in normal families, mothers would be more expressive than fathers.

Results of analyses of transcripts were interpreted as evidence that schizogenic families are more rigid in structure than normal families, a finding most compatible with a model that stresses the etiological importance of the quality of relationships (e.g., Wynne et al., 1958) over the content. Higher levels of instrumental and lower levels of expressive behavior were found in families of schizophrenic patients than in normal families. This pattern was assumed to reflect a collective defense against the expression of feelings resulting, in turn, in a more rigid structure of interpersonal and role relationships within the family. Paradoxically, the families of good premorbid patients were the least expressive in both female and male comparisons.

Power: Attention Control Strategies. Descriptions of schizophrenic families provide support for the hypothesis that there are major differences between these families and the normative pattern in terms of power structure. Schizophrenic families have been described (Lidz et al., 1965 and Haley, 1959) as having highly distorted or vague distributions of power and as maintaining early patterns far beyond their original usefulness. Two attention-control power strategies were evident in the families studied by Mishler and Waxler: family members attempted to control the interaction by using behavioral devices that maintain the focus of attention on the speaker; direct attempts at confrontation and control were used.

Data derived from indices of participation rate, who-speaks-to-whom, and length of speeches suggest that families having normal and schizophrenic children differed in the use of this strategy. In schizophrenic familes with sons (good and poor premorbid), the authors found a reversal of generational roles between father and son. Mothers and their schizophrenic patient sons took high power positions and the fathers exerted little influence. In contrast, the daughter patient in schizophrenic families was isolated from the parents, received little attention and respect, and attempted little control herself.

Attention control data support clinical observations (Wynne et al., 1958; Lidz et al., 1965) that link parental power roles with the development of the pre-schizophrenic child. These theories assume that normal development requires appropriate parental figures with whom to identify: a son needs a strong, dominant father, a daughter needs an expressive, supportive mother. Role ambiguity or reversal is thought to result in fragile or unclear self-identity in the child. Evidence from this measure supports these observations. In normal families, generational boundaries were clear and mothers and fathers were in relatively higher power positions than their children. In contrast, the father of male schizophrenic patients did not take the dominant role; it was assumed instead by the schizophrenic son in coalition with his mother. In families with a schizophrenic daughter, the mother was the dominant parent and the patient appeared to be isolated from both mother and father.

Power: Person Control Strategies.   Haley's (1959) analyses of the power structure in schizophrenic families suggest that these family members generally avoid direct, clear attempts at exercising control within the family. Mishler and Waxler hypothesized that normal families would, in contrast, be able to use control strategies directly to maintain the recognized power structure. Results of analyses of family interactions indicated that normal families preferred the direct mode of person control ("stop talking," or, "I won't listen to you anymore") to the indirect mode. Schizophrenic families—particularly the mothers—relied frequently on indirect controls. Families of good premorbid patients provided the greatest contrast with normals.

Mishler and Waxler concluded that the infrequent use of direct person control strategies by families of schizophrenic patients indicates that there are sanctions against direct confrontation of others within these groups. Attempts at influence are indirect, and take the form of questions rather than interruptions. The evidence suggests that the underlying power structure is more ambiguous in schizophrenic than normal families, and that norms for exerting influence are differential rather than equally applicable to all members of the family.

Disruptions in Communication. Mishler and Waxler hypothesized that normal families would evidence variable speech patterns—indicated by the use of incomplete sentences, pauses, fragments, repetitions, and laughter—and provide more opportunities for changing the course of a discussion, interjecting sanctions, and introducing new material. Schizophrenic patients were expected to evidence rigid, ordered patterns of communication requiring completed sentences, correct constructions, and allowing few opportunities for spontaneous changes.

Results indicated that normal families had the highest rates of disruption, poor premorbid families were in the middle, and good premorbid schizophrenic families were consistently lowest. Mishler and Waxler argue that even though normal families interact in a fragmented, disorganized way, these disruptions are not so frequent as to create chaos or unpredictability or to interfere with the members' ability to understand clearly and respond to one another. The families of good premorbid sons evidenced patterns of communication that provided few opportunities for alteration of the flow of interaction. They exerted strict control over all actions through the imposition of family norms. This control extended from content, or what can be talked about, to style, or how it can be discussed. These differences occurred only when the schizophrenic son was present, not when the parents were interacting with the well child.

Mishler and Waxler conclude that the rigid interaction pattern characteristic of good premorbid patients—speaking in complete sentences with little laughter and few fragments or false starts—suggests that the parents used a defensive pattern of communication to avoid uncertainty in any situation in which unacceptable or uncontrollable events might occur. In these families order and predictability were maintained to avoid discussion of forbidden topics or the expression of taboo feelings at the expense of spontaneity, challenge, and change.

Responsiveness. Schizophrenic families are frequently described as nonresponsive to each other's existence as independent persons. A recurrent theme in the clinical literature is that there is a lack of recognition of the particular qualities of the other person, an indifference or denial of his or her unique intentions and motives. Fromm-Reichmann (1948) introduced the concept of "imperviousness" to refer to the observation that the "schizophrenogenic" mother does not listen to or genuinely attend to the needs of the child, but responds to him or her on the basis of her own needs. In a similar vein, Laing (1971) introduced the term "mystification" to focus on the function and impact of communications where one person responds to another in terms of his or her own needs but acts as if it is really a response to the needs of the other.

Analyses of transcripts of family interactions indicated that normal families of children of both sexes were more responsive and more likely to focus their comments on the opinions of others. Poor premorbid families tended to orient toward the features of the immediate experimental situation, while the moderately responsive good premorbid families tended to introduce abstracted personal experiences. The authors interpret these findings as evidence that families of good premorbid patients are defensive and anxious about confronting others directly. This anxiety results in a discussion that appears clear and ordered but that lacks meaningful continuity and reference to each other's ideas. Normal families are more labile and nondefensive about discussing their ideas even when they disagree.

evaluation

Mishler and Waxler have conducted one of the few *experimental* studies of the interactions of normal and disturbed families. They have made an important contribution to the subtle process of translating clinical concepts and observations into researchable questions. This study, though limited in sample size and subject type (families of chronic patients were not included), lends important empirical support to many of the observations of family theorists. Findings indicate that good premorbid families are low on expressiveness, and are primarily instrumental in their behavior and negative in the quality of their expressed affect. Normal families were more flexible in their expression of affect, while poor premorbid families evidenced a concrete, particularistic mode of expression. Differences between the findings for sons and daughters were supportive of Lidz's distinction between skewed and schizmatic families. Family power structure contrasted most sharply between normal and good premorbid families. Important differences were observed between male and female patient families. Ritualistic, inflexible patterns of communication were more common in families of schizophrenic patients than in normal families. The Mishler and Waxler study can only be criticized for its limitations of sample size and the fact that it was conducted *ex post facto*. Inclusion of a wider range of subtypes of schizophrenic patients and a longitudinal design would provide more convincing evidence for the observations of family theorists.

Strengths and Weaknesses of Family Interaction Models

Mishler and Waxler (1968) have listed two major contributions family theorists have made to the general understanding of personality and social processes. First, focus on the family group as the unit of observation marks an important addition to traditional intrapsychic approaches to personality development. Second, through the introduction of such concepts as double-bind, mystification, pseudo-mutuality, and schizmatic conflict these theorists have sensitized clinicians to important aspects of interpersonal relationships that previously had been ignored.

Differences in emphasis which distinguish family theories from each other are associated with differing views of the schizophrenic process. Lidz and his co-investigators, for example, consider schizophrenia as a disorder of adolescence characterized by disturbed symbolic processes, disordered concept formation, and intrusions of primary process material. Problems in identity formation experienced during adolescence are thought to originate in a lack of adequate identity models in the family. Lidz postulates that the onset of an acute schizophrenic response is triggered by the collapse of a weak ego. The weak ego is a result of failure to form a sex-appropriate identity, and the collapse is precipitated by the fear of loss of control of hostile or sexual drives. Lidz later combined the problems of sex-role identification with the learning of distorted and maladaptive ways of thinking in his conceptualization of schizophrenia as a deficiency disorder, the end result of a series of failures of adequate acculturation.

Wynne and his group also view schizophrenia as the result of a failure to develop an adequate ego identity. The failure of ego development is attributed to a family learning environment which does not permit adequate reality testing or provide opportunities for the integration of flexible and appropriate roles into the developing ego. In pseudomutual relations roles are fragmented, dissociated from subjective experience, and not integrated into the active, perceiving ego. These distorted thought patterns and rigid, automatized role performances permit the individual to function adequately within the family until adolescence; they are, however, inadequate and inappropriate in the context of the general culture.

Bateson (1959) and Haley (1959) have attempted to develop an interactional description of schizophrenia that defines the "identified" schizophrenic as someone who avoids defining a relationship by stripping his or her communications of all metacommunicative meanings. Schizophrenic communications are understood as exaggerations of communications that are pervasive in the family of origin. The overt phase of schizophrenia is viewed as an intermittent behavior occurring in situations in which the individual feels required to break the rules of the family system and at the same time stay within them. Schizophrenic behavior is viewed as purposeful in that it enables the individual to avoid defining his or her relationship with another person, and at the same time is unavoidable, since the only solution to a double-bind communication is to respond in kind. Laing and his associates, in contrast, appear to reject the notion that schizophrenia refers to any kind of personal condition separable from the interactions of the families as a whole; if schizophrenia means anything, it refers to a communication disorder of the entire family.

The concepts and theories of family researchers can be criticized as representing little more than highly tentative constructs derived from poorly designed clinical studies characterized by the following methodological difficulties and omissions:

1. Much of the data upon which these theories are based are derived from retrospective studies, and so are subject to all the distortions of selective recall and biased reconstruction of events.

2. Most studies have been conducted on small, highly selected groups of young acute schizophrenic patients, yet family theorists rarely attempt to limit the application of their concepts to a particular subgroup of schizophrenics (process-reactive, paranoid, hebephrenic).

3. There is little supportive evidence for the reliability of the clinical observations which form the basis of the theories.

4. The researchers rarely attempt to study and compare matched control groups of families of schizophrenics, normals, and institutionalized individuals with different diagnoses (alcoholism, neuroses, affective disorders). Thus, it is not possible to determine the degree to which concepts such as mystification, marital schism, and pseudo-mutuality are specific to schizophrenics.

5. Family research has been conducted almost exclusively on upper-middle-class subjects, yet there is no acknowledgment of the possible biasing role of selective demographic or sociological factors in subject samples.

6. Family researchers fail to consider adequately the role of additional events (divorces, economic setbacks, and so on) or other groups (schools, churches, peer groups) in shaping personality.

Family researchers acknowledge the preliminary nature of their constructs, but argue that the traditional methods of science are not always adequate or appropriate to attempts to understand the relationships within the family system. Some also point to the prohibitive expense associated with intensive studies of family groups as the source of the methodological limitations of currently available studies. Still others question whether some of these criticisms, based on the assumptions and methodology of the natural sciences, are appropriate to family process research. Esterson (1970), for example, argues that many criticisms of family studies are based on the mistaken application of natural scientific standards and principles to the study of reciprocity between persons or groups. He maintains that this model fails to clarify the interplay of experience and action between the person and significant others, and suggests that the methods of phenomenological analysis and dialectic are more appropriate than those of natural science to the understanding of human behavior and experience.

Family theorists have contributed substantially to our understanding of the interpersonal origins of schizophrenia, but it is evident that these observations are of a preliminary nature and must eventually be considered in the broader context of evidence for the role of genetic vulnerability, of developmental issues, socio-economic class, individual experience, and contemporary sources of stress.

Family Therapy

Many clinicians have concluded that effective therapy, especially with young schizophrenic patients, must involve direct work with the family as well as—or in some instances rather than—the patient's psyche and behavior. Clinical experience and descriptive family studies indicate that families of schizophrenic patients are frequently characterized by contradictory metacommunications, inappropriate dependencies, symbiotic parent-child interactions, parental narcissism, and deviant beliefs and interactions (Henry, 1971). Family therapy has been widely accepted by therapists of diverse theoretical orientations as a technique that is a particularly useful means of bringing interpersonal and transactional problems into focus. Distortions of reality and deficiencies in the family environment that are not apparent in individual sessions or brief staff conferences are obvious in a family therapy setting. Open-ended parents' groups, in which parents talk to others with similar problems and are provided with opportunities to observe in others what they are unable to see in themselves, are another useful form of family therapy.

The concept of family has been expanded to include the patient's "network" of social and kinship relations (Speck and Attneave, 1971). *Network therapy* brings together an extended group or social network of between forty and one hundred persons who are involved in some way in the patient's life and are interested enough to want to help out during the acute crisis in a series of problem-solving sessions oriented around two goals: to alert relatives, acquaintances, and friends to the plight of the schizophrenic person and family; and to enlist the aid of network members in relieving their plight. This approach attempts to initiate experimentation with new patterns of relations among family members and others, and to broaden the social network of change agents.

The particular approach to family therapy adopted by any clinician is a function of his or her theoretical assumptions, but the goals of all approaches to family therapy are to change both the patient's behavior and the pattern of family interaction by bringing the interpersonal problems of the family into focus in such a way that family members are encouraged to separate themselves from the tangle of dysfunctional family interactions and to sever inappropriate dependencies and symbiotic bonds.

REFERENCES

ALANEN, Y. O. The family in the pathogenesis of schizophrenia and neurotic disorders. *Act Psychiatrica Scandinavia,* Supple. 189, *24,* 1966.

ARIETI, S. *Interpretation of Schizophrenia.* New York: Brunner, 1955.

BATESON, G. Cultural problems posed by a study of schizophrenic process. In *Schizophrenia: an Integrated Approach,* edited by A. Auerlack. New York: Ronald Press, 1959.

BATESON, G., D. JACKSON, J. HALEY, and J. WEAKLAND. Towards a theory of schizophrenia. *Behavioral Science, 1,* 1956, 251–264.

BOWEN, M. A family concept of schizophrenia. In *The Etiology of Schizophrenia,* edited by D. Jackson, pp. 364–372. New York: Basic Books, 1960.

CHODOFF, P., and W. CARPENTER. Psychogenic theories of schizophrenia. In *Schizophrenia: Biological and Psychological Perspectives,* edited by F. Usdin. New York: Brunner, 1975.

ESTERSON, A. *The Leaves of Spring.* London: Pelican, 1970.

FROMM-REICHMANN, F. Notes on the development of treatment of schizophrenics by psychoanalytic psychotherapy. *Psychiatry, 11,* 1948, 263–273.

GOLDSTEIN, M., and E. RODNICK. The family's contribution to the etiology of schizophrenia: current status. *Schizophrenia Bulletin, 14,* 1975, 48–63.

HALEY, J. An interactional description of schizophrenia. *Psychiatry, 22,* 1959, 321–332.

HENRY, J. *Pathways to Madness.* New York: Random House, 1971.

HIRSCH, S., and J. LEFF. *Abnormalities in Parents of Schizophrenics.* Oxford: Oxford University Press, 1975.

LAING, R. D. *The Divided Self: an Existential Study in Sanity and Madness.* London: Tavistock Publications, 1959.

————. *The Politics of Experience.* London: Penguin, 1967.

————. *The Politics of the Family.* New York: Vintage, 1971.

LAING, R. D., and A. ESTERSON. *Sanity, Madness, and the Family.* New York: Basic Books, 1964.

LIDZ, R., and T. LIDZ. The family environment of schizophrenic patients. *American Journal of Psychiatry, 106,* 1949, 332–345.

LIDZ, T. *The Family and Human Adaptation.* New York: International Universities Press, 1963.

————. *The Origin and Treatment of Schizophrenic Disorders.* New York: Basic Books, 1973.

LIDZ, T., A. CORNELISON, and S. FLECK. *Schizophrenia and the Family,* New York: International Universities Press, 1965.

LIDZ, T., A. CORNELISON, S. FLECK, and D. TERRY. The intrafamilial environment of the schizophrenic patient: II. Marital schism and marital skew. *American Journal of Psychiatry, 114,* 1957, 241–248.

LIDZ, T., and S. FLECK. *Family Studies and a Theory of Schizophrenia.* Unpublished manuscript, 1964.

————. Schizophrenia, human interaction, and the role of the family. In *The Etiology of Schizophrenia,* edited by D. Jackson. New York: Basic Books, 1960.

MAHLER, M. On child psychosis and schizophrenia: autistic and symbiotic infantile psychoses. *Psychoanalytic Study of the Child, 7,* 1952, 286–305.

MISHLER, E., and N. WAXLER. *Interaction in Families: An Experimental Study of Family Process and Schizophrenia.* New York: John Wiley, 1968.

————. Family interaction processes and schizophrenia: a review of current theories. *Merrill-Palmer Quarterly, 11,* 1965, 296–315.

SARTRE, J. P. *Critique de la Raison Dialectique.* Paris: Librairie Gallimard, 1960.

SEDGEWICK, P., and R. D. LAING. Self, symptom, and society. In *R. D. Laing and Anti-Psychiatry,* edited by Boyers and Orrill. New York: Harper and Row, 1971.

SPECK, R., and C. ATTNEAVE. Social network intervention. In *Changing Families,* edited by J. Haley, pp. 312–332. New York: Grune and Stratton, 1971.

SULLIVAN, H. S. Peculiarity of thought in schizophrenia. *American Journal of Psychiatry, 82,* 1925–26, 21–86.

WAXLER, N. The normality of deviance: an alternate explanation of schizophrenia in the family. *Schizophrenia Bulletin, 14,* 1975, 38–47.

WEAKLAND, J. The double-bind hypothesis of schizophrenia and three-party interaction. In *The Etiology of Schizophrenia,* edited by D. Jackson, pp. 373–388. New York: Basic Books, 1960.

WYNNE, L. The injection and the concealment of meaning in the family relationships and psychotherapy of schizophrenics. In *Psychotherapy of Schizophrenia.* Amsterdam: Excerpta Medica Foundation, 1972.

WYNNE, L., I. RYEKOFF, J. DAY, and S. HIRSCH. Pseudo-mutuality in the family relations of schizophrenics. *Psychiatry, 21,* 1958, 205–220.

WYNNE, L., and M. SINGER. Thinking disorders and family transaction. Paper presented at the Annual Meeting of the American Psychiatric Association, May 1964.

Chapter Ten

Psychodynamic Theories

Freud's Psychoanalytic Theory

Freud (1913, 1964) formulated the first comprehensive psychological theory of the origins of emotional disorders. Prior to this, emotional disorders were viewed as symptoms of unspecified neurological disease processes. Freud was strongly influenced by the positivistic model of the physical and biological sciences which prevailed at the end of the nineteenth century, and worked to construct a theory of psychology that would conform to the assumptions of the natural science model. His early clinical studies of female hysteric patients, his self-analysis, and his extensive studies of dreams and slips-of-the-tongue (paraprexes) convinced him that the unconscious is relatively independent of conscious experience and is crucial to the understanding of human behavior.

sources of emotional disturbance

Freud held an epigenetic view of personality development; each stage of personality growth must be experienced and built upon the foundation established during the previous stage. In his view, overindulgence or deprivation associated with infantile attempts to cope with the developmental issues at each psychosexual stage could result in a partial arrest of ego development. In this manner the ego may become partially *fixated* at one or more levels of development and never develop the capacity to appropriately discharge libidinal tensions beyond the level of primary fixation. These deficits in ego development are cumulative in effect, and may grossly impair the individual's ability to appropriately discharge instinctual tensions. Freud believed that instinctual energy is dammed up as a result of each ego fixation (arrest of psychological development at a particular stage) so that each occurrence leaves less energy available for coping with later tasks. He believed that past fixations have an unconscious prototypic influence on the present. In effect, the amount and levels of blocked libido are considered primary determinants of personality types and the associated predispositions to develop particular patterns of emotional disorder.

Anxiety is understood as a signal experienced by the individual when unconscious aspects of ego function recognize the threat of the buildup of unintegrated instinctual forces. The adult ego may be highly developed with regard to affectively neutral cognitive tasks but remain relatively primitive and undeveloped in those areas associated with the content of early fixations. Anxiety is a signal to the ego that it is in danger of being overwhelmed by repressed instinctual forces associated with the developmental issues left unresolved by earlier ego fixations. Freud described a number of *defense mechanisms* that characterize the ego's attempt to deny, block, distort, or re-rout these repressed impulses, the most important of which are repression and regression. In repression the ego (at a preconscious level) permanently diverts some of its energy in an effort to force a threatening impulse into the unconscious. Regression refers to the tendency of the ego to return to previously fixated levels of ego function in response to overwhelming anxiety.

Freud formulated a three-stage model of emotional disorders (Rychlak, 1973). In the first stage, unacceptable id wishes are repressed and countered by ego-defensive strategies designed to allow expression of the wish in disguised form. The ego is never aware of the actual meaning of the disguised expression, and anxiety is averted.

The second stage begins with pubescence. The surge of libido (sexual instinct) associated with the physical changes of adolescence gives increased impetus to inadequately repressed sexual and aggressive fantasies. This powerful resurgence of repressed impulses generates anxiety, and the ego must increase its efforts to control anxiety through the application of defensive strategies which either strengthen the repression or allow for the expression of unconscious forces in ways that allow the patient to avoid conscious awareness of the meaning disguised in the thought or action.

The third stage begins when a "compromise" is reached between the id wish and the antagonistic ego protective efforts. In Freudian theory, the "symptom" is a substitute expression, which allows for the disguised gratification of an id wish and at the same time protects the ego from conscious awareness of the meaning of the "symptom."

In the Freudian model the nature of the mental disorder is determined by: hereditary factors; the initial stage of fixation; the amount of libido originally fixated; and the extent of libidinal regression precipitated by contemporary sources of frustration and stress (Rychlak, 1973). In general, the *deeper* and more *extensive* the regression, the *more severe* the disorder. Individuals considered to be normal, neurotic, or psychotic may all be fixated at the oral level, for example; however, the extensiveness of the regression-fixation will determine the severity of impairment.

Psychoanalytic Theory of Schizophrenia

Since Freud was concerned primarily with formulating a theory of the neuroses, his contributions to a psychoanalytic theory of schizophrenia were incidental to his general theories of personality. He did incorporate schizophrenic behavior into his theory by considering these disorders in the context of the mechanism of regression. Specifically, he suggested (1924) that both schizophrenics and neurotics evidence ego regression, or withdrawal of libido from external objects. In the case of the neurotic this regression is temporary and partial; the ego eventually effects a relationship with the external world through the use of defense mechanisms. In the case of the schizophrenic the regression extends further back, to the period during infancy in which the ego was first developed. Freud postulated that the schizophrenic appeared to regress to a state of "primary narcissism" characteristic of a period of infancy during which the systems of mental functioning—id, ego, superego—were not differentiated from one another, and the distinction between internal and external did not yet exist.

The nucleus of the schizophrenic experience is considered to be the break with reality, following which the ego returns to its original undifferentiated state, in which it is dissolved wholly or partially into the id. Many psychoanalysts (Fenichel, 1945) consider the basic conflict to be the same in the neuroses and psychoses; in both cases the conflict is between the id (instinctual impulses) and the external world. The ego represses the objectionable demands of the id, which return distorted by one or several of the secondary defense mechanisms. In the case of the schizophrenic, the ego withdraws completely from the external world which limits its instinctual freedom, and attempts to regain the lost reality in distorted form. The difference between neurotic and psychotic patterns is explained in terms of differences in stages of primary fixation and regression. Regression in the schizophrenic is more extensive and goes back to a fixation point in psychic development which is considerably earlier than any observed in the neuroses. The primary fixation of schizophrenia is thought to be the early, objectless period which precedes the oral sadistic phase and occurs during the first year of life.

fundamental symptoms

Freud believed that most schizophrenic disorders involved two fundamental processes causing two categories of symptoms: (1) Symptoms of Regression and (2) Restitutive Symptoms.

Symptoms of Regression (four categories). These symptoms represent the inner perception of withdrawal of libido from external objects. Fenichel (1945) maintains that the *collapse of reality testing,* the fundamental function of the ego, causes symptoms such as fantasies of world destruction which symbolize the withdrawal of ego cathexes. These symptoms are interpreted as evidence that the schizophrenic personality is regressing to a time when the ego was not yet established.

The body image is said to be the nucleus of the ego. Since the beginning of the schizophrenic process is thought to be marked by regression to a state of narcissism, and the earliest stages of ego development are associated with the infant's discovery of his or her own body, hypochondriacal sensations and *alterations of body sen-*

sations are often associated with schizophrenic regression. *Feelings of depersonalization* and estrangement from direct experience are understood to represent a reaction of the disintegrating ego to narcissistic regression and the associated withdrawal of external libidinal attachments.

Delusions of grandeur or omnipotence are similar to day-dreams of nonpsychotic persons, except these narcissistic day-dreams are believed to be true. Freud explained these phenomena in the context of his assumption that regression to narcissistic omnipotence would result in the substitution of self-love or self-grandeur for attachment to external reality.

Schizophrenic logic and ideational content is *archaic,* similar to the magical thinking of primitives and small children, because the ego has partially disintegrated and the personality has regressed to an early stage of development.

Restitutional Symptoms.   These symptoms appear during and after the initial stage of acute ego collapse and regression, and are taken as evidence that the patient is attempting to re-establish ego control and reality contact. *Hallucinations* are considered to be projections of inner complexes which are experienced as external perceptions after total or partial loss of reality testing. The fact that many hallucinations are frightening rather than pleasurable is interpreted as evidence that some do not represent simple wish fulfillments, but result from the reappearance of part of the reality that was repudiated through regression. Hallucinations are considered to be expressions not only of the ego's escape from reality, but of the failure of this escape, represented as warded-off impulses returning in the form of projections of the superego. Delusions are viewed as attempts to reconstruct reality in ways that are less threatening to the ego.

Freud initially believed that psychoanalysis was useless in the therapy of psychoses, because psychotic patients were thought to have regressed to a state of narcissism which precluded development of the transference neurosis considered to be the key to all successful psychoanalytic therapy. (Many analysts used the term *transference neuroses* to refer to psychoneurotic classifications, and *narcissistic neuroses* to refer to the psychoses.) Analysts now believe that at least some schizophrenics can benefit from analysis because the regression to narcissism is never complete.

direct analytic theory

John Rosen (1952) developed a treatment approach rather than a complete theory of schizophrenia. He was impressed by the similarities between psychotic material and dream material, and based his technique on the dynamics of Freudian dream psychology. Rosen compares schizophrenia to an interminable nightmare, in which the unacceptable wishes or impulses are so well disguised that the psychotic does not awaken. The task of therapy is to "awaken the psychotic" by unveiling the real content of the psychosis in such a way that the patient must confront it. According to Rosen, schizophrenics live "under the shadow of the breast." He argues that the present aspect of their psychological existence is structured by needs characteristic of earliest infancy, and that the nature of the breast upon which they are so dependent is "life-threatening."

Rosen's therapeutic approach is based upon the principle that the therapist must be a "loving," omnipotent protector and provider for the patient, the idealized mother who now has the responsibility of bringing up the patient all over again. Once the initial relationship is established on the basis of loving protection, the patient is responded to as any other member of a family: anger, fighting, and withdrawal, as well as love, become important aspects of the therapeutic relationship.

Direct interpretation is the most important technique of Rosen's therapy. It is used to indicate to the patient that somewhere in his or her environment there exists a source of magical, omnipotent understanding similar to the earliest understanding exhibited by an adult in the neonatal environment. Direct analysis of the manifest content of the patient's verbalizations, gestures, mannerisms, posture, and day-to-day conduct gradually forces him or her to listen to its latent meaning. An example of direct analysis of psychotic content is presented in the case of a male patient who felt compelled to invent an auto transmission more powerful than any other transmission; he planned to do this by applying a fluid to gain power. This concern was interpreted by Rosen as, "How can you transmit mother's milk to your mouth?"

According to Rosen, schizophrenia has its inception prior to termination of the pre-verbal period, and is caused by the mother's inability to love her child. A paranoid patient is thought to be reliving the destructiveness of the frustrating early mother-child relationship which he or she now projects onto the world. Schizophrenic behavior functions to control magically those aspects of the inner and outer environment that are too oppressive to be faced as they are. The patient behaves in a manner we label schizophrenic because there is something he or she cannot get from the environment that he or she can find in the imagination. Rosen feels that only by the therapist genuinely "becoming" the loving mother and providing love, protection, and understanding will the patient dare to wake up from the nightmare of schizophrenia. Once the patient is "awake," he or she must undergo long term psychoanalysis to avoid a recurrence of the psychosis.

An Interpersonal Theory of Schizophrenia

Harry Stack Sullivan devised one of the few truly comprehensive theories of personality based on clinical experience with schizophrenic patients. Sullivan defined personality as a construct which manifests itself only in the process of interpersonal relationships. In his approach, the study of mental disorder is synonymous with the study of interpersonal relationships, for personality is thought to evolve almost entirely from the individual's relations with the people he or she lives with in childhood.

sullivan's theory of psychopathology

Sullivan viewed emotional disorders as inadequate or ineffective ways of relating to others which function to control anxiety. Anxiety originates through the process of empathy with an anxious, emotionally distant, or "malevolent" mothering person. Punishment, inconsistency, ridicule, brutality, and rejections also elicit anxiety. The developing self-system of the child attempts to minimize anxiety by selective inattention, avoidance, and, in extreme instances, dissociation. The anxiety-reducing maneuvers have severe consequences: they result in rigid, inflexible personifications which become less and less appropriate to the context of the person's interpersonal experience; they restrict the range of experience so that many aspects of the personality are not satisfactorily developed and integrated into the self-system. As a consequence, the person cannot integrate certain aspects of his or her personality into the interpersonal world and fails to cope successfully with the interpersonal issues associated with the various developmental eras. The result is a person who is threatened in interpersonal relationships, emotionally alienated, threatened by the competence of others, and dissociated from crucial aspects of his or her personal and interpersonal experience. Serious emotional disorders thus represent exaggerations of life-long patterns of dealing with anxiety.

In Sullivan's view, people who have learned to control and deny emotional needs through excessive religiosity and morality are predisposed to depression; those who control anxiety through superficial emotional contact, denial of needs, and narcissism tend to develop hysterical disorders; those who dissociate much of their experience become schizophrenic; and those who learn to project blame for inadequacies are most likely to become paranoid. Emotional disorders are *not* understood as processes residing within the person; they are essentially complications of an individual's interpersonal relationships.

Sullivan described four security operations as the primary strategies by which the self-system wards off anxiety: sublimation, obsessionalism, selective inattention, and dissociation. *Sublimation* is defined as the substitution, for a behavior pattern which arouses anxiety, of a socially more acceptable activity pattern which satisfies part of the motivational system that caused trouble. *Obsessionalism* refers to the use of language and speech as if words had magical potency to reduce anxiety. *Selective inattention* has its beginnings during the juvenile years, and becomes a source of trouble when it is used in such a way that the person must not and does not attend to large areas of information about himself or herself in order to maintain the security of the self-system. *Dissociation* is a security operation related to the "not me" personification which allows the individual to completely deny large segments of his or her personality. Dramatic changes in behavior, such as the drastic disruption of personality observed in acute reactive schizophrenics, are thought to result from the breakdown of the dissociative system and the emergence into awareness of the contents of the dissociated system.

schizophrenia as a human process

In Sullivan's view, the schizophrenic experience is characterized by the fact that the self-system has lost control of awareness, so that it can no longer maintain in dissociation the contents of the "not me" personification and restrict from awareness the chaotic mental processes characteristic of earlier periods of infancy and childhood. The emergence into experience of the previously dissociated "not me" in the context of increasingly chaotic, infantile modes of experiencing, and the collapse of the self-system, result in the feelings of terror, confusion, and urgency. Sullivan argues that the awesome feelings of vastness and smallness, and the chaotic confusion of categories of relevance characteristic of the schizophrenic, are part of the ordinary experiences we all have during very early stages of development.

The sense of urgency characteristic of the beginning of the schizophrenic disorder may result in either a pattern of frenzied, confused activity or concentration upon developing a theory or explanation for something. The purpose of a sense of urgency is to ward off a total collapse of the self-system which is sensed at some pre-verbal level of awareness.

Sullivan felt that the initial stage of acute excitement most resembles the catatonic subtype, and therefore regarded the catatonic as the "essential schizophrenic picture" out of which other subtypes are formed. According to Sullivan, the stupor and muteness typical of the catatonic schizophrenic emerges only after the period of urgent, undirected activity has resulted in such a series of exhausting frustrations that the individual actively inhibits tensions. Catatonic excitement is an interruption of the stuporous state by periods of intense activity and gesture which represent attempts to do something about the persistent feeling of urgency. The similarity between primitive dances and catatonic gestures and rituals was interpreted by Sullivan as evidence of attempts by patients to identify with and influence the cosmic power subconsciously identified with the uncontrolled psychotic experience.

Sullivan observed that in most instances some degree of control was gradually established by the person over his or her experience. In his view, the particular form of this control depends on the person's life experience and determines whether the essential catatonic state develops into a paranoid solution or further deteriorates into the hebephrenic style. Delusions represent attempts to establish a measure of control over chaotic mental processes through obsessional reconstructions of recent experience. These reconstructions impose meaning and reduce the confusion associated with recent experience, but are often strikingly primitive in logical structure, and so appear rather fantastic to others. Delusions are believed with unusual tenacity because they enable the self-system to regain control over the contents of consciousness by allowing the individual to deny responsibility for those "inhuman" aspects of himself or herself confronted during the period immediately following failure of the self-system. According to Sullivan, the rapid and unpredictable shifts in levels of consciousness observed in schizophrenia depend on what disadvantages the self-system is working under: "if the disadvantage becomes great the schizophrenic processes flow in and engulf all clear formulations" (1956, p. 24).

The paranoid dynamism is used by people who have learned to cope with interpersonal difficulties through the projection or transfer of blame to others, while the hebephrenic solution is attempted by those who have learned to despair that interpersonal contacts can ever be gratifying. Sullivan believed that the paranoid dynamism is rooted in an awareness of inferiority (real or imagined) of some sort which necessitates a transfer of blame to others. The paranoid transfer of blame is never stable because the real sources of insecurity, the roots of the self, date back to infancy and the empathic linkage with significant people during those early years, when the child was unable to discriminate the source or who was to blame for how bad he or she felt. The paranoid dynamism must not only transfer blame for feelings of insecurity to those who elicit or symbolize the origins of this insecurity, but must also explain why these people are so intent on victimizing the patient. At this point the origins of the grandiose quality of paranoid thinking become apparent through the application of the paranoid formula: "I am a very important person against whom certain more or less devilish people are engaged in a destructive plot" (1956, p. 149).

Sullivan believed that most schizophrenics are basically shy, sensitive individuals, possessed of an unusual proclivity for having their feelings hurt, who have erected enormous systems of defensive security operations to protect themselves from intimate contact with others. Schizophrenics have never developed the degree of self esteem and sense of ability to get along with other people that makes most human interaction safe. Specifically, Sullivan felt that anyone who achieved a truly satisfactory, intimate sexual interaction with another person of comparable status would not become a long-term schizophrenic. He believed that if the personality is well-developed in areas other than adjustive sexual intimacy, the schizophrenic break will be abrupt and acute in pattern, or reactive. If, on the other hand, life experience has been such that the adolescent avoids or retires from the realities of interpersonal peer and heterosexual relations to the juvenile world of submission to and dependency upon authoritarian adults, then the schizophrenic process is likely to be insidious.

sullivan's views on therapy

According to Sullivan, the essence of the schizophrenic dynamism is "a confusion of interpersonal relations by the appearance in awareness of referential processes ordinarily excluded from awareness" (1956, p. 361). The referential processes which appear are either incapable of being expressed in words or can be expressed only in terms of such unique word meanings that communication is difficult or impossible. The essential feature that distinguishes schizophrenic from nonschizophrenic is that the schizophrenic's self-system is unable to maintain control of awareness in those particular interpersonal situations in which feelings of insecurity are aroused because of extremely threatening dissociated impulses. Sullivan believed that the origin of the weakness of the schizophrenic self-system resulted from an "extreme lack of favorable opportunity," particularly early in life, because the idea was communicated to the child that he or she was a burden and "relatively infrahuman."

The goal of psychotherapy, according to Sullivan, is the same as that of other forms of education: "experience incorporated into the self" in an interpersonal context. The differences between good educative techniques and psychotherapy are related to the characteristics specific to the first several years of life, during which the basis for the self-system is formed. Therapy begins by removing the person from the stress situation into one in which he or she is encouraged to renew efforts at adjustment with others. The task of the therapist is to help the person feel that he or she is now one of a group, composed partly of persons who are having problems and partly of those who are paid to be of help. All thought and acts are considered valid to the person expressing them, and something he or she should understand. The emphasis of the initial phase of therapy is on removing the sense of mystery surrounding the psychosis and showing how all experiences are related to interactions with a small number of significant people in a relatively straightforward series of circumstances. Psychotic experiences recalled from the acute phase are related to personal relationships.

Sullivan reported good therapeutic results with young schizophrenic patients of the acute-reactive type, when received for care before they progressed into either hebephrenic dilapidation or durable paranoid maladjustments, and treated first in a context supportive of socialization and thereafter by attempts at more fundamental reorganization of the personality aimed at increasing the adequacy of the self-system's dynamisms for interacting with other people.

a psychological approach to schizophrenia

Silvano Arieti (1974) believes that a psychological approach to schizophrenia is presently most expeditious. At least fifty-four percent of identical twins of schizophrenic patients do *not* suffer from schizophrenia, which suggests that psychological factors play a larger role than genetic ones. He emphasizes the importance of early childhood experience in the development of the predisposition to schizophrenia. According to Arieti, the childhood world of the schizophrenic consists of interpersonal relations characterized by experiences of intense anxiety, frustration, inappropriate demands, inconsistency, and emotional detachment. In other words, the preschizophrenic child is born into a family that is unable to provide both an adequate sense of security and the interpersonal experiences essential to the development of a sense of "basic trust" in other human beings.

Arieti believes that traditional psychodynamic formulations unduly stress the effects of the primary family on the child; they view the child as a passive agent molded by family and social circumstances, and do not adequately consider what is happening to the child intrapsychically. He argues that psychoanalytic theory has focused on the impact of painful experiences on the personality development of the child, but has failed to consider the role of intrinsic qualities in the child and the effects of alterations in his or her development consequent to traumatic exposure that make him or her less able to cope with adverse circumstances.

Arieti has attempted to formulate a theoretical model which includes the influences of the interpersonal world, the manner in which the child experiences and internalizes the world, and how such internalization affects subsequent life events. In this view, the self of the pre-schizophrenic develops not as a simple reproduction of family circumstances but, because of particular sensitization to certain experiences and parental characteristics, as a "grotesque representation" of the family context and consists of all the defensive strategies developed to cope with these experiences.

development of schizophrenia

Arieti distinguishes four periods in the life of the patient from birth to the onset of psychosis. During the first stage (*early childhood*), the child cannot satisfactorily relate to and accept the other (primary nurturant) person, usually the mother, who is necessary for the adequate formulation of the child's sense of self. The mothering figure is perceived as a "malevolent thou" and the *I* as a "bad me." These experiences are distorted, and the conscious experience of the child is protected by such defenses as repression and denial. In the second period (*late childhood*), the child develops either a schizoid personality that avoids direct contact and feelings or a *stormy* personality, capable of a variety of intense responses. The *thou* then comes to be experienced as a "distressing other" during late childhood, and the "bad me" is transformed into a "weak, inadequate me." The child comes to experience himself or herself as weak and threatened in a world of overpowering, distressing adults.

The third period begins with *puberty,* and marks the beginnings of mature conceptual and sexual function. Arieti believes that, contrary to traditional psychoanalytic theory, ideas are of greater etiological significance than instinctual impulses in this stage. During puberty the self-image is composed of the adolescent's sense of personal significance, role in life, and self-esteem. The defensive strategies previously adopted to enable the child to adapt to the limited world of the primary family become markedly less useful now that he or she must begin to expand contacts with the broader social world. The pre-schizophrenic adolescent suddenly feels overwhelmed and unprepared for the challenges of establishing a life outside the family. He or she begins to feel unfit, unaccepted, alone, and without a future. These experiences provoke feelings of intense panic. They are caused by a resonance between memories of infantile experiences of the intensity of the threatening qualities of the interpersonal world and an increased awareness of a devastating self-image, facilitated by the expansion of sexuality and conceptual ability. Pre-schizophrenic individuals come to experience themselves as doomed to failure, without hope or possibilities.

At some point the patient enters the fourth stage, or *psychotic period.* Intense anxieties and despair overwhelm defenses that were at least minimally adequate during earlier developmental stages. The final self-protective measures available to the psyche are to dissolve or to alter cognitive functions so that external reality may seem difficult and strange but no longer emits a resonance with the preconceptual understanding of the self.

Arieti believes that the self becomes particularly sensitized to the negative characteristics of the person's relationships with family, particularly the parents. Sensitivity to the painful aspects of the parent-child relationship results in a partial awareness of the parent which emphasizes the negative and is based on primitive "primary cognition." The grotesque self-concept of the child which emerges from the unfolding parent-child interaction is particularly sensitized to interactions which elicit feelings of being unwanted, unloved, inadequate, unacceptable, inferior, awkward, not belonging, peculiar, rejected, embarrassed, guilty, confused, disgraced, remote, and suspect. This circular process results in increasingly intense experiences of anguish, anxiety, withdrawal, distortions and sensitivities, and produces two strategies: repression from consciousness of the reality of the parent- (mothering one) child relationships; and the displacement or projection of responsibility for this state of affairs onto the external world. These strategies are adopted because the person cannot accept this image of himself or herself and must represent the interpersonal world and his or her own self-image in less frightening ways. The strategies are representative of primary process thinking. Arieti argues that they are not learned or imitated habits, but innate, archaic, primitive ways of construing experience associated with early childhood.

Schizophrenic Cognition. The onset of the psychotic period is marked by a different type of cognition, one which alters the patient's view of the world and is largely responsible for the "symptoms" of schizophrenia. Arieti does not believe that these cognitive changes are learned or directly transmitted by other family members. In his view, they constitute structures of thought and language available to every person. Following Freud, he states that primary process thought has displaced secondary process. Arieti places a new and different stress on Bleuler's concept of thought disorder, but disagrees with interpretations that thought disorder is primarily the result of a disorder of attention, fragmentation of thought, or loss of the ability to abstract. In Arieti's theory schizophrenic cognition is based on: concretization of concepts; identification of concepts based on similarity of predicates rather than subjects (Von Domarus, 1944); and a changed relation between connotation and verbalization, so that the usual semantic value of the word is altered and the word itself becomes of special value and loses relation to its original meaning.

Confronted with overwhelming anxiety the ego of the patient succumbs, and the cognitive mechanisms of primary process thought enable him or her to escape the painful reality of living in the world. The presence of primary process dramatically alters adult cognitive function; inner reality becomes more important than external reality, internal-external, and self and other, become confused, consensual validation of beliefs is undermined, and paleological thought, archaic symbols, intercategorical content, and infantile psychological processes predominate. In general, the more disturbed the patient and his or her environment, the greater the influence of primary process cognition. Arieti believes that severe anxiety impairs logical cognitive function; in these circumstances a person adopts cognitive mechanisms characteristic of an earlier or lower level of integration. He has introduced the concept of *progressive teleological regression* to refer to the tendency of the psyche to purposively regress to successively lower levels of integration and function in order to reduce intolerable anxiety. In Arieti's view, a specific type of anxiety, one which injures the self-image and is experienced as an inner danger, induces schizophrenic regression.

Paleologic Thought.   As the patient regresses to escape anxiety, he or she can no longer tolerate a logical experience and comprehension of growing aspects of interpersonal reality. Isolated regions of logical thought may be retained, however, particularly in areas related to nonthreatening content. Logical thought may also be used, following the acute phase, to support views and conclusions reached with more primitive mechanisms. *Paleologic* thought is regressive cognitive function which reduces anxiety and forms the basis of the delusional structure that permits the patient to see reality as he or she wants to.

Arieti (1974) believes that paleologic thought is based on the principle of cognitive function enunciated by Von Domarus (1944), that schizophrenics accept identity on the basis of identical subjects. One patient, for example, believed she was the Virgin Mary. Her thoughts were: Mary was a virgin, I am a virgin, therefore I am the Virgin Mary. This delusion is based on the identity of the predicate of the premises (the state of being a virgin) which led the patient to accept the identity of the two subjects (Mary and herself). In Arieti's view, Von Domarus's principle helps explain the formal structure of many delusions; the content, however, is related to the specific life issues of the individual patient. The thought processes of schizophrenic patients appear bizarre, unpredictable, and incomprehensible because paleologic thought is based on identification by predicates. Since the number of predicates that may be applied to the same subject are often numerous, the observer is unable to predict or understand the schizophrenic process of conceptual identification.

Arieti believes, as did Freud, that primary process thought is present in the psychological life of every person, whether normal, neurotic, or schizophrenic. He believes, however, that its presence in schizophrenia is characterized by three distinctive features: it involves a relatively larger proportion of the individual's life than in nonschizophrenics; it resists or overpowers the influence of the secondary process and is therefore not corrected; it is usually not integrated with a secondary process to form a creative product.

Acceptance of patterns of cultural irrationality, such as shared prejudices, religious beliefs, ceremonials, and rituals, is not considered a sign of schizophrenic delusions so long as they are accepted by the individual from his or her social context and are not self-created.

Therapy. Arieti views schizophrenia as an abnormal way of dealing with an abnormal life situation. He believes that psychological therapy can effectively help many patients to re-establish human relatedness, to question delusional thought, to understand themselves in the context of life history factors, and to help the person discover nonpsychotic patterns of living. Unlike drug therapy, which Arieti believes treats only symptoms, psychological therapy attempts to change the person's self-image by undoing the destructive effects of the past and changing the patient's attitudes toward the present and future.

Evaluation of Psychodynamic Theories

Freud's theoretical formulations represent the first attempt to construct a natural scientific psychological theory based on internal or introspective data. Freud attempted to remain within the respectable confines of the physical sciences by constructing analogical ties between psychic constructs and biological drives. He accomplished this difficult task by postulating that conscious phenomena are understandable in terms of unconscious forces which, in turn, are reducible to the opposition of two instinctual forces: Eros and Thanatos. Freud attempted to avoid the pitfalls of dualism and the difficult issues of intentionality, will, and choice by reducing psychological explanations to substrates of physical energy (libido), thereby defining behavior as determined. In this model the psyche is conceptualized as an analogic physical energy system. Freudian scientific imagery is that of classical mechanics and hydraulics, a psychic analogue of the models of nineteenth century physics. According to many theorists (Bruner, 1956), Freud's model is not scientific theory in the conventional sense, but is a metaphorical way of conceiving human behavior that provides the fertile ground from which scientific psychological theory may eventually develop.

The numerous criticisms of psychodynamic theory are given their particular shapes by the theoretical assumptions of the critic. Empiricists, biophysical theorists, and behaviorists criticize psychodynamic theories as unscientific speculation, vaguely tied to empirical observation, and as philosophical metaphor that has generated few testable hypotheses and little validating research.

Phenomenologists are critical of psychodynamic theories because they transform the flow of human experience into static concepts and natural scientific causal principles, non-purposeful materialities devoid of consciousness or meaning to a self. Social psychologists criticize psychodynamic theories for imputing undue significance to intrapsychic and childhood factors, and for ignoring the important role of contemporary social and cultural variables in shaping human behavior and experience.

Sullivan was among the most influential psychodynamic theorists to reject Freud's metapsychology and instinctual model (libido theory). Thoroughly trained as a Freudian analyst, Sullivan became convinced that the biological metaphors of Freudian theory were not adequate to psychology. He focused on interpersonal events as the observational base for his constructs and attempted to create a model which views people as purposive and goal-directed rather than as objects driven by primitive instinctual forces. He believed that the personality manifests itself in interpersonal relationships and is nothing more than the patterned regularities observable in the individual's relations with other people, real or illusory (Carson, 1969). Sullivan attempted to integrate the concepts and clinical observations of psychodynamic theory with the empirical focus of the social sciences.

John Rosen pioneered in the adaptation of analytic concepts to the demanding task of psychotherapy with regressed schizophrenics. His primary importance is as an innovative therapist rather than as a theoretician.

Ego psychologists have also attempted to broaden psychoanalytic theory, and to avoid some of the pitfalls of Freud's model by emphasizing the theoretical significance of ego function (relations with reality) over instinctual forces (Hartmann, 1939; Holt, 1975). Ego psychologists have directed their efforts toward a reconstruction of Freud's metapsychology in terms of an action language, a theoretical system which translates Freud's static, structural constructs (id, ego) into descriptions of human action (Schafer, 1973).

Arieti's model represents one recent attempt to integrate the insights of the ego psychologists and a recognition of the importance of personal choice and responsibility emphasized by existential psychologists, into a revised psychodynamic formulation of the origins of schizophrenia. His theory represents an important addition to Freud's original formulations, yet retains his fundamental insights into the importance of unconscious motivation, psychic causality, ego defense mechanisms, infantile sexuality, epigenetic view of human psychological development, and the qualitative similarity of the psychological processes of normal and disordered persons.

Psychodynamic theories are largely *post hoc;* they focus on the past as a source of understanding the present. The epigenetic emphasis of these theories results in the tendency to ignore or minimize the significance of contemporary life events and to use analogized parallels across the life span as the basis for viewing adult behaviors as repetitions of unresolved childhood complexes. This focus leads to an emphasis on explanation rather than prediction, one which is unacceptable to many positivistic scientists. Psychodynamic theories are formulated largely in terms of after-the-fact explanations of clinical phenomena, and are based on case studies rather than empirical studies. Psychoanalytic theory has, nevertheless, led to a number of empirical studies of schizophrenic thought and function. Silverman (1976) and his associates, for example, have conducted research on schizophrenic patients which indicates that unconscious (subliminal) triggering of aggressive emotional stimuli results in increased evidence of disturbance, while supraliminal presentation does not affect the degree of psychopathology shown. This research is cited as support for the hypothesis that schizophrenic psychopathology is rooted in unconscious rather than conscious conflict.

Other investigators have attempted to test aspects of the psychoanalytic hypothesis that the symptoms of schizophrenia result from a regression to primary process thought characteristic of the infantile stage of psychic development. This hypothesis does not imply, however, that most schizophrenics will become childlike in all aspects of cognitive function; global or complete ego regression in schizophrenia is the exception rather than the rule. Studies of cognitive function suggest that schizophrenics tend to be similar to children on tests of abstraction (Vigotsky, 1934; Goldstein, 1941), and the capacity for logical justification is markedly deficient in severely disorganized patients (Cameron, 1938). The results of these investigations generally support the psychoanalytic regression hypothesis, but the results of each study are subject to alternative explanation (Chapman and Chapman, 1973). Empirical studies support some aspects of psychoanalytic theory. More predictive studies must be completed, however, before the theory is validated according to currently acceptable scientific standards.

Psychodynamic theorists appear to subscribe to a "coherence theory" of truth; explanations are considered valid as long as they are logically consistent and appear to illuminate the origins of otherwise puzzling clinical phenomena (Rychlak, 1973). The problem with this theory of valid scientific proof is that it does not lead to tests of predictions or comparisons of hypotheses generated by rival theories that appear to provide equally coherent explanations. Coherence theory produces a tendency for theories to remain relatively static once formulated, and for contradictory information to be ignored or explained away.

Experimentally oriented theorists, in contrast, subscribe to a "correspondence theory" of truth, which demands that psychological theories generate predictions and validating empirical evidence as well as coherent explanations in order to achieve legitimate scientific status. Many clinicians doubt that personality theories will ever adequately meet the criteria of correspondence theory, and believe that these criteria are restrictive and largely irrelevant to their goals. There can be little doubt, however, that many psychodynamic theorists have evidenced indifference to the need for and requirements of adequate validating evidence.

Psychotherapy for Schizophrenics

Psychodynamic clinicians believe that most schizophrenic patients, whether acute or chronic, require more than milieu therapy, hospitalization, medication, and/or family intervention if they are to reintegrate from schizophrenic disorganization without secondary personality deterioration and increased vulnerability to future breakdown. They take exception to the argument of the behaviorists and social psychologists, who maintain that the social environment and structure of mental hospitals causes schizophrenic behavior and/or schizophrenic deterioration. In their view, intrapsychic factors are the primary causes of schizophrenic disorganization, and this process can only be reversed in a highly supportive context that offers an array of therapeutic services. This view leads to criticisms of some aspects of the recent trend toward brief hospital stay and family intervention and/or outpatient chemotherapy.

Most psychodynamic theorists believe that individual psychotherapy must form the core of any "treatment" approach that attempts to effect lasting change in schizophrenic patients. Psychotherapy, when effective, is thought to enable patients to emerge from disillusionment and despair, to begin to trust and relate again, and then to rework their internalizations of significant persons and gain sufficient ego strength to adequately direct their own lives. Individual therapy is considered to be the central part of a total program designed not to treat a disease called schizophrenia but to help a person begin the task of coping with ego disorganization, anxiety, overwhelming emotions and confusion, regressed egocentricity, aggression and sexuality, faulty defensive strategies, and social isolation. The goals of therapeutic efforts are to provide adequate controls, appropriate reality orientation, and adequate identification figures to foster trust and a close relationship that will facilitate understanding of sources of anxiety and symptoms, allow for understanding the present in the context of the past, restore a sense of self, and allow the patient to put problems in perspective (Schulz, 1975). Lidz (1973) describes the basic task of the therapist as that of releasing the patient from the bondage of completing the unfulfilled aspects of a parent's life, or bridging the division between the parents, in order to enable patients to invest their energies in their own development rather than remaining tied to the problems of a preceding generation. The critical task of the psychotherapist is to encourage the (re)establishment of sufficient hope and trust in patients to enable them to seek meaningful relationships, to foster their latent desires for individuation, and to counter fears of abandonment and anxiety experienced as the result of growing independence so that patients learn to trust their own feelings and perceptions.

Research on the effectiveness of psychotherapy with schizophrenic patients is plagued by the many conceptual and methodological difficulties that have clouded the results of attempts to determine the effectiveness of all psychotherapy. Problems matching groups of patients in terms of personality characteristics, presenting problems, severity of psychopathology, involvement and motivation for therapy; matching therapists for experience, training, theoretical orientation, ability to empathize with a particular patient, congruence of understanding, personality type, and so on; and problems in determining adequate outcome measures render the results of available psychotherapeutic studies equivocal (Feinsilver and Gunderson, 1972).

The results of a large-scale study (Rogers et al., 1967) suggest that psychotherapy for schizophrenic patients can produce measurable differences from no-therapy control patients. This study further demonstrated that effectiveness is related to the establishment of a therapeutic relationship characterized by therapist empathy and congruence. The major findings of the Rogers study were that schizophrenic patients receiving psychotherapy demonstrated a decreased need to deny their own experience, evidenced greater appropriateness of emotional expression, and showed a higher rate (twenty-eight percent) of hospital release and post-hospital adjustment than patients who did not receive psychotherapy.

REFERENCES

ARIETI, S. An overview of schizophrenia from a predominantly psychological approach. *American Journal of Psychiatry, 131,* 1974, 241–249.

―――. *Interpretation of Schizophrenia.* New York: Basic Books, 1974.

BRUNER, J. Freud and the image of man. *American Psychologist, 12,* 1957, 463–467.

CAMERON, N. Reasoning, regression, and communication in schizophrenics. *Psychological Monographs, 50,* 1938.

CARSON, R. *Interaction Concepts of Personality.* Chicago: Aldine, 1969.

CHAPMAN, L., and J. CHAPMAN. *Disordered Thought in Schizophrenia.* New York: Appleton-Century-Crofts, 1973.

FEINSILVER, D., and J. GUNDERSON. Psychotherapy for schizophrenics—is it indicated? A review of the relevant literature. *Schizophrenia Bulletin, 6,* 1972, 11–23.

FENICHEL, O. *The Psychoanalytic Theory of Neurosis.* New York: Norton, 1945.

FREUD, S. *Interpretation of Dreams,* translated by A. Brill. New York: Random House, 1913.

————. *Letters of Sigmund Freud,* edited by E. L. Freud. New York: Basic Books, 1964.

————. *New Introductory Lectures on Psychoanalysis,* edited by James Strachey. Vol. 12. New York: Norton, 1964.

————. The loss of reality in neurosis and psychosis. *Collected Papers, 2,* 1924, 277–282.

GOLDSTEIN, K., and M. SCHEERER. Abstract and concrete behavior: an experimental study with special tests. *Psychological Monographs, 53,* 1941.

HARTMANN, H. *Ego Psychology and the Problem of Adaptation.* New York: International Universities Press, 1958.

HOLT, R. R. The past and future of ego psychology. *The Psychoanalytic Quarterly, 64,* 1975, 550–576.

ROGERS, C. R., E. G. GENDLIN, D. J. KIESLER, and C. B. TRUAX, editors. *The Therapeutic Relationship and Its Impact: A Study of Psychotherapy with Schizophrenics.* Madison, Wisc.: University of Wisconsin Press, 1967.

ROSEN, J. N. *Direct Analysis: Selected Papers.* New York: Grune and Stratton, 1952.

RYCHLAK, J. F. *Introduction to Personality and Psychotherapy.* Boston: Houghton Mifflin, 1973.

SCHULZ, C. G. An individualized psychotherapeutic approach with the schizophrenic patient. *Schizophrenia Bulletin, 13,* 1975, 46–69.

SILVERMAN, L. H. Psychoanalytic theory: "reports of my death are greatly exaggerated." *American Psychologist, 30,* 1976, 17–25.

SULLIVAN, H. S. *Clinical Studies in Psychiatry,* edited by D. M. Bullard. New York: W. W. Norton, 1956.

VIGOTSKY, F. S. Thought in schizophrenia. *Archives of Neurology and Psychiatry, 31,* 1934, 1063–1077.

VON DOMARUS, E. The specific laws of logic in schizophrenia. In *Language and Thought in Schizophrenia: Collected Papers,* edited by J. S. Kasanin, pp. 104–114. Berkeley: University of California Press, 1944.

Chapter Eleven

Existential Phenomenological Approaches

The Existential Dilemma

Existentialism is the branch of philosophy that attempts to understand human experience while avoiding the subject-object dichotomy that has been an issue in western thought since the Renaissance. Existential phenomenology is concerned with ontology (the study of being), and is a reaction against the western tendency to treat people as objects to be manipulated and quantified. The Danish philosopher Sören Kierkegaard was among the first to create a philosophy that recognized that "reality" or "being" cannot be comprehended as "truth" in a detached cognitive manner. Kierkegäard's philosophy is founded on the fundamental recognition that humans as subject can never be separated from the object they perceive; that humans and the universe are co-defining. According to Kierkegaard, humans experience their world as meaningful, and therefore experience freedom, choice, and possibility. Kierkegaard recognized two constitutive characteristics that distinguish humans from all other animals: they are condemned to freedom, and they are condemned to be aware of themselves as self-determining beings.

Self-consciousness—the capacity to be aware of oneself and the implications of one's actions, and to transcend the immediate situation—is the basic characteristic of human existence, according to existential philosophers, and is the basis for human freedom. Anxiety is understood as awareness of the possibility of freedom.

The terms *existentialism* and *phenomenology* are similar in meaning. Both refer to that branch of philosophy which attempts to derive philosophical underpinnings for a psychology that studies humans as beings rather than objects; both are concerned with ontology, the study of the being process.

The French philosopher Jean-Paul Sartre believes that the inescapable anguish of the human condition, of freedom and responsibility, leads to maneuvers to flee freedom, choice, and responsibility through various modes of self-deception, referred to as "bad faith." Sartre's modes of bad faith are descriptions of strategies used by people to attempt to dehumanize themselves in such a way that the issues of personal freedom and responsibility are denied, and anxiety is avoided.

The German phenomenologist Martin Heidegger has formulated a model that describes humans as process, as evolving systems of projects and understanding, continually struggling to understand themselves and whatever they encounter. This approach investigates that aspect of humans concerned with their awareness of their existence; to discover what it means for people to be, not what people are.

Anxiety, or dread, is understood as the experience of the individual in the face of the imminent dissolution into insignificance of the totality of his or her involvements, of the ultimate meaninglessness of his or her activities and understandings in the face of awareness of the possibilities of death, not-being, and nothingness.

Inauthenticity refers to the potential, in the face of dread, for the individual to turn away from ontological possibilities, from what is distinctive in human existence; to become absorbed in the world of objects, the instrumental world; to immerse his or her self into the world of "they," the "mass." *Authenticity,* in contrast, requires that the individual acknowledge his or her freedom to choose one's manner of existence and its meaning.

Existential phenomenology insists that psychology must expand beyond traditional causal-deterministic models and attempt to understand and characterize the individual's experience of world, of self, of being in the world. Existential clinicians eschew categorization, diagnosis, and other attempts to define, observe, and circumscribe the meaning of the person's life experience through what they consider the distortion of diagnostic categories, theoretical abstractions, or "aboutisms." They argue that humans viewed as organisms, diagnostic entities, or personality structures (id, ego, superego) are seen as complex organizations of things, of "its." Existential psychologists maintain that an objectified, scientific psychopathology, whether biological or psychological in orientation, is incomplete and cannot adequately or completely grasp the issues being lived out by the "patients" by their ways of being themselves in the world.

The existential movement in psychology, although it borrows heavily from the work of Freud, attempts also to study humans on a broader scale. This approach is based on the assumption that it is possible to have a science of human behavior that does not fragment and destroy the humanity of people as it studies them. Existential phenomenological theories do not attempt to explain so much as to understand and describe the state of being-in-the-world that characterizes individuals.

The Existential Theory of R. D. Laing

Laing (1957) has attempted to present an existential phenomenological account of schizoid and schizophrenic persons' experiences of their world and themselves. His book, *The Divided Self,* has had a considerable impact on the field of abnormal psychology; nevertheless, Laing has since renounced the point of view reflected in this work:

> I feel that in focusing upon and attempting to delineate a certain type of schizoid existence, I was practically falling into the trap I was seeking to avoid. I was talking too much about them and too little of us. In the context of our present pervasive madness, all our frames of reference are ambiguous and equivocal (1964, p. 11).

Laing uses the term *schizoid* to refer to individuals whose experience is split in two ways: a rent in their relation to the world, and a disruption of their relation to themselves. Schizoid individuals typically experience themselves as automata, machinery, or, as one person described it, "My feelings seem to be all rusty inside, so that

I can't feel, I can only think." In Laing's view, ontologically secure people encounter all life hazards from a secure sense of their own and others' reality and identity. They experience their presence in the world as real, alive, whole, and continuous, and can live out in the world and meet others who are experienced as equally whole and alive. Relatedness is threatening, on the other hand, to ontologically insecure people, who are preoccupied with preserving rather than gratifying themselves, and find the circumstances of living and personal intimacy threatening.

Laing has identified three forms of anxiety encountered by those who are ontologically insecure. (1) In *engulfment,* individuals fear relatedness as such with anyone, even themselves, because their uncertainty about their own autonomy generates the fear that they may lose their identity to someone else. In order to protect the identity from engulfment through relatedness the schizoid individual maneuvers to maintain the self in isolation. (2) *Implosion* contact with reality is experienced as dreadful, the world is experienced as likely to crash in unpredictably—*implode*—and obliterate all identity because the individual feels empty, a vacuum. In the case of (3) *petrification* (the dread of turning into stone, a machine, an "it," subjectivity resulting in the magical act of turning someone else into an "it"), depersonalization occurs in order to negate the threat of the other person's autonomy.

Persons who are ontologically insecure, who experience the three forms of anxiety described above, come to experience themselves as split, typically into a mind and a body. Laing has introduced the term *embodied* to refer to the experience of feeling oneself inextricably bound up in his or her body, to feel one's body as alive, real, substantial, and whole. A sense of being *disembodied,* characteristic of the schizoid state, occurs when people feel dissociated from their bodies. The body is experienced as one object among other objects in the world, rather than as the core of the individual's own being. Instead of being the core of the *true self,* the body is experienced as the core of the *false self,* while a detached, disembodied "true" self observes but never directly participates in life. Schizoid individuals are described as attempting to create a microcosmos within themselves, without recourse or direct relatedness to the outer world of persons and things. Since the self in a schizoid organization is disembodied, many of the person's actions are experienced as unreal or dissociated because they are actions of the false self. Out of fear of real intimacy and relationship, the schizoid individual creates a schism between self and body in an attempt to preserve a precariously structured being.

Schizoids are thought to enclose their beings through detachment, isolation, control, and independence to achieve safety for their true selves; but this detachment means that the true self is never directly revealed, that all transactions with others are delegated to a false self. The safety, control, and freedom from others experienced by the self is achieved at the cost of growing despair for the inner self which, unable to be enriched by direct, spontaneous outer experience, becomes increasingly impoverished. This impoverishment is expressed in the form of complaints of emptiness, coldness, despair, and worthlessness.

The false self system in the schizoid individual attempts to maintain its identity by remaining transcendent, as pure subject without objective existence, often through compliance with the expectations of others. This pattern is manifested in an excess of conformity, of being "good," of meeting others' expectations, of never asserting any will or making any choices of one's own. Laing has illustrated this point with a quote from a patient: "I am a response to what other people say I am" (1957, p. 98). Or: "I am nothing more than series of images, slides projected onto a circular screen, the center is empty."

Psychosis is, according to Laing, simply the sudden removal of the veil of the false self's outer conformity, so that the inner self begins to pour out accusations of persecution by the very persons with whom the false self has been complying. The model son, husband, or citizen may suddenly declare that his mother, spouse, or community agencies have been trying to poison him, steal his mind, or kidnap him. The false self system is understood as the basis for paranoid fears; since it is merely a mirror of an alien reality, it comes to be regarded as an alien presence, a persecutor, in possession of the individual.

The essential postulate of Laing's model is, "the reality of the self and the world are mutually potentiated by the direct relationship between self and other" (1959, p. 82); or, alternatively, "the sense of identity requires the existence of another by whom one is known" (1959, p. 139). In the schizoid condition the inner self grows increasingly unreal, empty, charged with fear and envy, while the false self becomes more extensive, autonomous, unreal, false, mechanical, and harassed by compulsive behaviors. The dissociation of self from body, and the close association between body and others, lead to the schizophrenic view that the body is in actual possession of others. From this perspective, the transition from schizoid functioning to overt schizophrenic behavior is always a gradual process, the natural culmination of the schizoid split. Abrupt schizophrenic "breaks," described in the psychopathological literature, are viewed as artifacts of a model which views people from the "outside" and the fails to consider their experience.

Schizophrenic psychosis is understood as an attempt at "the denial of being as a means of preserving being" (1959, p. 150). In schizophrenia, the self system undergoes a complete split. Hallucinations are considered to be thoughts belonging to the other self which have the quality of an as-if perception of the disintegrated false self by a part of the residual inner self. In chronic schizophrenia, the self has split into several fragments, each with a certain limited sense of self, and each experiencing the other foci, such as hallucinations and delusions of influence, as partially not-me. The inner phantom-self of the chronic schizophrenic is almost completely taken over by primitive, unconscious, archetypal forces.

Laing conceives of schizophrenia as an extreme defensive maneuver in which the false self system permits the schizophrenic to remain detached in order to preserve "being." The false self in effect allows schizophrenic people to experience themselves as dead in order to avoid the fear of being crushed, engulfed, or overwhelmed by the experience of being alive and free. Laing believes that the real self is aware of the false self in schizophrenia, but that pretense preserves the privacy of the self against intrusion.

Daseinanalysis

The Swiss psychiatrist Ludwig Binswanger has developed a clinical phenomenological approach based on Heidegger's philosophy, called *daseinanalysis*. The process uses phenomenological procedures to reveal phenomena in their own terms, without distortion by external constructs. This approach attempts to describe the alterations in the fundamental structure of existence that occur in schizophrenic persons. Daseinanalysis does not attempt to establish a theory of illness or system of diagnosis, nor does it attempt to speculate about underlying cause(s). It does try to discover the structure of existence and its transformations that underlie outward manifestations, or "symptoms." The aim is to "reclaim" the schizophrenic person from the conceptual structure of causal theories by discovering the critical moments responsible for the schizophrenic development of the existential structure. Such moments, according to Binswanger (1960), are associated with experiences of *failure* in the process of existence, during which the sequential character of experience becomes problematic. Interruptions in the natural sequence of experience create a vacuum to be filled; a void in which it no longer seems possible to conduct one's life.

The specific schizophrenic solution identified by Binswanger is the substitution of a set of *rigid alternatives* for the uninterrupted objective sequence of experience. Existence within the confines of rigid alternatives allows individuals to shut themselves off from others and from any possibility of loving relatedness. All schizophrenic modes of existence are understood as consequences of the breakdown in the sequential order of experience, and the resulting experience of an existence with no exits.

The task of the *daseinanalyst* is to apprehend the transcendental structure that makes it possible for phenomena to be phenomena for the patients, their world-designs. The world-design of the schizophrenic is considered to be particularly evident in delusions, where everything that makes the world significant is submitted to the rule of a single or a few categories that support the patient's world and being. In schizophrenia, that which is existentially *a priori* (makes existence possible) has been constricted so that existence is ruled by one or a few categories. The delusional meaning matrix within which all phenomena appear and take on relevance, and within which the world and self are constituted, are dominated by a few or, in extreme cases, only one theme. According to this view, the more simplified and constricted the world-design to which existence has committed itself, the greater the likelihood that anxiety will be experienced and thus, the greater the necessity of limiting one's life horizons. The major criterion of mental illness for the daseinanalyst is the degree to which the freedom of *dasein* is surrendered to the power of another, the choice of unfreedom.

Schizophrenic delusions are viewed as attempts, however inappropriate or inadequate, at coping with life. The existential structure is increasingly overpowered by a sense of the *dreadful,* of *existential anxiety*—the anxiety of not being able to cope with life after all. In delusions of persecution, the individual abdicates fulfillment and yields to one of the alternatives, to the feared alternative. At this point the experience of the dreadful becomes all absorbing; the physiognomy of the world is transformed into a world of malice and persecution. Existence is narrowed and anxiety is avoided.

Binswanger has described four situations that form the basis of schizophrenic experience:

1. *The consistency of natural experience breaks down.* The torment characteristic of the lives of schizophrenics results from the fact that when they are unable to come to terms with the chaos and disorder characteristic of their experience, they seek a way out of this chaotic world through delusions, so that some semblance of order can be re-established.

2. *Experiential consistency is split off into rigid alternatives, extravagant ideals.* The adoption of extravagant ideals and bondage to rigid alternatives (perfect-imperfect, beautiful-ugly) leads to the anxiety of giving in to the dark side of the alternative. The result is that the individual can temporize his or her self only in the mode of deficiency, imperfection, or "fallenness into the world."

3. *Covering.* The person engages in an extensive attempt to conceal or disguise the side of the rigid alternative that is unbearable to the *dasein.*

4. *Existence is worn away.* The person characterized by the above experience begins to feel worn away, resigned, no longer able to find a way in or out. He or she decides to end the hopelessness of experience by engaging in an existential retreat and renouncing life as an independent being.

Binswanger (1963) believes that the problem of schizophrenia "culminates" in delusions of persecution and that the origin of delusions of persecution may be seen in the self-surrender of the will to others. In such instances, *dasein* comes to see the enemy everywhere, sees hostile intentions in everyone, because the schizophrenic has surrendered his or her will to others and comes to experience himself or herself as a victim of those he or she has become dependent upon. By surrendering itself to the will of alien persons, *dasein* replaces the tension of disordered experience, and of being caught between irreconcilable alternatives, with a more one-sided, consistent experience. Binswanger refers to the process by which *dasein* abandons potentiality for being itself and displaces its own responsibility and guilt onto an outside "fate," or world-design, as *mundanization*. Through the process of mundanization existence escapes its actual task, meaning, and responsibility, but it does not escape anxiety.

Binswanger's existential-analytic model posits two phases of the schizophrenic experience. Through classic defensive measures, existence tries to protect itself against the emergence of the "uncanny" (anything which ought to remain secret and obscure but somehow has become manifest). Defensive measures having proved inadequate, the "dreadful" (the dread of loss of existence) is no longer felt as a vague internal threat; rather, it is transformed, and experienced as a concrete threat arising from the external world, from other people. Existential anxiety (the dread of loss of existence) is turned, through the development of delusions of persecution, into the certainty of being threatened by others, of being murdered (the mundanization of existential anxiety). The transformation of the dread of loss of existence into delusions of persecution is actually a relief. Through mundanization, the self need no longer exist as an independent, autonomous, responsible existence capable of taking a stand and making choices; it becomes instead a dependent ego, a victim of the superior power of the "enemies."

Existential Therapy

Existential therapists have attempted to retain many of the insights of psychoanalytic theory without transforming the experience of the individual into an impersonal system of unconscious forces and biological instincts. Psychiatric diagnoses are viewed as sociological statements, and "symptoms" of psychopathology are conceived of as disturbances in the framework of social relationships of which a given human existence consists (Boss, 1963).

The prime goal of the existential therapist (*daseinanalyst*) is to remain acutely aware of and adhere to the immediately given phenomena of the individual's world without distortion through objectification. These therapists stress the uniqueness of the individual and his or her life situation. Dreams, symptoms, slips of the tongue, transference, and other "irrational" phenomena are understood as reflections of the person's mode of being in the world, rather than as the result of unconscious forces.

The goal of existential therapy is to help the patients attain meaningful and purposeful lives within the context of their potential. This is achieved through gradual confrontation with self-imposed limitations of life, and with the possibility of a richer existence, in the safe context of the therapeutic relationship. The patients are encouraged to confront honestly their inauthentic ways of relating to the world, of becoming "adjusted," and of denying their own potential. Existential guilt (the result of failure to fulfill possibilities) is reduced as the patient discovers new, more authentic modes of being. Painful, constricting, or traumatic events in the life history of a person are not thought of as the "cause" of problems, but as conditions associated with the individual's initiation of inhibitions against fully carrying out all possible interpersonal and interworldly relationships.

Existential therapists have attempted to create small communities for "schizophrenics." These communities are designed to foster personal growth through the experience and understanding of the psychotic process lived through in a context of acceptance and support. Programs such as Kingsley Hall, founded in 1965 in London, and Soteria House in San Jose, attempt to provide a place in which individuals may experience their schizophrenic experience in a context of maximum freedom and acceptance. Professionalism, the medical model, and dichotomies between patients and staff are minimized. Staff is selected on the basis of their sensitivity and knowledge to help guide, support, and work with the patients as they go through the process of growth. Laing's (1967) later views of the schizophrenic process as potential breakthrough rather than failure or breakdown are the theoretical basis for such programs.

Striking case reports of the success of this approach have been published but it is too early to assess its range of effectiveness.

evaluation

Existential analysts have contributed greatly to our understanding of schizophrenic developments. This approach attempts to enrich and supplement traditional approaches, rather than to provide an alternative causal model of psychopathology. Existentialists maintain, however, that traditional psychopathology cannot incorporate their observations without simplifying or divesting these observations of their phenomenal contents. Existential analysis of schizophrenic developments is understood to stand in dialectic relationship to traditional theories. Existential analytic descriptions are intended to apprehend the fundamental structure of existence of schizophrenics as people rather than "things" or constructs.

Existential analysts have not, however, addressed the question of how delusional beliefs are thought to differ from culturally prevalent "nondelusional" beliefs (such as those which posit an afterlife, immortality, political salvation, or longevity). Delusional beliefs constitute integral portions of the schizophrenic's worldview, just as "normal" beliefs constitute integral portions of the normal individual's worldview, and existentialists have not adequately differentiated between such beliefs. Their view of delusions as intentional phenomena (as means by which the individual adapts to an unbearable existential situation by reducing himself or herself to an entity with limited or unreal possibilities and responsibilities) illuminates the functional, purposive aspect of schizophrenic thought, but does not consider possible predisposing factors, or how such beliefs differ from the functional maneuvers of "normal" individuals, which also serve to reduce existential anxiety.

It is an open question whether the existential analytic descriptions of Binswanger and Laing are equally applicable to all persons labelled schizophrenic, whether hebephrenic or reactive paranoid. It seems likely that differences in education, culture, genetic background, life history, and social circumstances are also important to the understanding of the particular manner in which an individual experiences and attempts to reduce anxiety. The case illustrations provided by existential analysts suggest that they have formulated descriptive models on the basis of clinical experience with a select group of intelligent, highly verbal adults with good pre-breakdown social history. Existential phenomenological theories have added a new dimension to our understanding of the complex, multifaceted phenomena called schizophrenia, that supplements, rather than competes with or supplants other theoretical perspectives.

REFERENCES

Boss, M. *Psychoanalysis and Daseinanalysis.* New York: Basic Books, 1963.

Binswanger, L. Existential analysis of schizophrenia. *Journal of Existential Psychiatry, 1,* 1960, 157–165.

Heidegger, M. *Being and Time.* New York: Harper and Row, 1962.

Laing, R. D. *The Divided Self.* London: Pelican, 1959.

————. *The Divided Self,* second edition. London: Pelican, 1964.

————. *The Politics of Experience.* New York: Pantheon, 1967.

Index

Author Index

Subject Index

253